Dear Reader:

The book you are about to read is the latest bestseller from the St. Martin's True Crime Library, the imprint *The New York Times* calls "the leader in true crime!" The True Crime Library offers you fascinating accounts of the latest, most sensational crimes that have captured the national attention. St. Martin's is the publisher of John Glatt's riveting and horrifying SECRETS IN THE CELLAR, which shines a light on the man who shocked the world when it was revealed that he had kept his daughter locked in his hidden basement for 24 years. In the Edgar-nominated WRITTEN IN BLOOD, Diane Fanning looks at Michael Petersen, a Marine-turned-novelist found guilty of beating his wife to death and pushing her down the stairs of their home—only to reveal another similar death from his past. In the book you now hold, CRAZY FOR YOU, Michael Fleeman examines a case of obsession and delusion, where things aren't often what they seem.

St. Martin's True Crime Library gives you the stories behind the headlines. Our authors take you right to the scene of the crime and into the minds of the most notorious murderers to show you what really makes them tick. St. Martin's True Crime Library paperbacks are better than the most terrifying thriller, because it's all true! The next time you want a crackling good read, make sure it's got the St. Martin's True Crime Library logo on the spine—you'll be up all night!

Charles E. Spicer, Jr.
Executive Editor, St. Martin's True Crime Library

CRAZY FOR YOU

MICHAEL FLEEMAN

St. Martin's Paperbacks

CRAZY FOR YOU

Copyright © 2015 by Michael Fleeman.

For information address St. Martin's Press, 175 Fifth Avenue, New York, NY 10010.

EAN: 978-1-250-03638-4

Printed in the United States of America

St. Martin's Paperbacks edition / February 2015

St. Martin's Paperbacks are published by St. Martin's Press, 175 Fifth Avenue, New York, NY 10010.

10 9 8 7 6 5 4 3

CHAPTER 1

Early one crisp fall day, rush-hour commuters got their morning pick-me-ups at the drive-through windows at Starbucks and Dunkin' Donuts, then slogged down Mount Vernon or Chamblee Dunwoody Roads toward the Interstate 285 freeway that circles Greater Atlanta. Women in brightly colored tank tops and gym shorts power-walked to music from their iPods along the wooded trails that ran next to the traffic-clogged roads. The Dunwoody Village shopping center in the heart of Dunwoody, Georgia, was quiet but for the distant sound of a leaf blower and an impact wrench at the Goodyear store. The Village Barbershop waited for its first customer; a training car from Taggart's Driving School sat alone in the nearly empty parking lot. The post office would open within minutes, and people lined up outside in front of the glass door with the sign reading, WE APPRECIATE YOUR BUSINESS.

Shortly before 9 a.m., on Thursday, November 18, 2010, a silver Infiniti G35 pulled into the shopping center and came to a stop next to a red-brick wall in front of the Dunwoody Prep preschool. Russell "Rusty" Sneiderman, thirty-six years old, boyish looking with glasses, had his three-year-old son, Ian, strapped in the car seat in the back. The preschool run had become the morning routine ever since Rusty lost his CFO job, and his wife, Andrea, took her first full-time employment in the corporate world. Andrea usually took their five-year-old daughter, Sophia, to kindergarten on the way to her office at GE Energy in Marietta. Later in the day, Rusty would pick up both Ian and Sophia and take Sophia to ballet. In between he would squeeze in work on a voice-mail company he was trying to start up.

Rusty brought Ian to his classroom and returned to his car. His schedule this day called for an 11:30 a.m. meeting with a potential business partner. Based on his casual dress, it appeared that Rusty had planned to make the short drive back to his large house on Manget Court and change clothes.

By all accounts Rusty never saw the silver minivan following him into the parking lot, and if he did it didn't mean enough for him to do anything about it. Nor did he seem to recognize the driver, a bearded man in a hoodie sweatshirt who had waited behind the wheel until Rusty emerged from the school.

Rusty opened his car door, and the bearded man approached. If they exchanged words, nobody heard it. Without any apparent warning or provocation, the man pointed a handgun at Rusty's head.

The gun was large and chrome-plated, the morning sun glinting off the polished surface.

Four times the man pulled the trigger.

* * *

"Did you hear that?"

Fifty yards across the parking lot Craig Kuhlmeier, a chiropractor with a practice down the street, and his wife, Aliyah Stotter, were standing outside the post office to buy stamps when they heard four popping sounds from the direction of the Dunwoody Prep preschool and saw the silver minivan. Kuhlmeier thought it might have been a Chrysler. A man was "casually walking" toward it, Kuhlmeier would later say. The man stood medium height, between five foot nine and five eleven, and wore blue jeans. He turned and stared at the couple. In his hand was the silver gun, in Kuhlmeier's estimation a semiautomatic of some sort, definitely not a revolver.

The man started the van but struggled to get it in reverse, the gears grinding, as if he were unfamiliar with how to operate the vehicle. The van jerked away and peeled out of the parking lot, the tires screeching, raced straight down the street, made a U-turn, then continued on Mount Vernon Road into the rush-hour traffic.

On the pavement next to a silver luxury car a man lay dying.

The couple rushed across the parking lot and found the man horribly wounded and barely alive. Blood snaked from his head like a small stream across the parking lot. Brass shell casings lay beside him. The scene was surreal, like a movie scene. Kuhlmeier kept waiting for the director to yell, *Cut, do it again.*

The man gasped for air. Kuhlmeier checked his pulse. It was weak.

"Are you okay? Can you hear me?" Kuhlmeier asked. The man didn't respond.

Calling 911 on her cell phone, Stotter told the operator that a man had been shot outside the Dunwoody Prep preschool in the Dunwoody Village center. As a crowd began to converge, the bleeding man struggled for air. Panic overtook Stotter, and she later said she wished she'd had the presence of mind to have started CPR.

Across the street, Chris Lang had taken his daughter to the doctor at Dunwoody Pediatrics for an 8 a.m. appointment. Returning to his truck, he put the child into her car seat and was pulling out of the parking lot when he, too, heard the popping noises. He U-turned and heard another pop. That's when he saw the man in the hoodie, and what he'd later describe as a "noticeable" beard, firing at least twice more into the man on the ground before getting in the van and peeling off.

Through the rearview mirror, Lang watched the van exit onto Mount Vernon and race away before he drove up to the wounded man and saw Kuhlmeier talking to him and Stotter on her cell phone. Lang went to Dunwoody Pediatrics for help.

Dr. Terrence Gfroerer had just finished seeing a patient when one of his staff members told him that there had been a shooting in the parking lot across the street. He and a staff member went to the Dunwoody Prep lot, where he saw the victim on the ground slouched on his side, blood pouring from him. Dr. Gfroerer rolled the man onto his back and saw what appeared to be multiple gunshot wounds. He checked the vital signs. The carotid artery revealed a faint pulse. Gfroerer began mouth-to-mouth resuscitation while his staff member did chest compressions. The vital signs didn't improve.

Although not a trauma doctor, Gfroerer had been a physician for ten years. He didn't think he could save the man.

Inside Dunwoody Prep, school assistant Colleen McNulty had taken six three-year-olds from a classroom to the playground on the other side of the brick wall when she saw a flock of birds take flight. A fraction of a second later she heard loud noises, four in succession. Peering over the wall to the parking lot, McNulty saw a minivan race away and several people gathered over a man on the ground with blood pouring from his head.

She recognized him as Rusty Sneiderman, a parent whose son, Ian, attended the preschool and whose daughter, Sophia, had been a student a few years previously. McNulty ushered the children back into the classroom and tried to dial 911 on her cell phone but got busy signals. She told another teacher to go into the office and call for help.

In the office, Donna Formato at first thought it was a bad joke. She had worked at Dunwoody Prep for fourteen years and now was the assistant director, supervising a staff of about three dozen, including teachers, assistants, and support personnel. She went outside to find a crowd gathering around a prone man with what she later described as "very gray" skin. She did not immediately recognize him. Beside the man was an Infiniti, the driver's-side door still open, as if he had just gotten out or was about to get in when he was shot.

With somebody attending to the man, Formato went back inside the school to first check on the students. None apparently had seen the shooting. If any had heard the gunshots, they didn't make the connection between the loud pops and something horrible happening. An office worker told her the victim was Ian Sneiderman's dad, Rusty. Formato pulled the family emergency contact information card and dialed a work number for Ian's mother, Andrea Sneiderman.

The 911 call was relayed by the dispatcher at the DeKalb County emergency call center to the patrol car of Dunwoody Police Department officer Brian Tate, who this morning had been cruising around town in one of the department's gleaming new black-and-white patrol cars. Officer Tate was three hours into a twelve-hour shift that had started with a 5:45 a.m. roll call. Somehow the details of the incident had gotten garbled. The dispatcher initially sent him to the RBC Bank in the Dunwoody Village shopping center for what was described as an armed robbery. The suspect was said to be a Hispanic male, the victim a non-Hispanic white man. According to the dispatcher, the Hispanic male had a gun pointing at the white male, who had his hands in the air. Tate sped to the shopping center. A minute later the dispatcher changed the call to a person being shot at Dunwoody Prep in the same mall.

Tate arrived in just two minutes. It was an impressive response time in keeping with the three-minute-or-less goal of the Dunwoody Police Department. Aliyah Stotter flagged him down and directed him toward the entrance to the school. As he got out of his patrol car, he could hear the siren from the approaching paramedic. On the pavement Tate saw the victim on the ground with what Tate later described as "very serious" gunshot wounds. Dr. Gfroerer and a woman the officer took to be a nurse were performing CPR.

Within seconds, emergency medical technician Rhoda Berkeley from the DeKalb County Fire and Rescue was on the scene. She and her crew took over CPR from Dr. Gfroerer for another five to ten minutes, then transported Rusty Sneiderman fourteen miles to the Atlanta Medical Center.

It was about 9:15 a.m. when the phone rang at Andrea Sneiderman's desk. "I told her something had happened at the school, that Ian was okay and that she needed to come to the school right away," Formato later would say. Formato said nothing about people hearing gunshots or having seen the ashen-faced Rusty, who was Andrea's husband. She didn't want to alarm Andrea any more than necessary, presuming she'd be driving to the school. She later recalled, "I didn't want her to have an accident on the way to the school. I was worried about her safety, too."

Andrea started screaming into the phone. She demanded more information. Had something happened to Rusty? Formata refused to say more until Andrea got there. Andrea ran out of her office and down to the parking lot and drove off in her black SUV. Going against rush-hour traffic, she likely took Cobb Parkway South to Interstate 285 East— the northern tip of the Perimeter—and exited toward Dunwoody. Along the way, she made a number of calls on her cell phone. She called her parents telling them that she was on her way to the daycare center. She also called her brother with the same message. Her parents and her brother all lived nearby and would meet her. She also called Rusty's father, Donald Sneiderman, a retired accountant who lived in Cleveland. And she called her boss, Hemy Neuman, on his cell phone. She later said she intended to tell him she had to leave work abruptly for an emergency, but she got only voice mail.

She tore into the school parking lot, flung open her door, tumbled out, and ran toward the crime-scene tape. Behind it sat Rusty's parked Infiniti.

"What happened?" she screamed. "What happened?"

Detective Jesus Maldonado from the Dunwoody Police Department intercepted her as she headed toward the crime-scene tape. She was in her business attire, long dark skirt, black jacket, glasses. Repeatedly she asked what happened, and Maldonado didn't tell her anything.

"Calm down," he told her, leading her away from the crime scene and toward the front door of the daycare center. "You gotta relax."

Her knees buckled and Maldonado caught her from

falling. He had no intention of saying anything about the case while she was in this condition. The crime scene had not been processed; witnesses had not been interviewed. The victim had been taken away by ambulance, condition unknown. Maldonado half carried her to the door where she was met by two women who worked at Dunwoody Prep and another detective, Sergeant Gary Cortellino.

Aliyah Stotter, already shaken by hearing the gunshots and seeing the bloodied man on the ground, had seen Andrea arrive. The screaming grief-stricken woman only made Stotter more upset and she started, in her words, "bawling." Stotter pulled up her hoodie, shielding her tear-soaked face from the woman.

In the daycare center, a teacher embraced Andrea but neither the teacher nor anybody else would tell her what had happened. "No one was talking, no one was saying a word," Andrea later recalled. Brought into a glass-enclosed office, Andrea was joined by several other people, including Sergeant Cortellino. The ranking officer on the scene, Cortellino had arrived twenty minutes earlier, after Rusty had been taken away, and he temporarily took charge. He told officers to look for witnesses, called in crime-scene techs to collect evidence, including the shell casings in the parking lot, and sent a detective to the hospital to talk to family members. He later acknowledged being taken by surprise that one of those family members would be right there in front of him. "I really didn't know she was coming," he later said. "I wasn't prepared for that."

Andrea continued to ask what was going on. Cortellino wouldn't tell her. Instead he asked if she knew where Rusty had come from and where he was headed. Andrea told him she had no idea, and she'd later express frustration that she had answered questions when nobody would answer hers. She would also claim that Cortellino refused to tell her where Rusty had been taken; Cortellino would say that he wanted a detective to drive her to hospital—"She didn't need to be at the school," he said. When it looked like she would get herself to the hospital, Cortellino called a friend who headed security there and "told them the family was coming down and to look out for them."

At some point while inside the school, Andrea spoke on her cell phone to her parents. They were driving to meet her from their home in Roswell, thirteen miles to the east.

Eventually, her parents arrived, as did her brother. Among the four of them they somehow ascertained that Rusty had been taken in an ambulance to an unidentified hospital after some sort of incident. Any more information—from the school, from the detectives, from anybody—would not be forthcoming. "We were instructed to go home," Andrea later said, but she couldn't remember by whom. "A police officer, I presume," she would recall. "I was in a fairly catatonic state."

At the recommendation of Donna Formata, Andrea left Ian at the school, feeling it was better for him there while everybody sorted out what had happened to his father. Andrea's parents drove her to her house, and then her father called all the local hospitals. The Atlanta Medical Center confirmed that a Russell Sneiderman had been admitted but wouldn't say why or what his condition was. Andrea and her parents piled into the car and headed for the hospital while Andrea worked her cell phone, calling a long-time friend, Shayna Citron, Rusty's father, Donald, and her boss Hemy Neuman, again.

The paramedics continued to perform CPR as they wheeled Rusty into the emergency room to attending physician Dr. Mark Waterman. A quick assessment told him the prognosis was grim. The man had suffered multiple gunshot wounds to his neck, near the carotid artery, and chest. It would later be determined that the first bullet entered the left side of the jaw, traveled through his jaw, and hit his right shoulder, ending up just below the skin in his back. The gunman fired at point-blank range; Rusty had stippling burns to the face from the gunpowder grains that shot out with the bullet. The second bullet came from farther away, probably while he lay on the asphalt. It entered the right side of his abdomen at the bottom of his rib cage and pierced his liver, diaphragm, and right lung, lodging itself just under the skin of the back, causing serious internal bleeding. Two more bullets went into his abdomen, slicing through his intestines and exiting from his back, causing more internal bleeding. Rusty also suffered a graze wound to his forearm, either from a separate fifth shot or more likely from one of the other bullets hitting him just below the elbow as he tried in vain to fend off the shots.

Dr. Waterman checked his patient's pulse and breathing. All vital signs were flat.

Within minutes he declared Rusty Sneiderman dead.

CHAPTER 2

The parking lot where, just minutes before, parents had delivered their children to preschool had become a staging ground for patrol cars and other emergency vehicles with lights flashing. Men and women in uniform could be seen inside and outside the school. Crime-scene techs spray-painted orange circles around brass bullet casings and set up little yellow markers; they took measurements and snapped photographs. A pool of coagulating blood was still visible from beyond the crime-scene tape. Police officers fanned out looking for witnesses.

The first newsperson to arrive was Dick Williams, publisher of the weekly *Dunwoody Crier*, whose offices were across the street from the preschool. A phone call to his home got Williams to Dunwoody Prep minutes after the paramedics took away the victim. "It's unheard of," he said later. "I've had this paper for sixteen years and that's probably homicide number four in all that time." A former writer and editor for the *Atlanta Journal-Constitution* and a news director for several TV stations, Williams had seen his share of crime scenes, but nothing like this. "There was a chalk outline," he recalled. "The real impression it made on me was how much blood the human body had. The blood was still there. It covered a large area. There was a slight incline and the blood ran down fifteen feet and four feet wide."

Soon the parking lot was teeming with reporters. The *Atlanta Journal-Constitution*, the region's leading daily newspaper, is located in Dunwoody, its office a couple of miles away from the school. News helicopters circled over the preschool, and vans from Atlanta's local TV stations rolled into the parking lot, telescoping up their transmission poles for live satellite reports. Somewhere in the newsroom of CNN's world news headquarters, producers at crime-centric HLN took first notice of a story fifteen miles away that one day would be a big part of their programming.

The early coverage was breathless.

"A father shot and killed minutes after dropping off his children at preschool," the anchor of Channel 2 Action News ("Live. Local. Late-breaking") announced to lead the afternoon newscast. The co-anchor added: "We talked to worried parents," then tossed to reporter Erin Coleman in the field. "I just got off the phone with Dunwoody police. They tell me right now they are out actively searching for the man that shot this father."

"And now—panic outside a preschool," began Fox TV affiliate anchor Tom Haynes on that night's telecast. "A man murdered after dropping off his young son . . . Tonight a shooting suspect is still at large." The account in the

Atlanta Journal-Constitution echoed the tone of disbelief. DUNWOODY MAN WAS UNLIKELY VICTIM, read the headline over a story that began, "Russell 'Rusty' Sneiderman didn't see it coming." It called the murder a "sensational crime" that "offers few obvious avenues for investigation."

Quiet, leafy Dunwoody represents all that locals savor about life Outside the Perimeter, where suburbs, shopping centers, and office parks dominate the landscape. The world within the I-285 Perimeter loop is considered more urban— downtown Atlanta's gleaming skyscrapers are at the center—with closer access to corporate offices, fine restaurants and bars, the theater and college and professional sports. Georgia Tech is ITP (Inside the Perimeter) and so are the stadiums for the Falcons and Braves. Much debate rages on whether one should live OTP or ITP (that is, if one has a choice), and in many places the differences are not distinct. Dunwoody and neighboring Sandy Springs, with their sprawling office complexes and the large Perimeter Mall anchored by a Nordstrom, are said to have an "ITP feel"; the mansions and estates of ITP Buckhead that the pro athletes and music stars call home could seem OTP.

Carved out of farmland beginning in the 1970s, Dunwoody's residential streets wind through old groves of pine and oak. The houses are built on large wooded lots set back from the street in the "five-four-and-the-door" design: five windows on the top story and four windows on the bottom with a door in the middle. Nearly every subdivision has tennis courts, and the Atlanta Lawn Tennis Association is located here.

"There's a joke here," says Dick Williams, the *Crier*'s publisher. "What do you wear to a funeral in Dunwoody? A black tennis dress."

Dunwoody is symbolized by its favorite son, Ryan Seacrest, who grew up here and developed his broadcasting skills by giving morning assemblies over the PA system at Dunwoody High School before working at a local radio station. Seacrest has lost none of his boyish good looks from his 1992 senior high school prom picture, and he maintains local ties. An old high school friend, now the assistant principal, arranged to fly a Dunwoody mass media class to the *American Idol* set in 2011 for a backstage visit with Jennifer Lopez, Randy Jackson, and Steven Tyler.

It's the kind of place that people want to get transferred to. "Dunwoody was the first suburb of Atlanta essentially created by Yankees," says Williams. "I've never figured out the chicken-and-egg part of it, but for some reason it became the suburb of choice for business executives transferred to Atlanta from other places." IBM, which has offices all over Atlanta, has drawn many people, as has GE in nearby Marietta. The schools are top-notch, the mall the best in the region, the weather never too cold in the winter, and the brutal southern summer heat and humidity are tempered by the shade from hundred-year-old trees and the air-conditioning in every home. With several churches, a large Jewish community center, and a powerful homeowners' association, life in Dunwoody is dominated by God and city planning. A tree can't be cut down here unless a new one is planted to replace it. Trash and recycling pickup comes four times a week.

Residents follow community issues with the zeal of the recently converted. A fiercely fought incorporation battle raged to unshackle Dunwoody from sprawling DeKalb County government—and what locals long complained were DeKalb's unresponsive bureaucrats and ineffective police who ignored Dunwoody's concerns over higher-crime areas to the south ITP. Dunwoody was accused of siphoning off tax revenues, particularly from the lucrative Perimeter Mall, from other DeKalb County communities, and every argument seemed to be shaded by the issue of race. Dunwoody is 80 percent white while the rest of DeKalb County is a majority African American.

Incorporation ultimately prevailed—and a city and a police department were born in 2008. With incorporation came great promises of a better and safer Dunwoody. Now, after a few short seconds of gunfire, Dunwoody Prep had become that all-too-familiar American tableau: the school-shooting scene.

Dunwoody Prep promotes itself as a mini-Ivy, a first literal baby step to Harvard, promising "an environment where students are exposed to a rich balance of academic and social skills that afford them a bright future in an increasingly competitive world." Infants receive care in "small developmentally appropriate groups" with a "home-like atmosphere where babies are rocked, cuddled and surrounded by love." Toddlers then are nudged to "make the transition toward independence" and begin the "language experience" through creative movement, art, outdoor play, music, and singing. By age two, students "begin the preparation for the academic skills needed" to advance to the older levels. They develop "their individual self-help skills while promoting self-worth and self-esteem." By preschool—ages three to five—they're immersed in a dizzying array of experiences: math, "pre-reading and pre-writing activities," science, social science skills, art and music, computers, Spanish, sports, and "social and play skills."

The school assures parents that "the safety and security of our students and staff is something we take very seriously." It installed what the website calls a "state of the art security system" with "cameras monitoring every class-room, every entranceway, all of our playgrounds and all over the exterior of our buildings." Security locks protect every entrance.

Within minutes of the shooting, school staff scrambled to clear the premises. Parents receiving calls off their emergency cards converged on the school—or sent their nannies—to pick up their children. One of the few parents left by the time the media arrived was a woman named Natalia Kelly, who was interviewed by several stations while she carried her young child, who was wearing a paper hat. "The last place you'd think that a child may be in danger is at a school, especially a preschool," she told reporters. "There are children there that are only three months old. And the fact that any parent could just happen to have been dropping off their child in a car seat and could have been hit by accident, or a child on the playground. And so I don't understand even if this was intentional." Another parent, Katie Ackerman, told a TV reporter, "I was terrified to think that something could have happened to a child. It's very scary."

The Dunwoody Police Department whisked its public information officer to the school to offer what little investigators knew. Sergeant Mike Carlson said that shortly after 9 a.m. a bearded man opened fire with four shots on a parent dropping his son off at school, then fled in a silver minivan heading west on Mount Vernon Road. He stressed that no children were harmed. By evening, the victim was identified as Russell Sneiderman of Dunwoody.

Within hours, interviews with Rusty's friends and colleagues and a scan of social networking sites, online databases, and company and government websites produced a glowing biography. Rusty was by all accounts a successful man of business with a background in finance and insurance. Raised in the Cleveland area, educated as an undergraduate at the University of Indiana before pursing a graduate degree, he came to Dunwoody from Boston to take a position as the CFO of a large Atlanta company. He'd recently struck out on his own as an entrepreneur. He had no known enemies, no criminal record, was active in local charities and in the Jewish community. Nearly every media account took note that he possessed a Harvard MBA.

"It's like everybody lost a brother," a former schoolmate, Abby Stadlin, who attended kindergarten through high school with Rusty, told the *Cleveland Jewish News*. "Many of us have taken similar paths [in our lives], and we're all connected. That's why it's so shocking." Words like *kind*, *caring*, *professional*, *focused*, and *thoughtful* filled the early news reports. Rusty served on the boards of the Osteogenesis Imperfecta Foundation, a medical charity in Atlanta, and the Autism Society of America–Greater Atlanta. "For someone as young as him, that was unusual and impressive," ASAGA president Claire Dees told a reporter. "He definitely had a heart for other people." Ken Finkel, a former board president of the OI Foundation, added: "Some people walk into a room and carry themselves in such a manner that you know they are well educated, sharp, attuned and soak up information quickly. That was Rusty."

"None of this makes any sense," Rusty's friend Jonathan Ganz told the *Atlanta Journal-Constitution*. Another friend, Matt Davidson, who was Rusty's college roommate, added, "I can guarantee you no one would have predicted this was going to be the way his life would end."

The early speculation was that Rusty was the victim of some sort of hit. Casey Jordan, a criminologist and professor at Western Connecticut State University, told Pete Combs's radio show AM 750/95.5 FM News/Talk WSB not long after the incident that the shooting looked like "an organized hit"; the killer was either somebody who had a vendetta against Rusty or a shooter hired by somebody who did. Everything about the murder said professional assassin, she said, from the nondescript attire to stymie identification, to the getaway vehicle without plates, the firing of multiple shots to make sure the job was done, and the fact that the victim's luxury car was left at the scene. "This man took precautions to make sure he fit the description of thousands of people and thousands of cars," Jordan said.

The *Dunwoody Crier* also saw the possible work of a professional assassin. "The person who did this wanted this guy dead," a source told the paper, "and he made sure that he did the job." Publisher Dick Williams later said, "My personal theory was that it was a mob hit. I looked at Rusty's business background—he started a lot of companies, and I could see maybe some disgruntled investors could have been there. And look at the way it was done: the two shots at close range, the van engine still running, the guy jumps out of the van and bam! Bam!"

The crime scene offered few answers and little evidence: a dead body and four brass shell casings scattered on the blacktop near Rusty's car. This told police the shooter used a semiautomatic, either a .40 or a .44 caliber, but ballistics couldn't narrow it down to a make or model of gun, much less where or when it was purchased. If a murder weapon was ever found, the casings and slugs could be compared to make a positive ID. Rusty's car wasn't stolen.

Eyewitnesses all told a similar story: a man, a van, and a gun. Nobody caught a license plate number, and most believed the van didn't have plates. Nobody recognized the shooter though most agreed the beard looked fake. Security cameras trained on the parking lot captured the van entering and leaving but didn't show the actual shooting. The footage went to a private technician for analysis, but a quick viewing showed the same thing the witnesses had already described. The van had no license plates; the shooter's image was obscured through the vehicle windows. An alert went out for the van, but with Interstate 285 so close, the vehicle could be anywhere by now, either hundreds of miles away or blending in with thousands of family vans just like it in the Atlanta suburbs.

Shortly after 9 a.m., Detective Andrew Thompson of the Dunwoody Police Department heard the original radio call mistakenly alerting police to an incident at the bank. When word came across the radio that the getaway car was a silver van heading down Mount Vernon Road, he drove farther ahead and parked at an intersection in the hope of intercepting the suspect. But no silver vans appeared, and Thompson was relieved by police from neighboring Sandy Springs. He then went to Dunwoody Prep. His boss Sergeant Cortellino handed the case to Thompson, making him the lead detective, while Cortellino went to the impound lot where Rusty's car was being processed by crime-lab techs.

Previously an officer with the Atlanta Police Department for eight years, Thompson had only two years' experience as a detective, working narcotics, before coming to Dunwoody. This was his first turn as lead investigator for a homicide. He was pacing around the crime scene, getting the lay of the land, when he saw Andrea arrive. He didn't know her then but assumed she was close to the victim. He would recall her behavior as "very loud, very dramatic." Her mother and father later drove up and were about to go under the crime-scene tape when Thompson directed them inside the daycare center. "I told them that Rusty had been hurt," he would recall later in court. "That was the extent of what I told them." He hadn't spoken to Andrea, who by now was inside with Cortellino.

Thompson spoke briefly to the eyewitnesses—Craig Kuhlmeier, Aliyah Stotter, and Chris Lang—and the pediatrician, Terrence Gfroerer, who had attempted to resuscitate Rusty. He took down their contact information for longer follow-up interviews. He called in the crime-scene technicians to take measurements, photograph the scene, and collect evidence. Rusty had few personal effects when he died—an envelope in his jacket, a wedding ring, and a watch. Nobody could find his wallet. The witnesses hadn't seen the gunman take the wallet—the presumption was Rusty had raced out to drop off his son and perhaps go to the post office and had simply forgotten it.

A call to another detective at the Atlanta Medical Center confirmed that Rusty had arrived in grave condition. After spending an hour at the crime scene, Thompson made the half-hour drive south to the hospital. In the family waiting room he met Andrea and her family—her parents and her brother Todd. By now they had been notified of Rusty's death and appeared in no condition to speak to police. Thompson asked Andrea a couple of questions, seeking any information to tell him where to begin the investigation. She said only that Rusty had planned to have a lunch meeting with his partner in a business venture. She gave Thompson the partner's name.

Thompson returned to the Dunwoody Police Department and drew up two search warrants, one for Rusty's car, the other for his house.

It was dark when Thompson and Cortellino pulled up to the Sneiderman house on Manget Court. The Sneidermans lived on a cul-de-sac in a nine-hundred-thousand-dollar house that a Realtor would later describe as an "impeccable luxury home in a great Dunwoody neighborhood." It sat on a half-acre wooded lot against a forest traversed by walking paths. When they rang the doorbell, a couple who identified themselves as Andrea's parents opened the door. Thompson told them he had a search warrant and wanted to come in.

"We are a house in mourning," said Andrea's mother. Andrea's father told them they couldn't come in, according to Thompson.

Thompson told him that police had a warrant and to get out of the way or go to jail for obstruction when Sergeant Cortellino interjected. Cortellino said they would come back tomorrow. In the paramilitary culture of police departments, a detective on his first murder case would never argue with a supervising sergeant. Thompson would later leave little doubt that he disagreed with the gentle handling of the family.

"I don't normally tell them I'm coming out to serve a search warrant to preserve the integrity of the case," he said later in court. "If you give a person notification, [it] gives them the opportunity to destroy or hide or move the evidence." (Later, Cortellino would say he didn't remember going to the house at all that night; he also said they never had a warrant until the next day.)

Dunwoody has a special relationship between its citizens and police, one born from the founding aspirations of the city. Under DeKalb County rule, Dunwoody residents complained about what they saw as a law enforcement agency distracted by higher-crime areas to the south. A Dunwoody resident reporting a burglary or stolen car radio could wait an average of seventeen minutes or more for a patrol car, if one showed up at all. Many reports were taken over the phone. Paying more taxes than others in DeKalb County, Dunwoody residents found this unacceptable, and after incorporation made the police department the centerpiece of the city plan. More than a third of the initial fourteen-million-dollar budget went toward a department with thirty-five sworn officers and five civilian assistants and technicians. "We are committed to developing a top-notch Police Department that interacts daily with the residents and businesses of Dunwoody," the newly hired chief of police, Billy Grogan, said at the time, according to a report in the *Atlanta Journal-Constitution*. "People need to see police cars out there."

The former deputy chief in Marietta, Grogan was a perfect fit for Dunwoody. Even-tempered and politically astute, he worked well with the new city council and business community. He had his pick of officers and his selections won praise from the locals—among them many officer-of-the-year recipients and veteran cops who had avoided any taint of the scandals that seemed to plague Atlanta-area departments. The Dunwoody jobs paid better, the department had the best and latest equipment, the cops could take their official cars home. The department was housed in a nondescript office building with dark-tinted windows in an office park hidden among the pines, not far from the Perimeter Mall. Even after the department's performance in the Sneiderman case would raise questions, the town's newspaper publisher, Dick Williams, says support remained high at home. "I think people in Dunwoody were pretty certain of this: They loved their cops."

The next day, Thompson and Cortellino again rang the doorbell at the Sneiderman house in the late afternoon or early evening on November 19, 2010, a copy of the search warrant in hand. The detectives were welcomed into the dining room, where they took their seats at a long table. The house was spacious and modern. It had five bedrooms, four bathrooms, walk-in closets, a sitting room, fireplace, gourmet kitchen, deck off the back porch, and three-car garage with a remote-operated door. Andrea was at the table, along with her parents, Bonita and Herbert Greenberg, Rusty's mother and father and, in time, Rusty's brother, Steven. A tape recording of the interview picks up more voices in the background. Andrea and Rusty's children would be heard on the tape; at one point, the interview would be interrupted by Ian crying and Sophia saying she was going to take him for a walk.

The detectives later said they wanted to build rapport with the family, gather information about the case, and search Rusty's computer and other belongings. Throughout, the detectives would treat them with deference. "Part of my job for this interview is I need to get to know you and your family, like a relative," Thompson said at one point. "Your family," he went on, "is a very prominent family." He called them "very well known" and assured them he had no doubts that he'd find evidence that Rusty was, as Andrea and the rest of the family insisted, "very well liked."

The problem, Thompson was trying to impress upon the Greenbergs and Sneidermans—people unaccustomed to dealing with police or crime—was that not everybody might be inclined to view Rusty and his family so positively. "When it comes time to make an arrest, a defense attorney is going to want to paint a very bad picture about his life," Thompson said, "and we want to be able to counter anything he has to say."

For the next two hours, the detectives got to know the Sneiderman family—and its secrets.

She was born Andrea Greenberg and grew up with her brother, Todd, in the northern Ohio city of Sylvania. A bright student with an aptitude for math and science, she went to the University of Indiana in Bloomington, majoring in computer information systems and technology. In September 1994, she visited the campus's Hillel chapter, the "Jewish home away from home" as the Helene G. Simon Hillel Center calls itself, with a big-screen TV, pool table, gym, and, according to its website, "lots of comfortable couches to relax on," plus an "open refrigerator policy for students to grab a snack or a to-go box." The Hillel offered a weekend retreat twice a year. "It's just a time for the Jewish kids to get away," Andrea would later say. There were activities, religious services, and socializing with other students. She started talking to a junior named Rusty Sneiderman whom she'd seen before on campus but hadn't spoken to until now. Rusty asked her about her sweater—it had the logo of the summer camp she had gone to with her brother, Todd, for years. Rusty had a friend who also went.

Later that evening, with the retreat over, Rusty called Andrea. They went out together for the first time that same night.

The son of an accountant, Russell Sneiderman was, like Andrea, from a close-knit Jewish family in northern Ohio, just 125 miles to the east of Sylvania, in Cleveland. An overachiever still well remembered at Beachwood High School, Rusty served as the editor of the school newspaper and played on the golf team. His good-bye column his senior year, reprinted in full after his murder more than fifteen years later, revealed the traits that would later serve him well in business: He was self-deprecating, charming, funny, optimistic. He reminisced about his hapless freshman year in which his locker was "already assigned to a very popular senior girl who was not interested in a 'four-eyed' freshman," his golf team won only a single match, and he got the three hardest teachers three periods in a row. He joked about speaking before a thousand people at the North American Invitational Model United Nations only to have a stink bomb go off ("My partner, from the class of '91, said, 'Maybe it was just your breath' ") and how he finally got his groove by his junior year. "I had figured out how to get good grades without working too hard and could devote my remaining time to after-school activities," he wrote.

Both bright and ambitious, the young couple explored the quaint towns surrounding the university, Rusty's obituary would say, and soon found they shared a family history—their grandparents on both sides had founded the same synagogue in Florida.

Rusty graduated in 1996 and returned home to Cleveland to work at an accounting firm; Andrea followed him there for the summer after her junior year, living in an apartment and visiting Rusty and his parents frequently. Donald and Marilyn Sneiderman were fond of their son's girlfriend, and Donald later remarked that they seemed very much in love. For the next two years, they had a long-distance relationship. When they weren't putting thousands of miles on their cars going back and forth between Cleveland and Bloomington, the technologically savvy couple used early incarnations of social networking sites and experimented with a videoconferencing precursor to Skype—"not an inexpensive thing at the time," Andrea would recall.

After Andrea graduated in 1998, they found a small apartment in Chicago, both working at Deloitte Consulting, which helps businesses improve management practices and technology. Andrea's parents frowned on them living together before marriage but Andrea was certain it was only a matter of time before they were husband and wife. "I wasn't going to move in with him unless I knew we were getting married," she later said. At Deloitte they worked in different divisions of the company, Andrea in technology, Rusty in finance. "The stock market was doing well then," she said and Rusty set aside money regularly in what they called their "ring fund," watching it grow until it reached the right amount. Andrea picked out a design for an engagement ring and Rusty ordered it. The only surprise for her was when it would happen and how the ring would turn out. She found out when Rusty proposed in 2000 while they vacationed at a resort in Laguna Niguel in Orange County, California.

Over the next hectic months they planned a wedding while Rusty applied to business schools. In rapid succession, Harvard Business School accepted him, and on December 30, 2000, they tied the knot in a ceremony in that same Florida synagogue co-founded by their grandparents. The newlyweds settled into an even smaller apartment in Boston—the closet was so tiny they couldn't use hangers—while Rusty attended business school and Andrea worked at a struggling start-up company. When the company went under, Rusty found a posting for a job at the business school in the information technology department. Andrea was hired as a liaison between the technical people who wrote the software and the Harvard professors and faculty who used it. She saw Rusty every day, and they socialized with his classmates.

Andrea was in the midst of a major project when Rusty, after graduation, got offered a business development position for Siebel Systems' offices in Atlanta. He had worked previously in wealth management and insurance in Boston but, wanting a less expensive place to live and more house for their money for when they had children, the couple agreed he should take the position. After three months in a comfortable company apartment at the San Mateo, California, headquarters while Rusty trained, they moved to Smyrna, Georgia, northwest of Atlanta, into a neighborhood with other young couples who would become their longtime friends. Andrea telecommuted from her home for her job with the Harvard Business School, traveling to Boston about once a month for meetings. She later became an independent contractor for the business school's publishing unit, billing hourly.

After their first child, daughter Sophia, was born in August 2005, the Sneidermans sought a new neighborhood with better public schools. They found it in Dunwoody. Rusty would move to another company, this time doing wealth management at J. P. Morgan in Atlanta. Their two incomes and savings got them a nine-hundred-thousand-dollar house on a quiet cul-de-sac. As members of the Congregation Or Hadash synagogue, they were active in Atlanta's Jewish community. Dunwoody was home to the new site of the Marcus Jewish Community Center—named after its major donor, Home Depot co-founder Bernard Marcus. Sophia would be enrolled in Dunwoody Prep preschool, and when son Ian was born in October 2007 he stayed home with Andrea while she worked out of the home. The Sneidermans made extra payments on their home to build equity and earned enough to buy a second house on Lake Oconee, in Eatonton, Georgia, an hour-and-a-half drive away, where they spent weekends boating and waterskiing with family and friends.

Their lives as busy young professionals with small children were not always easy. As the country sank into a recession, Harvard had less work for contractors like Andrea. Soon her remaining duties—developing online courses—dwindled. Then in late 2007, Rusty was laid off from J. P. Morgan, a victim of the hit on financial institutions. Property values throughout the Atlanta region plunged, including the mini-mansions of Dunwoody, where some residents found themselves owing more than their houses were worth. Unemployment inched up, and so did crime. This was when Dunwoody's drive to break away from DeKalb County built steam. The Sneidermans now had two mortgages and two children and neither Andrea nor Rusty had a full-time job. But they had time and resources.

"We're savers, always have been," Andrea later explained. "Whenever everyone else was going out to fancy dinners we were eating peanut butter and jelly at home so we saved our money. We had a lot of money saved up in the bank. I worked many successful jobs myself, Rusty has made a lot of money over the years. We saved it. Our financial situation was just fine. We work and live based on what we earn. That's our style of living. We don't live beyond our means. So the times Rusty was unemployed, I was always making consulting income at that time or he himself was making consulting income."

Even during the worst of the recession they had nearly a million dollars in the bank in cash and retirement accounts. Characteristically self-confident, Rusty set out to find another job without having to settle for the first opportunity that came along. He explored several ventures— businesses he could purchase or start up—but none panned out. He eventually took another salaried position, this time as chief financial officer for Discovery Point Child Development Centers, a daycare chain based in Duluth, Georgia—fifteen miles from Dunwoody—with schools in Georgia, Tennessee, and Florida (Dunwoody Prep was not part of the chain).

Almost immediately, Rusty clashed with the owner. His days at Discovery Point seemed numbered. By late 2009, with Rusty on the brink of unemployment and Andrea's contract work with Harvard petering out, she ventured into the job market. She commiserated with a friend, the wife of one of Rusty's college roommates who was trying to return to the work world after having children. She led Andrea to a woman in her book club named Ariela Neuman who was married to a top-level manager at GE Energy in the same technical/computer field as Andrea. Andrea didn't know Ariela or her husband, Hemy Neuman, but they had mutual acquaintances. Andrea's friend got Hemy's contact information, and Andrea sent him a résumé.

After an interview Hemy hired Andrea in March 2010 as a quality systems manager in the product creation department. The engineering teams developed complex integrated systems in the aerospace, healthcare, and energy industries. Job descriptions were so technical that a person unschooled in technology and engineering would struggle to understand what anybody even did at GE Energy. But for Andrea it meant a solid job in a rough economy, full benefits, and a salary of $125,000 a year.

She was to report to work in April. That same week, Rusty was fired from Discovery Point. "I asked him to quit Discovery Point," Andrea would later say. "We realized that it was really just making him unhappy to work for other people and he really was an entrepreneur in spirit and needed to do it on his own." Rusty seized the moment with characteristic enthusiasm, putting his schmoozing skills to work to strike out on his own as an entrepreneur. "He was probably the best networker that this city has ever seen," Andrea would say.

Rusty finally had the freedom to fulfill his dream of building a company that he could pass on to his children. Meetings were held and funding was sought. He explored buying a company that installed radios in police cars, but his group's offer came in too low for the sellers. Then at a party he met a man with an idea for a voice-mail service with a celebrity twist. In a filing with the Georgia Secretary of State, Rusty named the business Star Voicemail and described it as a service providing "custom voicemail greetings featuring notable sports, movie, music and TV personalities. He registered a domain name and began building a website. Andrea helped with the technical side and became one of its most enthusiastic supporters.

"Imagine if you were to call someone else's phone who didn't answer," she would later say. "Instead of saying, 'Hi, this is Susie'—and if Susie was fifteen, you heard, 'Hi, this is Justin Bieber. Susie is out with me shopping. She can't get to you right now, but, hey, have a great day.' So it's Justin Bieber's voice for example, saying Susie's name." Software programs made it possible for a celeb's voice to utter any number of names, and the service would be sold as an app with a celebrity menu. "So you could purchase the George Clooney or the Justin Bieber or whomever your favorite star was and that person was giving a quippy message," Andrea would say. "It's their voice instead of yours. That's the business."

The start-up showed promise. Meetings were held with investors. They got interest from Bieber's manager. But with Andrea now holding down a full-time office job, Rusty had taken over the bulk of the childcare duties. "It was a difficult transition," Andrea would acknowledge. At times Rusty "would be annoyed with the situation," she said, particularly when home life cut into the time he wanted to spend on the voice-mail start-up. Complicating things were Andrea's unexpected travel demands for GE. "That was an issue of mine when I took the job," Andrea later said. "I didn't want to be away from home very often so we came to an agreement that it would only be about 20 percent of my job. It turned out to be more than that. But it was pointed out to me that I should visit all of the sites that I manage and that it was important for me to meet the people in those locations and for some reason it was important for me to do it soon." Within days she was on the road, and her travel schedule would call for one trip a month on average.

When she wasn't on the road or staying late at the office, she had to take work home with her. Rusty saw the demands on Andrea and began to feel guilty. "He was supportive of me working," she would later say, "but he didn't want me to feel the pressure to work." Out of the tension came a solution. They hired a part-time nanny to give Rusty more time for work. Andrea became the "science parent" at Sophia's elementary school. They played softball in a cystic fibrosis fund-raiser. They traveled with the children to Washington, DC, for the ninety-fifth birthday party for Rusty's grandmother; then Rusty and Andrea left the kids with relatives and the two of them took a five-day cruise, returning on November 15. Rusty's parents planned to spend Thanksgiving with them in Dunwoody, and the six of them were to travel to Disney World in March. "They had a happy, hectic life," a lawyer for Andrea would later claim. "They were enjoying each other. They were enjoying their kids. It all came crashing down on November 18, 2010."

Most of these details came out in Andrea's interviews with police, some later, but the story represents the substance and tone that emerged in the days after the murder. The Sneidermans looked like just about any other two-salary couple in Dunwoody, their challenges shared by thousands of families in every subdivision Outside the Perimeter. As the media had reported, nothing on the surface suggested why Rusty would be targeted for murder.

Thompson asked Andrea if anything unusual had happened recently. Minutes into the interview, she pointed to two events that had left her and Rusty shaken. The first occurred a month earlier on October 20 when she was upstairs at home with Rusty and heard the garage door open.

"I panicked," she said. "I screamed that the garage door opened, somebody opened the door."

They called 911 and a Dunwoody police officer took a report. Nothing had been stolen, and it didn't appear that anybody had entered the garage or house. Police suggested that it may have been a technical glitch—somebody with

the same garage remote code activating the Sneidermans'
opener by mistake.

Three weeks later they got a second scare. Around 8:30
a.m., on Wednesday, November 10, Rusty was getting ready
to take Ian to Dunwoody Prep when he thought he smelled
gas. Walking around to the side of the house to check the
meter, Rusty saw a man lying facedown on the ground near
the air-conditioning unit.

"He thought he was sleeping," Andrea told Thompson
and Cortellino. "But then the person stood up, and Rusty
asked him some questions. One, he asked this person, 'Are
you okay?' And two, 'Are you supposed to be here?' Like
he would ask a two-year-old. There was no response. Rusty
got smart, ran into the car in the garage, backed up the
driveway into the street, and called 911."

Andrea was at her desk at GE at the time, having
dropped off Sophia at the elementary school on the way
to work. Recounting what Rusty later told her, she said that
the man appeared to be Hispanic. The man fled across
the lawn and into the woods behind the house. As he
ran, he held something in the small of his back. Rusty
didn't see it but feared it was a gun.

Their concern was deepened by the fact that the man
seemed to know the layout of their property. Had the man
run down the other side of the house, he would have plunged
into a deep gully. Instead, he went toward a pathway so
secluded that only people who lived there knew it existed.
Rusty later took Ian to daycare and returned to talk to police and firefighters who had come to make sure there was
no danger from the leak. Gas had in fact been released,
though it appeared to a gas company employee that the meter had only been falling apart through age and manufac-
turing defect and not from tampering.

"The gas guy, when Rusty told his story, said the [man]

was probably not just looking for a place to sleep but was stealing copper," Andrea said.

Thompson asked if her neighbors had a similar problem with a suspicious person.

"The neighbors didn't even know it happened," Andrea said. "I don't talk to these neighbors. I'm not a chatty individual. I didn't go out that night and say, 'Guess what happened.'"

Assuring Andrea that he'd follow up on the reports, Thompson next asked Andrea about Rusty's business dealings.

"From what I understand Rusty decided to stop working for a paycheck so he could focus solely on getting his own business started?"

"That's not what happened," Andrea said. "Rusty was fired from his last job."

"Which job was that?"

"He worked at Discovery Point."

"What was he fired for?"

"The bosses were assholes," said Andrea. She spoke at length about Rusty's rocky stint at Discovery Point—how the owners didn't appreciate his ideas, how he clashed with them over the future of the company, how the bosses came to distrust Rusty. He was let go in April but able to collect unemployment. Thompson took down the names of the bosses and other contacts at Discovery Point. Andrea portrayed the firing as a blessing in disguise.

"He finally agreed he can't work for anybody else," she said. "He's the kind of guy who needs to do it for himself. He's tried many times to work for companies and it's never really worked out for him."

Rusty spent the next several months looking for a business to buy, including the police radio company deal, before plunging himself into the Star Voicemail project.

Andrea spoke about the project, saying it had the usual fits and starts. One potential investor didn't work out, and Rusty and his business partner were pursuing other money sources. Rusty and his primary partner also parted ways with another partner.

As Andrea appeared frustrated at the extent of the questions, Cortellino said, "We're going in every direction we possibly can."

"I want you to do that," Andrea said, "but I want you to understand where I'm coming from and this is: I think you're barking up the wrong tree. The people that Rusty deals with and the way we do business is not what you're thinking, it's not what maybe the movies have in it, or all this other shit is."

Instead, she reminded them of "this Mexican," as Andrea described the man whom Rusty saw behind the house. "This man on the side of my house, yes, I could see that man wanting to kill Rusty because he saw his face and he was worried that he might get in trouble. I can see that. That makes sense to me," she said. "Do you understand? I have no problem with you looking into all this [business]. That's lovely. You want to ask fifty people looking into our business dealings, great. It kind of makes me feel better. Rusty has done such great work."

"We're going to look into that," said Cortellino.

"I see you sitting there," Andrea continued, "and I want to help you, but I want to know that that other thing is being investigated with the same amount of—"

"Energy?" offered Cortellino.

"Energy," Andrea agreed, "because if you're not then I think you're barking up the wrong tree and you're wasting time. So you understand where I'm coming from?"

Thompson said, "Yes, absolutely." He told her that "everything is being done at the same time" in the investigation and warned her against drawing conclusions based on their questions. It was at this point that Thompson spoke of how her family was prominent and how he wanted to get to know them to thwart a smear by a defense attorney later on. He assured her another detective was well positioned to follow up on the mysterious man lead.

"Our gang officer knows a lot of good snitches . . . He's going to help out with anything with the Hispanic side of it."

Andrea repeated that the man "had to know" the neighborhood, had to "have been here before." She suggested it may have been a construction worker from a project on a house behind theirs. Thompson said her information was helpful and he'd pass it on to the gang officer, then asked her more about Rusty's businesses. They talked more about his wealth management jobs, Discovery Point, and Star Voicemail.

"Is there anybody in Rusty's past that you could imagine would want to do this to Rusty?" Thompson asked. As Andrea paused, he added, "Even if you can't imagine that person doing it himself or hiring someone?"

"I understand," she said.

"He had a lot of wealthy clients—someone with that kind of money?"

"I understand, but Rusty had the best relationships with all of these wealthy people he's worked with. Really, I can't think of one person. I will definitely think about it, but there's not one—not one—person that comes to mind that could—in his life—that he's ever rubbed the wrong way like that."

As Thompson asked who would know about Rusty's daily routine, Andrea drew a blank. In the background, a family member said, "We do," but nobody else came to mind. Then her phone rang.

"By the way, this is my Baco exterminating guy," she said reading the number. "He comes into my house fre-

quently, sprays for bugs. I mean I love him, he's actually
great, but I'm telling you that he knows our schedule."

Thompson spoke on the phone with the exterminator
and set up a time to talk to him before hanging up.

They were more than an hour into the interview when
Thompson broached a subject he had stayed away from because of its sensitivity. The group at the table had now
grown to include Rusty's brother, Steven, a civil lawyer
from Ohio. The voices of children and adults could still
be heard in the background.

Thompson asked, "Has there been anybody recently,
and when I say recently, within the past year, that has expressed interest in you?"

"Yes," she said without hesitation.

"Who?"

"My boss."

"Your boss?"

"Yes."

"What's his name?"

"Hemy," she said, and she began to cry.

"How do you spell it?"

She spelled his name and Thompson asked, "You know
what his last name is?"

"Neuman," she said, and spelled that.

"How old is he?"

"Forty-six. I have no idea. In his late forties."

"What does he look like?"

"Shortish," she said. "Todd's height." She gestured to
her brother, who gave his height.

"How much did he weigh? Is he fat or is he thin? Is he
healthy looking?"

"Todd's size," she said.

"Does he have white hair, black hair?"

"Gray and black."

"Is he balding?"

"No."

"Does he wear glasses?"

"Yes."

"Is there anything real distinctive about him?" She shook her head. "No? Now, how is he trying to—"

"He expressed his feelings for me," she said.

"Has it been as a flirtation or has he specifically said: 'I'm interested in you'?"

"He specifically said that, yes."

As Andrea became upset, Cortellino asked, "You want to continue in private?"

"No," she said. "It's fine. Go ahead."

"Has there been anybody else?" asked Thompson.

"No."

"Has there been anybody that's been interested in Rusty in the same way?"

"I don't think so."

"You don't think so," Thompson said. "Okay, anything else to add?"

Andrea's mother said, "You didn't ask if that was reciprocated?"

"Was it reciprocated?" asked Thompson.

In a quiet voice barely audible above the household din, Andrea said, "I made it clear that I am not an individual that would do something like this."

After Andrea gave Hemy's title as an operations manager, her mother added, "I just want to explain that she [was] one of the only females amongst a group of males."

"That's not necessarily true," Andrea told her mother, appearing embarrassed by her interjection.

Her mother continued, "She's conducted herself aboveboard. She's extremely professional."

The detectives looked at the woman questioningly.

"This is Andrea's mother," she said, identifying herself

for the tape recorder. "I just need for you to know that as soon as that happened she said that to me. She said: 'I made it very clear to him that I wasn't interested in him, that this wasn't going to go anywhere.'"

Cortellino asked, "You knew about this?"

"I'm close," said Andrea's mother. "She said, 'I'm going to handle this.' What are you going to do? Go to someone in HR?"

A man's voice, apparently that of Andrea's father, said, "We don't need to talk about it as a family now, okay?"

Her mother continued, "She was just a professional."

"I'm not judging," her father said.

Thompson made a mental note to continue this line of questioning in a follow-up, one-on-one interview with Andrea at the police station later.

Thompson and Cortellino segued to the search warrants. The detectives were authorized by the courts to seize the family's computer and personal and financial papers. Andrea's mother became particularly animated about it, as did Andrea. They worried about losing the computer and everything on it, including family pictures. They acknowledged that overnight they had already taken some pictures off the hard drive. The detectives said this would be a problem—one that that could be exploited by a defense attorney—and told them they'd have to sign a document saying that the photos were the only things removed.

Rusty's attorney brother joined in the discussion, saying that while he wasn't a criminal lawyer he remembered from his law school classes that the search warrant did provide the power to take everything listed in it even over the objections of the owners. He suggested that the best course of action was for the family to cooperate. They grudgingly agreed, and the house was searched. As the detectives went through the couple's papers in the upstairs office, they found a document that Donald Sneiderman—as the family accountant—recognized. It was for Rusty's life insurance policy in the amount of nearly two million dollars, payable to his beneficiary, Andrea.

When her father, Herbert, saw the bill, he told Donald that Andrea had no idea Rusty was insured for that much.

CHAPTER 3

Arlington Memorial Park covers over a hundred acres of rolling hills, nearly a century old and catering to all faiths, with Catholic and Jewish sections. With forested areas, two lakes, and streams, the cemetery is located just off Mount Vernon Road in Sandy Springs, next to Dunwoody. On Sunday, November 21, the casket was lowered into the rich Atlanta soil. Per Jewish custom, mourners took turns shoveling dirt onto the casket, a final sign of respect, though it's not for everybody. "I can't do it," Rusty's father would later say, "because I don't have the stomach for it." He certainly couldn't do it this day. He watched as others dropped dirt on his son's coffin.

For Donald Sneiderman, the last three days had brought a torrent of emotional upheaval, the events blurred. At the funeral, Donald would shake hands, accept offers of condolences, meet friends and business associates of his son, all the while remembering little if any of it in detail. The nightmare had begun that previous Thursday morning with a phone call to his Cleveland home from Andrea at about 9:30 a.m. "She called and said Rusty had been shot," he would later recall in court. "She was so, so sorry, and . . . she was going to Dunwoody Prep to find out what had happened."

For the next fifteen to twenty minutes, Donald and his wife had waited anxiously for an update from Andrea. Finally, Donald called Dunwoody Prep. "I identified myself and asked them again what had happened, and the lady who answered the phone there said Rusty had been shot." Donald was told that Rusty had been taken to the Atlanta Medical Center. Donald sent an email to Rusty's older brother, Steven, who was traveling to Hawaii for vacation. Donald figured Steven's BlackBerry would pick up the message faster than a phone call since he was in transit.

"Rusty was shot outside Dunwoody Prep this morning," Donald wrote. "We don't know the details at this time other than he was shot." He sent the message at 10:38 a.m., ending with: "I don't know what else to tell you."

Donald waited a few minutes for Rusty to arrive at the hospital, and then called. He spoke to a physician who at first wouldn't tell him anything, but then got permission—Donald presumed it was from Andrea. The doctor told him Rusty had arrived with multiple gunshot wounds, that he had not survived.

Numb, Donald sent another email to Steven at 11:06 a.m.: "Rusty passed away this morning. Don't know anything else."

Plunged into a fog of shock, Donald and his wife made arrangements to go to Atlanta. He called a friend asking to pick up the mail. He called to cancel newspaper delivery. He sent an email to his brother, a teacher, telling him

Rusty had died. In the middle of everything his stockbroker had called. An emotional Donald hung up on him when the stockbroker was in midsentence. Donald called back later to apologize.

At one point, Andrea called him asking for permission to bury Rusty in Atlanta so she and the children could visit the grave. Donald said that would be okay.

When they first heard something had happened to Rusty, Donald and his wife started packing. Now they repacked to include funeral clothes.

They took an afternoon flight to Atlanta, rented a car and drove to Andrea and Rusty's house in Dunwoody, and stayed there for a time with Andrea and the children before checking into the Marriott Perimeter Center, where Steven's wife, Lisa, had made a reservation. The next day they returned to the house for the police interview and search. Steven canceled his Hawaiian vacation and flew back with his wife to Atlanta.

Jewish tradition calls for the body to be buried quickly—but the police investigation trumped tradition. Rusty's body was released to the funeral home within days and Donald placed funeral notices in the *Atlanta Journal-Constitution*, the *Cleveland Plain Dealer*, and the *Cleveland Jewish News*. The notices said that Rusty Sneiderman, a "devoted and loving husband, father, son and loyal friend," had "died unexpectedly." The obituary cited his educational and professional accomplishments and charity work. It noted that he was an entrepreneur "in the process of developing a new product for the entertainment industry." Mourners were asked in lieu of flowers to send donations to the Cystic Fibrosis Foundation. "Rusty was known for his big heart, and large circle of friends," it said. "We miss him dearly."

His death sent shock waves through the Jewish communities in Atlanta and Cleveland. His murder garnered regular coverage in Jewish publications and become a hot topic of discussion on message boards. Remembrances flooded an online guest book for the funeral. A Harvard Business School classmate remembered Rusty as "being a happy, upbeat, friendly, thoughtful contributor to the school experience." A family friend described him as a "wonderful(!!) man with a huge warm smile and caring heart" and said his children would always feel their father's love. One of Sophia's teachers wrote that the child was "a living reminder of the great and powerful caring force" of Rusty and Andrea.

Even those who didn't know Rusty personally were moved by his death. "Please know that you are in my thoughts and that there are people in the Jewish community who are in grief with you," said one post from the Hillel at the University of Texas at San Antonio. "May you be consoled with the other mourners of Zion and may Rusty's memory be a blessing for our People and society at-large."

The funeral began at 11 a.m. Two rabbis, Rabbi Bortz and Rabbi Mario Karpuj, spoke to a crowd of hundreds. Several of Andrea's co-workers came in carpools arranged by her boss Hemy, who had previously explained to the non-Jewish employees the customs and traditions at a Jewish funeral. Hemy was among those who shoveled dirt onto the coffin. Mourners then gathered at the Sneidermans' house to sit shiva, the period of mourning that can last several days. People brought food and offered condolences. Hemy introduced himself to family members, including Rusty's brother Steven, and spoke to Rusty's father. "My wife introduced him to me," Donald Sneiderman later recalled. "I talked to him for about thirty seconds. I recognized the name . . . It was about thirty seconds or so." The family asked Hemy to sit up front and say a prayer, which he did. He shook hands and embraced mourners.

Like Donald, a dazed Andrea would only recall some

of the day's events. Although a shiva is supposed to be a solemn and quiet affair—people are expected to speak in low tones—a house packed full of people and two confused children made for a more chaotic reality. "My children were running around like Indians during that time," Andrea would later say in court, "not really sure what five thousand people were doing in their house. They were being cared for by most of my cousins and family and not being distracting." She vaguely recalled Hemy being there, but didn't know how long. Andrea described the days after her husband's murder as being one long blur of activity and crowds and little time to properly grieve, much less process the surreal notion that she was in the middle of a murder case. "I was," she later said, "in a fairly catatonic state."

Rusty's brother, Steven, and Steven's wife, Lisa, spent time with Andrea and other relatives, sharing memories of Rusty as they went through old photo albums showing pictures of Rusty and Andrea when they were dating, their honeymoon, and the arrival of their children. Lisa described Rusty to the *Cleveland Jewish News* as "Harvard-educated, brilliant, very caring and loving and super-ethical," and said, "He's not the kind of person who ever got in any trouble, even as a kid."

The day of the funeral, while everybody was at the cemetery, police searched the Sneiderman house again, still trying to find Rusty's wallet. Andrea said he sometimes kept it tucked away in places she didn't know about. Instead of obtaining another search warrant, Thompson reached an agreement with Andrea that the search would be conducted while everybody was away to avoid disruption. A neighbor was assigned to monitor police to ensure that nothing that Andrea deemed inappropriate was taken. "Andrea set the ground rules," Thompson later said.

The department was eager to keep relations with Andrea good and lines of communication open. But it wasn't an ideal way to operate. With Thompson and Cortellino turned away from the house the first night, then given resistance the next night about taking the computer, "It did not arouse my suspicions," Thompson later recalled. "It irritated me that they weren't cooperating."

CHAPTER 4

"There's a man who was sleeping in my backyard," Rusty Sneiderman was heard telling the emergency operator. "He's running. I think he has a gun in his back pocket and now he's running away. I don't know who the hell he is and I don't want him by my house."

This was a recording of the 911 call Rusty placed on November 10 after he stumbled on the man on the side of his house. As promised, police followed up on Andrea's suspicions that this incident may have been linked to Rusty's murder. Detective Thompson not only reviewed a police report but listened to what in all likelihood was the last time Rusty's voice would be recorded. It was touched with fear.

"This is a house, you said?" asked the operator.

"The house," Rusty replied.

"What did he look like? Was he black? White? Hispanic?"

"He looked Hispanic with a mustache. He was wearing a hat and earmuffs, black mustache. I walked around the side of my house this morning—"

"What sort of shirt and pants did he have on?"

"Jeans and it looked like a gray jacket. He's running now. He ran past Manza Court down the hill towards—I don't know what the name of the street behind us is. Hold on, I can tell ya. He looked like he was drunk and passed out. He's running towards Valley View Court."

"You can still see him right now?"

"No, he just ran off into the bushes. I'm in the car right with my son. He's two—".

"When did you last see him?"

"Twenty seconds ago."

"Okay, did you see a gun?"

"No but he was holding the small of his back just above his pants and I don't know if it's a gun or what, but I think it's unusual to be running away from something holding on to that. But it scared the hell out of me. I walk around the side of the house, there's some guy laying there sleeping on the side."

In the background Ian can be heard crying.

"I know, bud," Rusty comforted him. "I didn't get your water bottle. I'm sorry."

"Okay," said the emergency operator, "we'll get an officer out there as soon as possible. What's your last name?"

"Sneiderman." Rusty then spelled it. "Should I stay here? I'm in my car."

"It's up to you if you want to stay and make a report. If not, they'll post an officer in that area to check on the subject."

"Well, I want to make a report because we had a problem." This was a reference, Thompson knew from Andrea, to the October 20 call about his garage door being opened.

"Just stay there and a Dunwoody officer will be out there with you," the operator said. "Are you still at home now?"

"I'm in front of my house right now in a silver car waiting."

"A silver what?"

"A silver four-door Infiniti."

Impatience now crept into Rusty's voice. "I'm in a cul-de-sac. I'm the only car on the street, ma'am."

After reviewing the police report and the recording, Thompson canvassed the neighborhood asking if anybody else had seen the man. Thompson walked the path through the woods that the man had apparently used. He spoke to people at the construction site. But nobody else had seen the man or anything else unusual around that time. The lead seemed to be a dead end, one of what would be many in the early days of the investigation.

But the possibility that Rusty's killer may have been somebody familiar with his house—and probably Rusty's routine—still had credence. Lawrence Minogue, a Dunwoody resident, heard about the shooting on 680 The Fan, Atlanta's sports radio station, on his car radio at about 1 p.m. on November 18. He called police to report he had seen the silver van mentioned in the news report at about 8:15 a.m. that morning in front of the school as he dropped off his son. Minogue didn't believe the van belonged to a parent because it had no car seat. He thought it might have been a delivery van. The driver appeared to be in his mid- to late thirties of Middle Eastern descent with a bushy beard so jet black that it had to be fake and what appeared to be short hair sticking out of the hood of a sweater. The van pulled out of the parking lot and turned onto Mount Vernon Road.

A few minutes later, another witness, Jack Gay, who lived on Manget Court near Rusty's house, was taking his recycling can to the curb when he saw the silver minivan. It was around 8:30 a.m., he guessed. The van barreled toward him well past the twenty-five-miles-per-hour speed limit, then slowed down as it neared, the driver turning and facing him for three to five seconds. From about twenty-five feet away, Gay saw what he described as a dark-complexioned man, either Latino or Middle Eastern but not black or Asian, clean-shaven and wearing a hooded sweatshirt. The van then left the neighborhood more slowly, going toward Chamblee Dunwoody Road in the direction of the preschool, where within minutes the security video would again pick it up following Rusty's car into the parking lot.

The day after the shooting, Minogue went to the Dunwoody Police Station and worked with artist Marla Lawson to draw a sketch of the man who may appeared to have been staking out Rusty's house before the murder. Lawson—who got her professional start by drawing Atlanta subway commuters in early 1970s—would create police sketches in a number of high-profile cases for local agencies and the Georgia Bureau of Investigation. Of the hundreds of pictures of killers, rapists, and thieves in her portfolio, her most famous picture was a sketch of the Atlanta Olympic bomber in 1996. Working off Minogue's descriptions, Lawson created a drawing that Thompson would distribute to the public after rejecting sketches from two other witnesses. To Lawson's artistic eye, it was the wrong choice. "They didn't circulate the one I thought was best," she'd tell the *Atlanta Journal-Constitution*. But on the evening news the night after the shooting, Atlanta residents were presented the black-and-white image of a swarthy man with a beard and no mustache, a cap, broad nose, and full lips. The effect was sinister. If anybody could put a name to the face in the sketch they did not come forward. None of Rusty's friends, business associates, or family members recognized the man in the drawing.

It was a rocky start to the investigation. The man and the van both seemed to vanish. Taking his cues from the interview with Andrea, Thompson focused most of his efforts in the first few days on Rusty's business history. Aside from the man on the side of the house, Andrea spent the most time talking about Rusty's various employers and financial deals, with one job ending in a layoff and the other in an acrimonious firing. The detective interviewed several people at Discovery Point as well as Rusty's partners in Star Voicemail, looking for evidence of animosity, checking out alibis. It was a time-consuming effort and in the end fruitless. Nobody provided any information helpful to the investigation, and one by one everybody Thompson talked to was eliminated as a possible person of interest. The exterminator was interviewed and also cleared.

Follow-up interviews with Rusty's family and in-laws generated no leads. The questions touched on everything from Rusty's finances to his social activities, even his sexuality. His parents and father-in-law sat in horror as they were asked whether they thought Rusty could have been gay or bisexual. "The questions were just to figure out if Rusty had a secret lifestyle," Thompson later explained. Everybody insisted that Rusty was a dedicated father and husband, as straight as they come.

On Tuesday, November 23, five days after the murder with Thompson getting nowhere, the police department summoned reporters to headquarters for a press conference. It started just after 4 p.m. and local TV stations cut away live to carry it. Dunwoody police chief Billy Grogan, all authority in his crew cut and dark uniform, three gold stars on his epaulets, began by summarizing the stark facts about the murder of Rusty Sneiderman.

"This does not appear to be random in nature," he began in his smooth southern accent. "The victim was shot multiple times at what appears to be point-blank range. We do have several witnesses that actually saw the shooting and from those witnesses we were able to get a composite, or a sketch, of what the suspect may look like. And this is the sketch."

He pointed to the drawing tacked to the wall behind him.

"We also, in talking to our witnesses, have been able to get a more accurate make and model of the vehicle," he continued, pronouncing it "vee-hickle" in the local fashion. "The vehicle appears, according to one particular witness—who has some knowledge about automobiles—that vehicle was a Dodge Caravan, a newer-model Dodge Caravan." He then gestured to a photo of that car on the wall.

The chief then got to the point of the press conference. "The Dunwoody Police Department is asking for the community's help in finding Rusty's killer," he said, calling out for anybody in the Dunwoody Village shopping center area between 7:30 and 9 a.m. that previous Thursday to contact the department "if they saw anyone matching this description, saw a silver Dodge Caravan." He noted that at the time of the crime the van may not have had license plates but could have them now. "Any information would be greatly appreciated and needed."

He then announced that the Sneiderman family was offering a ten-thousand-dollar reward for information leading to the arrest and conviction "of the person or persons responsible for this terrible crime," before introducing the next person to address reporters: Rusty's brother.

Like all of the family members, Steven Sneiderman had spent much of the three days since the funeral sitting shiva, speaking only to police and refraining from any public comments. He appeared nervous as he gazed at the reporters through his glasses.

He took a deep breath, exhaled with a sigh, and said, "Thank you for this opportunity. I'm here today to speak for my brother who can't speak anymore, and I'm here today to speak for my family and to reach out to this great community to help us. My brother was murdered. No one should have to face that. Our family has been devastated. My niece and nephew will never know their father. My sister-in-law has had an entire lifetime of dreams ripped from her."

Overcome with emotion, he struggled to continue, his voice breaking, tears welling. He breathed rapidly. "Our whole family has lost its brightest light, and we don't know why. Can you imagine that? Put yourself in our shoes for just one moment. It's why I'm here. We need your help desperately. Any information, anything at all could help. We don't know what we don't know, and we need every shred of information that we could get to help us solve this crime."

He urged the public to look closely at the sketch and the photo of the Dodge and "search your memory and help us to find the killer. Our family will be forever grateful. Thank you."

As Steven stood red-eyed and sniffling, Grogan took questions.

"Chief, what leads you to believe, what evidence do you have to lead you to believe this was a targeted crime, not a random crime?" asked one reporter.

"We don't want to get into any details of our investigation too much at this time, but there doesn't appear to have been any exchange of words between the suspect and the victim. From our witnesses' accounts the suspect just walked up to the victim and started shooting."

"Mr. Sneiderman," the same reporter asked, "is there

anything that would lead you to believe that somebody could have targeted your brother for any reason?"

"That's what's so hard to understand," said Steven in a soft voice. "To know my brother was to love my brother. He just had an energy about him that drew people in, and he would do anything for anybody, and I can't fathom for a moment what could drive someone to do this. We're just grasping and were devastated. You never think something like this could happen to your family. It's something on a TV show. It's not real. But this is real. We need help from the community."

Another reporter asked, "Could you talk about what makes your brother special, something that will stick out to friends and family that they will always remember?"

A smile came to Steven. "It's hard to say. It's just—I mean, he's Rusty," Steven said. "If you talked to anybody who knew him, you're hearing that. He was Rusty. And he just, he had such a giving heart, he would do anything for anybody. And it haunts me. But I see that smile and that light in his eye. He was always there for everybody. That's all I can tell you."

Steven then addressed his comments directly to the public. "Imagine if it was your brother and come forward," he said. "I would like to think that if I wasn't in this spot, and I had that information, I would have that courage to come forward. We would be so forever grateful."

The press conference and the sketch brought a torrent of leads. Police tracked them down, no matter how far-fetched. Tips came in that Rusty was targeted by al-Qaeda or the Taliban. One call came from as far away as California. A Beverly Hills detective wanted to compare notes with Thompson on an unsolved case with vaguely similar details. Ronni Chasen, a Hollywood publicist who as far as anybody knew didn't have an enemy in the world, was gunned down on November 16, two days before Rusty's murder, in her car on the way home from the premiere of the movie *Burlesque*. Both were Jewish, both had been killed for no apparent reason, both had Hollywood connections, though Rusty's were tenuous. Thompson and the Beverly Hills investigator would find nothing tying the cases, and Chasen's murderer would turn out to be an unemployed felon who opened fire from a bicycle in a robbery.

The leads kept Thompson busy—and distracted—and brought him no closer to solving the case. He admitted as much the day after the press conference when he interviewed Andrea for the second time. Thompson wanted to get Andrea away from her relatives and the distractions in her house. He spoke to her in a designated interview room with a wall-mounted video camera that he activated with a switch outside the front door. Sitting across from Andrea, he had taken off his coat and wore his dress shirt and jacket. Andrea dressed in a long-sleeved sweatshirt and appeared tired.

"This tragedy has never happened to me personally," he began by telling her. "I would be ignorant to think that I know what you're going through . . . however, I can sympathize knowing what it's like losing a family member in general."

"I wish he could have died of a heart attack," Andrea told him. "I wish it was just a heart attack. Then I would have the answer."

"It's the not knowing that drives people crazy," Thompson agreed. "It's driving me crazy because I don't know what exactly to focus on."

Thompson told her that six days into the investigation, police had made little progress. "This is not going to be a quick process," he said when the interview was interrupted by Sergeant Cortellino, who poked his head through the interview room door to say that Andrea's mother had arrived at the station and was sitting outside.

Thompson continued, "I can't tell you how long because I don't know. Somebody could walk through the front door tomorrow . . . Could be the person who did it who had a sudden crisis of conscience. That's movie stuff. This is a real-life movie that you had no intention of being a character in. My feeling right now is that this is going to be a lot longer than anybody whose dealing with this wants to take. I am not at the point going to say this is a cold case and we have to close it until we get some information from some source. The department is far from that."

He told her about the Beverly Hills detective with the Ronni Chasen case, and Andrea noted, "This Star Voicemail is all about celebrities. We had just started sharing this publicly."

He told her about a Philadelphia detective "that has a case that has similarities to this" and how they were comparing files.

"What we're going to be talking about today, some of it is going to be hard questions," he said. "They're going to be hard for me to ask. I just don't like to ask certain kinds of questions regardless of the situation. They're going to be hard for you to hear. You may end up walking out of this interview hating my guts because of the questions I need to ask. The reason I'm asking a lot of these questions is because this is still a fishing expedition. There might be something you might not have thought of."

He assured her that the interview room was soundproof and that nobody in the station could hear or see them. When Andrea asked if it was being recorded—"I've seen a couple of crime shows," she said—he acknowledged that it was. "My memory is not that good," he said.

"Any kind of sensitive information that you tell me is going to remain in the inner circle of this investigation,"

Thompson continued. "I'm not going go talk to your parents about it, I'm not going to talk to Rusty's family about it. They have no need to know. The reason I'm saying that is I need to know things that you may consider embarrassing to the family, things that may be disgusting to some people . . . I'm sure every couple have little secrets that they do that they don't want their parents to know about."

Once again acknowledging her standing in the community, "I know that you're a very educated woman, you're very intelligent. You're not the normal person that we get back here. That is the whole thing. If I come across like—"

"If you're attacking me?" interjected Andrea.

"It's not personal," he said.

"I understand," she said.

After covering some of the same ground from the previous interview, he began by asking about her relationship with Rusty.

"If you don't tell me something voluntarily or in response to specific question and I end up finding out later down the road from somebody else, it could be an issue. So I have to come back and ask you why didn't you tell me this."

"I get that," she said.

For the next half hour, he brought her through the entire story of her marriage, from meeting Rusty at the weekend retreat at the Hillel at the University of Indiana, through their moves to Chicago, San Mateo, Boston, and Atlanta, their wedding in the synagogue founded by their grandparents, having children, and settling in Dunwoody for the good public schools. Andrea was effusive and seemed to enjoy sharing her memories—until she suddenly stopped.

"I still feel unsafe," she said.

The fear after the murder had her considering hiring private security.

"This is akin to a terrorist act," Thompson said, urging her to continue with her life. "One way to let the terrorists win is to stop doing your routine. That makes me angry."

She then continued with her life story, talking about her difficult pregnancy with Sophia, how her daughter was born with health problems and had to be on a heart monitor for six months. "Rusty was a mess, I was a mess," she said. "I was exhausted, I was probably a raving lunatic." But Rusty, she said, "has been a great parent, a great husband."

She talked about her easier pregnancy with son Ian and how she worked at home while taking care of her son until Rusty's job at Discovery Point was ending and she started working at GE Energy. It gave the family a steady income and health benefits, even if her travel put a strain on Rusty.

"There was a period this summer, I was gone one or two weeks in a row, and he was responsible for taking them and picking them up everywhere," she said. "When I got back from that trip, he was an ass. He couldn't get any work done." They spoke about it and sometimes he raised his voice, though she added, "He didn't raise his voice at me, he raised his voice out of frustration. We did argue and then we made an agreement and said we need more help in the house." They hired a part-time nanny and "the past couple of weeks it's been great."

They talked about the Sneidermans' lake house, the weekend trips boating, the parties with friends. Andrea broke down. Her voice shaking, she said, "I want to have the memories that we're talking about and not the four times that we've fought."

Thompson changed the subject, taking her through the family's daily routine. He asked about the cruise the couple took shortly before the murder and took down the names of the people they met on the ship. He asked her about work on the house and got the name of her "rain-gutter guy" and the contractor. He got more names of business associates. He took down her passwords for the social networking site Facebook and her email.

An hour into the interview, he finally got to the questions he'd warned her about.

He asked if Rusty ever dated women before meeting Andrea. She assured him he was monogamous—"just the kind of guy who wanted a girlfriend around."

Thompson then asked, "People do things to experiment: Has he ever talked to you about experimenting about being with another man? Has he ever talked to you about a desire to do that?"

She shook her head no.

"Has he ever shown to you as possibly being bisexual or having some sort of unexplored homosexuality?"

"No, never."

"Since he has been with you, has he ever expressed to you a desire to experiment with having another person with you, a threesome, sex parties? Have you ever expressed an interest in trying that with him?"

"No."

"Same thing for you: Have your ever experimented with another woman?"

"No."

"You told me about your boss: Has there ever been another woman that approached you?"

"Woman? No."

"Let's talk about your boss," Thompson said. "This is your current boss?"

"Yes."

"How did he approach you in expressing an interest?"

"We traveled for business together and we were at dinner."

"On one of your trips?"

"Uh-huh. And he said—what I think I said to you—which is that he thinks I'm fantastic and that was kind of it. [He] would love to have a relationship with me but knows that that's probably unlikely. That was sort of—"

"So it was a sort of polite come-on?"

"Very," she said. "That's right. He really respected me as a person."

"Was it out of respect for you as a person or out of fear for keeping his job?"

"I don't have an answer to that."

"That's a fair answer. That's reasonable. Is he married?"

"Oh, yes."

"He has children?"

"Yes."

"Did he go into any other further detail about how he would want to work [a relationship]?"

"Not really," said Andrea. Her tone now changed. She became business-like. "Let me describe this to you. I feel like you're asking me a question—I want to tell you. We're close friends, he and I. Even once he said that, and I said no, and we worked together a lot, traveled together a lot, I enjoy his—I admire him as a professional. I enjoy learning from him. I learned a ton. We talked a lot, talked a lot of business. He talked about his family, I know. We're friends. I want it to be clear, it wasn't just that 'You're great and I'm interested,' and it's that or nothing. Am I saying that the right way? We continued our relationship."

"It sounds to me like you had a strong enough friendship beforehand that this didn't disrupt anything, was a blip on the radar and got past it?"

"Exactly."

"How often do you do business trips?"

"I went on them once a month. Maybe July I went twice.

I went to a training class one week. I went to a site, a software location where we build software. Minden. And the next week I had auditor training—I trained to be an auditor as part of my job. Longmont, Colorado. Those just happened to be back-to-back because of poor timing. That was the July where Rusty was like: Are you kidding? Two weeks of kids?"

"Didn't have time to work?"

"Exactly. But you asked how often I traveled? That was a long trip. In September I went to England."

"How was the trip?"

"England was great. I hadn't been there since with Rusty."

That trip lasted a week. She had also traveled to Melbourne, Florida, where software was built, and to Greenville, South Carolina, where GE made turbines.

"How many of your business trips does your boss go with you?"

"All of them."

"All of them?"

"Besides Longmont, Colorado, for some training," she said, "he went to all of them and I'll tell you why. He hadn't been to the sites, either. And it was part of his goals and objectives, and he'll tell you that from his boss, and he needed to get out there more, and he wanted to introduce me to people also. And so he went with me. I could have shown up to those places by myself, but I'm not sure I would have gotten the respect or the attention. Does that answer your question?"

"Yes, it does."

"And, of course we travel together, so we became friends, right?" she said. "A million hours, you're in the car or you're on the plane."

"You can't help it," said Thompson. "If you don't get along it's going to be a very long trip."

"And we saw eye-to-eye from a business perspective on a lot of things," said Andrea.

"Did the company pay for hotels, or it came out of your own pocket and got reimbursed?"

"Corporate cards."

"What hotels did you guys normally stay at?"

"I like Hilton points so I would stay at Hiltons. Maybe all of them were Hiltons."

"To be convenient, did you have rooms on the same floor?"

"Sometimes," she said. "We didn't control it, you know what I'm saying? We didn't always control where the hotel put us. I have no problem being next door to each other. It's neither here nor there. Again, we were friends. It didn't bother me, I guess."

Moving on to another topic, Thompson returned to a question he had asked her at her house.

"Anybody you can think of that would be interested in pursuing your husband? Your reaction was a little odd. You laughed, you smiled, and you said no one would be interested."

"I'm laughing now," Andrea said. "He doesn't have time to go to the bathroom, let alone have an affair. It's one of those things. Of course, through this whole thing people bring that up—vengeance or revenge, I have no idea. Honestly, he didn't have time to pee. I can't imagine him fitting that in. He loved me so much, and made that clear a million times a day, so I laughed because—"

"It's so absurd?"

"It's absurdly ridiculous," she said. "There's actually more words I can use."

Thompson chuckled and said, "Understood."

Without prompting Andrea then said, "My mom knew about this Hemy thing. I mentioned it to her—he expressed an interest. I needed to tell someone."

"She's the only one that didn't jump up," Thompson said, a reference to the family's reaction when he asked the question during the interview at Andrea's house.

"There you go," said Andrea. "There's no point in telling the rest of the family."

"There is no point," the detective agreed.

"No one needed to know."

"I was sort of surprised you said it with everybody around."

Speaking in a whisper, so softly the interview room microphones barely picked it up, Andrea said, "I'm not hiding—"

Thompson assured her, "I don't get the impression that you're hiding anything."

"And I don't think that this Hemy thing is anything. I really don't," she said, her voice louder. "If I did, I'd sit here and give you fifty other reasons why. I don't know, that's up to you to figure out, I guess. Or decide if that's on your list. I don't know how you guys figure out what your priorities are."

"It's one of those things that we have to look into and prove it one way or the other," Thompson said, "so that when it comes to a trial, if a defense attorney brings it up, if they happen to get their hands on the information, we can say we investigated it, this is what we found, this is why we didn't do anything with it."

Andrea said, "Okay."

Thompson and Cortellino would agree on priorities; looking into Hemy Neuman could wait, favoring other avenues of investigation. Thompson changed the subject "You guys met in 1994, you got married in 2000 . . ."

And on it went. The interview lasted a few more minutes before Thompson ran out of questions and sent Andrea on her way.

CHAPTER 5

At Dunwoody Prep, forty-seven security cameras peered into almost every corner of the grounds. The day after the shooting, CDs of the footage from the two cameras with the best view of the scene—those trained on the parking lot—were submitted for analysis to Walter Pineda, a former Pinkerton detective who went on to start his own company, Video Enhancements, that specialized in analyzing security videos. He could adjust the contrast, color, and darkness of the moving images in the hope of getting a better view of the shooter. He could also lift the best images from multiple cameras and edit them together like a movie to provide a better sense of movement and time.

In this case he created an eerie sequence that began about an hour before the crime, when the van pulled into the parking lot at 8 a.m., left, then returned about an hour later. The effect implied that the shooter either was casing out the school, looking for the best location to kill, or had shown up at the wrong time, since the van went back to Rusty's neighborhood then reappeared on the security footage at 9:10 a.m. Rusty's Infiniti could be seen approaching the school, with Ian in the backseat and the van on his tail.

Nowhere in all the footage could any part of the actual murder be seen; it all occurred in a security camera blind spot. Nor could Pineda generate a better image of the shooter; in all the frames the assailant remained a bearded blur. But what did come through clearly—better than any of the descriptions provided by eyewitnesses—was the van. Witnesses had variously characterized it as a Chrysler, Kia, and Hyundai. Chief Grogan went public calling it a Dodge. It was silver or gray and probably new. The security cameras captured the van from different angles, the enhanced images providing police a strong hope of narrowing down the getaway vehicle.

Detective Thompson brought the photos to Chrysler, Honda, and Ford dealerships, but none said the van looked like one of theirs. A colleague, Officer Brian Tate, the policeman who had gotten the first call to the crime scene, suggested the van looked like a Kia. Looking at photos on the company's website, Thompson compared the body shape, hubcaps, side-view mirrors, and lights. It all added up to a Kia Sedona, a family minivan. The general manager of a local Kia dealership examined the enhanced photos and confirmed that the murder van was in fact a 2011 Sedona, on the market for only weeks. A call to Kia headquarters found that sixteen hundred of those vans had been sold in the United States in black, burgundy, white, dark blue, light green, and silver. But only thirteen were sold in Georgia and South Carolina.

So began the time-consuming process of hunting down

the van. Working off Kia's list, police visited every buyer, then took pictures of the vans and checked alibis. All the Sedona owners were cleared.

But before police had to expand the search to other private buyers outside Georgia and South Carolina, Thompson got an idea. The enhanced photos from the security cameras revealed what looked like white stickers on the van's windshield and driver's-door window. A friend told Thompson that rental car agencies use window stickers with bar codes to keep track of their vehicles. Could the killer have rented the van?

Police refocused the search for 2011 Kia Sedonas sold as fleet vehicles to rental agencies in Georgia and North and South Carolina. This meant tracking down fewer vehicles than the more than nine hundred sold to private buyers outside Georgia. As investigators logged miles and hours tracking down vans, Thompson continued to chase leads to the tip line and from other law enforcement agencies and interviewing Rusty's business associates and family members.

Adding to the workload was the fact that this was not the only murder investigation under way. Although the Sneiderman case attracted all the media attention, Dunwoody police actually had two other recent homicides. In July, an elderly couple's bodies were found in the rubble of their home, apparently set on fire to conceal evidence of the murders.

"Certainly, there is pressure to bring some closure," Chief Billy Grogan acknowledged to the *Atlanta Journal-Constitution* in December 2010. "But these incidents are not related, so there's no need to believe that Dunwoody is not safe." He urged residents to have reasonable expectations. "Just because we have the Dunwoody Police Department doesn't mean crime is going to disappear," he said. Sergeant Gary Cortellino attributed part of the problem to new apartment complexes going up—the newspaper noted that the slain-and-burned couple lived near a "cluster of apartments."

In the past, a small department like Dunwoody's could have reached out for help to the Georgia Bureau of Investigation, but the state police force had its own staffing issues. Two years into the recession, budget cuts, hiring freezes, and furloughs had trimmed the GBI's head count to its lowest level in a decade. The GBI would be able to provide police lab support, but for more investigators on the ground, the Dunwoody Police Department would have to look elsewhere.

By mid-December, a month into the investigation, it was all hands on deck for the Sneiderman case, with supervisors like Lieutenant David Barnes, who headed the detectives, pitching in. The department finally got outside help from the DeKalb County District Attorney's Office, which provided investigators to track down the van leads and perform other tasks. Sergeant Cortellino obtained a list of fleet Kia Sedonas sold in the Southeast, then sent word to all the rental agencies in the region to hold on to their rentals until police could go out and inspect them. For each Sedona that Cortellino found, DA investigator William Presnell would head to the lot and take a photograph for comparison.

When a Kia Sedona was returned to one Enterprise Rent-A-Car, Presnell headed out to take a look. The lot was located on Riverstone Parkway in Canton, twenty-five miles northwest of Dunwoody in the foothills of the Blue Ridge Mountains in the heart of Cherokee country. By the time Presnell got there, on December 14, the van had been rented out again. Presnell left his business card asking for a call when the van was returned. His phone rang a week later.

On December 21, he returned to the agency and saw the

Sedona—silver with a sticker on the window—with South Carolina plates. The van looked like the one in the security video stills and was impounded. Forensic technicians conducted a thorough search, recovering small dark synthetic hairs. Working off Enterprise records obtained by subpoena, Thompson tracked down the people who rented the van over Halloween and asked if anybody had worn costume wigs or beards. They said they had not. The records showed that the van had been rented from another Enterprise Rent-A-Car agency in Marietta on November 17 and returned on November 18. The contact number was a cell phone.

Sergeant Gary Cortellino called it on December 26. Hemy Neuman answered.

CHAPTER 6

For all the discussion of Hemy Neuman, he had not become a priority of the investigation. Nobody went looking for him. Nobody tried to call him or compared the sketch to Hemy. Nobody looked into whether he drove a silver Dodge Caravan or even wondered where he was the morning that Rusty Sneiderman was murdered or if he had an alibi, despite Thompson's assertion to Andrea that due diligence would require investigating Hemy

Instead the investigation went in other directions, primarily back to Rusty's career history and business dealings. Why it happened this way would become a nagging question for the police department and one they would have to answer for in court. "Well, if you could go back in time, immediately when we'd had his name, we'd have went and talked to him, but that's hindsight," Chief Grogan would later tell WSB-TV in Atlanta. "We have practices in place so the right hand knows what the left hand is doing, and we certainly learned from that."

Thompson would later acknowledge he should have taken down Hemy's contact information from Andrea as he had that of the exterminator and various business associates of Rusty's. "I made a mistake," he said. But he would lay much of the blame on Andrea. He interpreted her comments to mean Hemy's romantic advance was a fleeting moment that they both quickly put behind them. Had she made more of it, "I would have, as soon as the interview was done, found him and got him for an interview," Thompson would say. She didn't, so he didn't.

At Thompson's instruction, a routine background check was run on him on December 15, as was done with all the names that arose in the investigation. It raised no red flags; Hemy's record was spotless. He had no arrests, no lawsuits, nothing that would draw any attention to him. He was put on the back burner.

The hand-wringing would come months later. For now, police had the biggest break in the case.

When Hemy answered, Cortellino introduced himself as a Dunwoody police detective. "I told him that I was investigating a hit-and-run accident occurring in Dunwoody involving a silver van and I had traced that van back to him and that I had some questions I'd like to ask him in person," Cortellino later said.

If Hemy caught on to the deception, he said nothing about it. Calm and cooperative, Hemy said he would be happy to meet with the police but that he was in Florida for a few days to attend the funeral of his father's wife.

"I'll call you when I get back to Georgia," he said.

Cortellino waited about a week. It was a calculated risk. Police could have swooped in immediately to prevent him from fleeing or they could take their time, learn more about

Hemy, and see if he crossed himself up. They chose the latter. Cortellino would later claim that all he knew about Hemy at the time came from the background check: that Hemy was clean and that he worked at the same GE office as Andrea. Though he had sat at the Sneidermans' dining room table the night Andrea was first interviewed, he later said he never heard her mention Hemy and that she may have brought him up when Cortellino was outside the house; due to a communication breakdown at the police department he didn't learn what Andrea had told Thompson in the follow-up interview. Cortellino left a message on Hemy's voice mail asking if he was back in town.

On the morning of January 4, 2011, Hemy did call back. After Cortellino thanked him for returning the call, Hemy affected the same anything-I-can-do-to-help tone. He said he had returned to Georgia and was willing to set up a time to talk to police. Cortellino said he wanted to do it that day. Hemy had a doctor's appointment, but thought he could reschedule that. He provided an address in the tony Buckhead community south of Dunwoody.

It had been decided that Cortellino and his boss, Lieutenant David Barnes, would approach Hemy. They were among the most experienced members of the Dunwoody PD, Barnes with twenty-five years of experience before joining the department as a lieutenant, Cortellino with thirty years, all of it with the DeKalb County police. While Barnes had come from the South and spoke that way, Cortellino was a native New Yorker—and he still sounded like one, three decades in Georgia failing to penetrate his eastern accent.

They would drive separately, Cortellino heading to an address provided by Hemy, while Barnes inexplicably went to an address listed on the background check in East Cobb, an Outside the Perimeter suburb not far from Dunwoody.

It would never be clear why they didn't have the same address, if this was another instance of a communication breakdown. Also, Barnes would later say that he learned Hemy was Andrea's boss when a Google search turned up his résumé, not from any reports or word from his own detectives. Either way, while in his car, Barnes got a call from Cortellino telling him to turn around and meet him south in Buckhead. Barnes got there first.

About seven miles south of Dunwoody, Buckhead is the jewel of Inside the Perimeter living, often called the Beverly Hills of the South. Mansions and sprawling country estates house the titans of business, music, and sports. The address provided by Hemy turned out to be more modest accommodations, a condominium building on Andrews Place. Barnes went to Unit 139. The man who came to the door bore little resemblance to the bearded killer in the police sketch. Hemy Neuman looked very much like the GE Energy executive of his résumé and Andrea's description: shortish, middle-aged, with mostly gray hair and glasses. He let the detectives in and they made "casual conversation," Barnes said later, while they awaited Cortellino. Hemy said the apartment was owned by a longtime family friend named Ruthy whom he knew as far back as when he was attending Georgia Tech. When she still had a house, she'd give him a place to go for the Jewish holidays. Repeating what he'd said on the phone, Hemy noted that his doctor's appointment that day was a follow-up for recent minor surgery and that he wasn't feeling 100 percent. When Barnes asked if he could try to postpone it, Hemy agreed.

Within ten minutes, Cortellino arrived. Introductions were made, and the detectives asked Hemy if he would be willing to speak with them at Dunwoody Police Station so they could get his statement on tape. Once again agreeable, Hemy got in the passenger seat of Cortellino's

unmarked 2010 Ford Fusion and Barnes sat in the back—
he would make arrangements for somebody to pick up his
car at Hemy's place later. Cortellino drove them north on
Georgia 400 and crossed the Perimeter.

The Dunwoody Police Department is located at 41 Perimeter Center East, occupying the first floor of this office
building about a twenty-minute drive from Buckhead. It
looks nothing like a police station. Identified only by a sign
outside the front door, Dunwoody Station has no bars or
security windows. It doesn't have a jail. The trio walked
down a small hill and in through a side door hidden from
view of the parking lot and Hemy was led into the same
interview room where Andrea had given her second statement. Hemy was pinned in the corner flanked on both sides
by the detectives.

"There's no beating around the bush," Cortellino began.
"You know why we called you in. I've been trying to get
you." Cortellino asked for his driver's license and wrote
down his full name.

"You don't have any weapons on you, do you?" he asked.

Hemy fidgeted.

"You okay?" asked the detective. "You all right?"

"It's unnerving to be in a room like this," he said.

Cortellino tried to put him at ease. "I hope I don't make
it unnerving for you because I'm not the nervy type," he
said. "It's not you, it's the situation."

The detective expressed his appreciation for Hemy calling back after returning from Florida. "I mean that was
nice of you," he said. "Some people don't like calling back.
As you said, it's unnerving but I thought you seemed to
be okay with it because you called me back."

The detective explained that talking in the apartment
"didn't seem conducive with Ruthy there so I thought coming here would be better." Seeking to build a rapport, as

Thompson had done with Andrea, Cortellino asked Hemy about his background. Hemy related how he'd graduated from "Tech," as locals call Georgia Tech, with a degree in aerospace engineering. He spoke of working for General Dynamics in Israel, then another company in Israel that was bought by GE, "so that's how I ended up at GE."

The interview began pleasantly enough despite the claustrophobic confines of the room. Hemy was dressed casually in a dark long-sleeved shirt or sweatshirt and jeans. A cup of water sat in front of him. The detectives both had on sports coats and were heavier-built than he was. Cortellino sat to his left and would lean forward and increasingly push closer to him, and ask most of the questions. Across the table sat Lieutenant Barnes, reviewing documents and rarely making eye contact with Hemy, seemingly preoccupied with paperwork while Cortellino asked the questions.

Cortellino urged Hemy to call him Gary, which Hemy did. They joked about Cortellino's New York accent. Cortellino made self-deprecating remarks about not being as smart or highly paid as Hemy, and affected a wide-eyed interest and envy in Hemy's corporate world. All the while Barnes loomed silently across the table, poring over papers with a seriousness that suggested he knew a lot more than he was letting on.

"So General Dynamics was GE at one time?" Cortellino asked. "My cousin worked for them in New York."

Hemy squirmed again.

"You okay?" asked Cortellino.

Hemy looked around. "Again, I'm feeling great. The setting is just—"

He didn't finish the thought. Cortellino jumped in with more questions about Hemy's time at GE, and Hemy reluctantly answered them, recounting his rise through the executive ranks. Now a quality and operations manager, he supervised twenty-two employees who in turn oversaw a total of thirty-five hundred engineers.

Cortellino then asked, "Andrea is one of your employees there?" The question came out of the blue. Up until now Cortellino had said nothing about Rusty's murder.

Showing no surprise at the question, Hemy said only, "Uh-huh."

"How long she been with you over there?"

"Since April."

"What is her title?"

"She's the quality manager for our software team."

"Pretty good employee?"

"Yes."

"She's got the credentials to do that?"

"She's doing great work."

Hemy explained that he knew not only Andrea but also her late husband, Rusty. He said he had visited their house.

"How long have you known the family?" Cortellino asked, all this information new to him.

"I met Rusty in, I think it was August. We ate lunch. Went to their house. And then went to their house again."

"What is the reason? Just socializing?"

"Yeah, they're Jewish. Good guys."

"What about the other employees? Did you do the same for them? Or was Andrea just because she's Jewish and you tend to follow—"

"Yeah, pretty much—again because of tradition and everything."

"You said you saw Rusty a couple of days before he was shot?"

"Yes."

"And where was that? What were the circumstances?"

"We were working on a project and we had a deadline," Hemy explained, "and Andrea needed to go home to take care of the kids, so we agreed that we would break it up.

She would go home and basically put the kids to bed and I would come."

When Cortellino asked the date that Hemy visited the Sneiderman house, Hemy checked his iPad and said it was November 16—two days before the murder.

"Was Rusty there?" the detective asked.

"He came around nine," said Hemy. "We were working at the kitchen table and he did some work at the kitchen table. Half an hour later, he went upstairs. I left there about ten thirty."

"What did he do?"

Hemy described the same celebrity voice-messaging project that Andrea had sketched out for Detective Thompson. Hemy revealed that he, too, was involved in Rusty's enterprise, if only tangentially. Cortellino and Barnes would later find out this was just one of many things Andrea had not mentioned to Thompson. Hemy said Rusty would bounce ideas off him about the business plan. Rusty had also talked to Hemy about another possible project, something involving communications for police cars.

As Barnes listened and took notes, Hemy shot him nervous glances. Cortellino inched closer, pushing Hemy tighter into the corner. He asked how many times Hemy had spoken with Rusty.

Hemy said it was maybe twice in person, other times by phone. He described Rusty as a "really, really smart guy—Harvard Business School." Rusty had told him about a meeting with business partners in the messaging service who met in Atlanta, one from California—Nate somebody, Hemy didn't know the last name—who was in charge of the technical end. Rusty told Hemy that the other partners didn't like this Nate. After the meeting, Nate got kicked off the project.

"Did Rusty have a lot of money involved in that?" asked Cortellino.

"I don't think he did. I don't know. I have no idea."

"Did you put money in it?"

"Oh, no," said Hemy. "I'm broke. I'm bankrupt."

When Cortellino was asking Hemy about his job, he described himself as an upper manager pulling down $170,000 a year, Cortellino joking that this was a lot more than a small-town detective made. The detective would return to the subject of Hemy's finances, but first asked how much money Andrea was making.

Hemy said $125,000.

"So you and Andrea were working for GE. GE's all over the world, right?"

"Right," said Hemy, explaining that the company had one hundred sites under Hemy's supervision alone. Hemy spent a lot of time on the road—"It's part of connecting with people," he said—while also keeping close tabs on GE's empire.

"Does she go?" Cortellino asked.

"Her team has eight different locations so she might go," Hemy said.

Cortellino asked how frequently she traveled with Hemy.

"We went a few times," said Hemy, listing plants in Florida, Nevada, and the United Kingdom. He said that he and Andrea had made the UK trip together in September.

"So how long are these trips usually?" asked Cortellino.

"The ones here in the US, it depends."

"Could it be two, three days?"

"Nevada, she went for three days. I didn't go. I went—I had another trip with my boss at that time."

"You hired her in April and in September she's traveling?" asked Cortellino. "You felt that comfortable she can go handle what she had to do?"

"She's good."

"She's that sharp?"

"She's very sharp," Hemy said. Her listed her qualities

as being able to quickly develop contacts and connect with people, just like him. For the most part she did this on her own without supervision.

"I did a couple of trips with her as an introduction," Hemy said, "and get her up to speed, show her the facilities."

Cortellino asked, "You were still with your wife at the time? Was everything going all right with you or were things happening with you at home?"

Hemy said, "There's conflict," without elaborating.

"Did it interfere with your work performance?"

"No."

"Not at all?"

"No."

"How long has that been gong on?" asked Cortellino. "Home-life problems?"

"Well, I wouldn't say problems," said Hemy. But he did say he had moved out in October.

Cortellino asked: "When was the last time you guys traveled together, you and Andrea?"

"In October," said Hemy. "I don't remember the exact date. We went to Greenville, South Carolina."

"Was that a day trip?"

"It was overnight because the meetings were early in the morning."

Barnes interjected a rare question. He asked where they stayed in Greenville. Hemy said the Hampton Inn.

"In your name or Andrea's?" asked Barnes, writing notes.

"Each of us has our own," Hemy said. "She had a room in her name and I had one in mine."

Cortellino asked: "Are these trips planned or do they just happen?"

"They're typically planned. I mean, that one was ten days before, something like that."

"Why did she have to go? Was it concerning her aspect of the company?"

"Right, what we're doing, we're developing a new process, we were developing a new process for developing product, how we develop a product," Hemy said. "And it was very integral with work that she was doing with that process. So we had to tie that together and so we went to Greenville to work with a team over there."

Cortellino asked the question that had been floating out there: "And what's your relationship? Be honest. What's your relationship with her? It sounds like more than business."

"Not that close," Hemy said.

"Did you call each other after work, before work?" pressed Cortellino. "Did you talk to each other on weekends other than work? She must be concerned about your well-being."

"My job is 24/7," he said.

"Does the rest of the group know you've got problems at home?"

"They know now," he said, naming a couple of employees in his working group, his boss—and Andrea. "My performance didn't slip."

Barnes asked, "What was the decision to actually step out and get out on your own? What was the catalyst for that?"

"It's a silly thing, actually," said Hemy. "It's always the straw that breaks the camel's back. We went to Lowes and we're broke. Again, I owe money up the quazoo [sic]. It's crazy."

Hemy, who through most of the interview had sat still in his chair, hands in his lap, became animated. He waved his arms and raised his voice. "I'm in a debt consolidation plan, I have a personal loan of sixty-five thousand dollars."

"Then you have the Georgia Tech loans?" asked Barnes.

"I have the student loans, which is like fifty grand or something," Hemy said. "So we were way over our means. I mean the mortgage is three thousand dollars. We have all these expenses, and we have no money. I told my wife, I said, 'We just don't have any money. We're broke.' Not only are we broke, but I think I'm going to maybe have to declare bankruptcy. Or foreclose on the house. I don't know how we can continue to afford this. And I'm telling her this and we went to Lowes and she says, 'Oh, you know, there's patio furniture on sale. Our patio furniture is old.'"

Hemy continued, "Say what? I said, 'You realize that we don't have a dime. We cannot buy anything.' But she says, 'It's on a sale. A really good price.' I said, 'I don't care if they're giving it away. We can't afford it.' And that's when I realized, the relationship became destructive. I was trying to please her. She was never happy with what we have. I kept trying to please her with buying things."

His wife wasn't working, he said. She had been trained as a teacher in Israel. "She has a teaching credential, not that she ever worked," he said, then added, "She knows Hebrew. She's a good person." He said she has recently gone back to work "out of need," as a teacher's assistant. The Neuman family had amassed a mountain of debt. They owed $450,000 on their house in East Cobb, $77,000 in credit card balances.

Barnes asked: "What were you using the credit card for?"

"Trips, just buying things. We were spending sixteen hundred a month on food. My wife loves to cook. You know, Jewish. I mean, we would have twenty-five people in and serve them filet mignon. It was crazy. I mean we have twenty-five people over, dinner would cost six or seven hundred dollars. We were spending four thousand or five thousand a month more than I was making."

Cortellino asked, "Sounds like you were spending more on socializing?"

Hemy paused.

They had now been in the room for thirty-eight minutes and neither detective had asked about the rental car or Rusty's murder. With exasperation in his voice, he asked, "Where is all this going?"

Cortellino answered vaguely, "I'm just trying to get a basis on Rusty. How you and Andrea and Rusty can cross."

Although two detectives had him pinned into the corner of a small room, Hemy technically wasn't in custody or under arrest. He had not been read his rights. He was theoretically completely free to leave at any time. The law covers statements made by custodial and noncustodial people in different ways; Cortellino would need to tread carefully.

Hemy didn't press the issue and Cortellino resumed his questions. The detective asked again about the night Hemy had visited the Sneidermans. Hemy explained that he and Andrea were scrambling to finish a project. The late hours became necessary. The project had a year-end deadline.

Hemy was asked if he noticed whether the long hours had caused issues between Andrea and Rusty. Hemy said he began to sense tension between the two. Before joining GE, Andrea had worked from home. Now going into the office each day, leaving Rusty with the children, created "some conflict between them," Hemy said. "She's got a little bit of pressure."

Cortellino asked: "Did she share what was going on in her home as you shared with her?"

"She talked about it," he said. "She's not at home with

the kids. Rusty is at home. He doesn't have an office. He's trying to set up his business. He becomes the dad, has to go take them to school, bring them back, all of that stuff."

"So the roles pretty much reverse?"

"That caused some stress, but you know, again, it's not anything that you wouldn't expect," he said. "She indicated that, yeah, they were having problems over who has what priorities."

Casually, Cortellino asked Hemy where he happened to be the morning of the murder.

"I was at work," he said.

"And Andrea?"

"Andrea was at work."

"And Rusty? You don't know what Rusty was doing?"

"No, I don't."

Cortellino then asked: "What time did Andrea get into work because I thought she was able to work out of the home and come to the office?"

"When she joined the agreement was that a couple of days of the week she would work from home, which she didn't do, which was part of the stress between Rusty and Andrea. When you're training and you're learning and you're trying to develop your relationships and all that it's hard if you're not in the office."

Cortellino paused before asking his next question. In a more serious tone, he said, "Listen, I'm going to talk to you about the day of the shooting, but I'm going to read you your rights on it, your Miranda rights."

Hemy was taken aback. "Why, am I—?" he asked, not finishing the thought.

"Well, you never know," said Cortellino. "I mean, I just want to talk to everybody about that day and I'm asking everybody to be honest and truthful with me and just re-call the day as you remember it."

"Do I have to worry?"

"I don't think so," said the detective. "Okay. I'm not worried. I'm not going to worry. You're fine."

Cortellino's voice dripped with a just-between-us-guys sincerity. "Listen, you're helping. You got the information. You're flowing with it. For a guy that says, 'What do I know?' you're giving me a lot."

Cortellino gestured to Barnes, who had resumed silence but busily took notes. "He's up to five pages already, he's writing."

Hemy lifted his palms in a what's-going-on-here pose: "You asked me about a car and you're asking all these questions?"

"I'm asking you questions about Rusty and Andrea. I'm trying to get into their lives," said Cortellino. "Andrea's not at a point right now, I'll be honest, she's not at a point where I can sit down and talk to her. You know, she's got so many emotions going on and let's face it. You probably could tell we're not the most congenial guys. That's the nature of the beast. I can't sit there and console her. I'm not a rabbi, I'm not a therapist. I'm just somebody looking into why this happened to her family. She wants to know why her family is destroyed, why her kids don't have a father, why she don't have a husband. That's all she keeps asking. And I'm hunting around asking all these people that they know and they want to know."

Hemy dropped down his head, shaking, hands in his lap. "Am I suspect?"

Before Cortellino answered, Hemy asked if the detective had read Miranda rights to everybody else he had interviewed.

"If I have to, yeah," the detective said, not letting on that so far nobody had been read their rights in the case. "I mean, do what I got to do. I mean talk to everybody I have to and it is."

Cortellino slid a piece of paper to Hemy.

"You can read English pretty well, right? These are the statement of Miranda. I'm going to read them."

He cited the familiar refrain from countless TV shows: the right to remain silent, the warning that everything he said could be used against him in a court of law, the right to an attorney.

"Do you understand?" asked Cortellino.

"Am I going to need a lawyer?" asked Hemy.

The detective evaded. "Do you need a lawyer?" said Cortellino.

"I don't know," said Hemy. "I'm asking you."

"This is what you need to ask yourself," said Cortellino. "These questions. Do you feel like being asked questions about Rusty?"

"You're reading me—I've never been in a situation like this."

"This is plain English. You're an intelligent guy. You're college-educated. You've been around the world more times than I have. You're more attuned to what's going on than I am."

Cortellino read Hemy his rights again.

"Do you understand those that I've just read you?"

"Yes."

"You need to sign right over here."

Hemy signed, though the process didn't end there. The detective had a second piece of paper for Hemy. Now that Hemy acknowledged understanding his rights, would he waive those rights?

"Are you willing to talk to me right now to help me find the person who did this to Andrea and her family?" asked Cortellino.

"Yeah," Hemy said, "but I'm not going to waive rights. I'm not—I don't know where you're going with this."

"We're looking into what's happened on that day."

"I mean, I have these rights, and now you're saying that I'm waiving them? What does that mean?"

"Having these rights, what I've just read to you, are you wiling to give up these rights and willingly talk to me, to make a statement? Are you willing to talk to me?"

"Okay, so, why didn't you give this to me an hour ago?"

"Because I wanted to see what you knew," said Cortellino. "Did you know Andrea? Did you know Rusty? How well do you know him? See where we're going with it?"

"I don't know where you're going with this."

"It's just a conversation. This is a conversation. You have information. You know Andrea. You know Rusty better than I do," the detective said. "And I've got a task ahead of me to find out who did this. And all I'm doing to is talking to all their friends, all their business associates, anybody that knows—neighbors, friends, I don't care if it's a waiter or waiters, I'm going to talk to everybody that knows them. Everybody. And God only knows how long it's going to take me to do that. When I say me, I'm talking to all of us."

"I don't know again, my comfort—I'm in this setting."

Cortellino spread out his arms. "This is a comfortable setting."

Hemy said, "You call me in about a car—"

"I want to talk to you about a car. I want to," said Cortellino. "Maybe you got something that can help me. You worked in the same environment with Andrea. That's as close as I've gotten to her so far. I'm not going to get any closer to her working over there than you. You work there. I'm looking into the family. I've got to get insight on the family."

The more they talked, the more agitated Hemy became. Cortellino said he just wanted a simple conversation, talk about Andrea's family, Rusty's family, their friends—"A simple thing," the detective said.

"I am talking to you," said Hemy. "I'm talking to you right here."

"Hemy, this is not rocket science. You are a smart guy. You're not signing away your mortgage."

"No, I'm not signing away my mortgage but this is very uncomfortable."

"Well, I'll make it comfortable again. Why is it uncomfortable? You were doing so well up until now. I put a piece of paper in front of you—you say it's uncomfortable. That concerns me, to be honest."

"No."

"That concerns me," said Cortellino, his voice rising.

"I know, but you read Miranda rights and it seems like as if I'm a suspect."

Cortinellino locked eyes with Hemy: "Are you a suspect?"

Hemy looked away. "I don't think I need to be a suspect. I shouldn't be a suspect. There's no reason why I should be a suspect. But you're reading me my rights."

Hemy shook his head back and forth as if trying to get a crick out of his neck.

"I mean, you're shaking like a leaf," Cortellino said. "I got to wonder about that."

"Again, I told you everything. Last night, I wasn't feeling well. My head is about to explode."

"Maybe it's the conscience," suggested Cortellino. "You got a lot on your mind."

"It was a crappy day the last couple of days with my twins," said Hemy. His two daughters had blamed him for the breakup of the marriage, he said.

Cortellino said ominously: "Every day could be crappy for the rest of your life."

Hemy didn't seem to hear him. "It's not great if your daughter is telling you that you're an asshole."

Cortellino told Hemy a story about a friend who lost a

daughter to a drug overdose and now wishes every day the daughter was still alive if only to call her an asshole. He urged Hemy to stop thinking about himself, to think about his family. "Think about Andrea," the detective said.

"Yeah," said Hemy.

"Think about what she's going through."

"Right."

"And help them, help them all. Help them all in any way you can, whatever way you can," said Cortellino.

Hemy then mentioned his doctor's appointment.

"You're fine, just make it tomorrow," said Cortellino. "I'm trying to bring these people peace in 2011. I'm trying to bring Andrea closure in 2011. I failed in 2010. I'm trying to bring some peace, some resolution, let this family know what happened. They deserve it. They need to know what happened that day."

Hemy took a long sip of water from a foam cup.

Then Barnes spoke quietly in his southern accent. "This is going to be the last chance to help yourself."

"And if we stop now," asked Hemy, "what happens?"

"Then we'll have to make a decision," said Barnes, "decide how to proceed without you. It's that simple."

Hemy asked: "Can I go to the bathroom?"

"Absolutely," said Barnes.

"I can try and absorb everything."

Two minutes later, Hemy returned. Barnes handed him another cup of water. Hemy picked up a pen and signed the rights waiver. Cortellino added his signature. Barnes sat back, quiet again.

Cortellino then asked again where Hemy was and exactly what he was doing on the morning of November 18, 2010.

CHAPTER 7

"We've got four buildings and she's in a different building, employees spread all over." Hemy Neuman was explaining the layout at GE Energy in Marietta.

"You were at work?" asked Sergeant Gary Cortellino.

Hemy nodded yes.

Cortellino asked: "If she was there she would be at her own desk in her own building?"

"If she was there?" Hemy asked, stressing *if*.

"Right. Is there any way we can verify that? Knowing what you know about GE, is there any way we can verify she is sitting at her desk on November 18."

"We have badges with electronic—"

Cortellino cut off his answer. "Who can we contact to check?"

Hemy reminded silent.

"Hemy, am I talking too fast for you?"

"No."

"Simple question."

The interview, going on for an hour, had taken a more confrontational tone, Hemy's evasive answers met with ever-sharper questions from Cortellino.

"There's a facilities manager," Hemy said. "I guess with reports, I don't know."

"What time did you get there on the eighteenth?"

"Around five thirty. I got in early."

"Is that a normal hour to get in there?"

"No. I've done it in the past, not normal, but we had, I had several—not the project with Andrea, but another big project I'm working on."

"So on the eighteenth, five thirty you get there, six thirty you're working, seven thirty you're working, people starting to come in? People seeing you, saying hello?"

"Yeah, normal day."

"So Rusty gets shot sometime in the morning. How does the news hit?"

"Again, the first thing I knew was when Andrea contacted me."

"How did she do that?"

"She sent me a text and called me."

Barnes asked, "What did she say in the text?"

"It was—there was an accident."

The text actually went to another employee named Alan who worked in the office next to hers, said Hemy. Alan then texted Hemy saying, "I need to make contact with you. Andrea has a family emergency."

It was later in the morning, Hemy said, when he heard directly from Andrea. She had tried calling him on his cell phone, but he hadn't picked it up. When he saw the missed call he dialed her back, reaching her in a car as she was going to the hospital with her parents.

"When you talked to her on the phone, how did she sound?" asked Cortellino, resuming the questioning.

"Very distressed."

"Have you ever heard her in a distressed moment before?" the detective asked.

"Not really. She was sort of shaky."

"Did you say: *Let me talk to your parents to find out what's going on?*"

"She didn't give me much of an opportunity to say anything," said Hemy. "Again she said, 'There's been a serious accident with Rusty' or something like that. 'I need for you to handle the office. I ran out.' "

"And later on in the day you learned that Rusty had died?"

"Yeah, somewhere around twelve thirty."

"And how did you learn that?"

"Again, Alan came to me," said Hemy. "He was in our building and he came up to me and said Andrea had called him and said Rusty died. Now, we didn't know how or what."

Hemy said he went to the human resources manager with the news that Andrea Sneiderman's husband had died. An hour later, Alan called to say that another employee had seen an online news report that Rusty had been shot.

"What were you guys thinking at that point that he's been shot?" asked Cortellino.

"What we were trying to do is keep the information to what we know," said Hemy. He sent around an email saying that Andrea had to leave the office due to personal reasons. "I didn't even say that her husband had died."

He said he left the office at about 6 p.m. and went to Ruthy's apartment. He returned to work the next day, Friday.

"You were able to carry on?" asked Cortellino.

"It was difficult," Hemy said. "I don't think I was very functional at that point."

The detective asked if Andrea had called Hemy that Friday night.

"No," he said.

"Did you try calling her that night?" asked Cortellino.

"No, no. I'm her boss, but I mean, she's dealing with a tragedy. What am I going to do?"

The next time he saw her was two days later, Sunday, at the funeral for Rusty, but he didn't talk to her. "She was in bad shape."

Returning to the day of the murder, Cortellino asked Hemy a second time to retrace his actions. Hemy said that while it was a normal day at work, he had left at one point to run an errand.

"My car was in the shop," he said.

"What shop was that?" asked Cortellino.

"Ed Voyles Honda," said Hemy, referring to a dealership about two miles away.

"They had a safety recall that they needed to do. It was going to be like a day job or something and, stupid me, I asked them if they would give me a car because Ed Voyles is pretty cheap and they're—my wife has a Lexus and they always give her a car."

Cortellino asked what the recall was for.

"The transmission or something," said Hemy. He said he had gone to Ed Voyles on Wednesday, the day before the shooting. When the garage wouldn't give him a car, he went to a rental agency.

"What did you rent? Did they give you another Honda?"

"No."

"What did you get?"

"It was a Kia minivan," said Hemy, "white or gray."

"Where'd you pick it up at?"

"Enterprise," he said, giving an address across the street from the garage.

Hemy said he drove the Kia to work the next day—the day of the shooting—and returned it around 11 a.m.

Cortellino asked: "I want to ask you a personal question, man-to-man, just between us."

"Okay," Hemy said.

"What was your relationship with Andrea? Be honest."

"Andrea and I are friends," he said.

Cortellino locked eyes with Hemy.

"She works for me, of course," Hemy said. "So the first part of the relationship is she's my employee. Umm, we connected. We're friends. I find her attractive and, and I indicated that to her and she—but again, you know, I'm her manager, so we—"

"You gotta be careful?" asked Cortellino.

"You don't want to play those games," said Hemy, "and I said, you know, in the future, when I have a different job, you know, I'd like to continue to develop the relationship. And she basically said no, I'm committed to Rusty and it ain't gonna happen."

"Did she tell you that?"

"Yeah," said Hemy. Then added: "Why?"

There was suspicion in his voice, the new line of questioning appearing to rattle him.

"I'm asking, that's why," Cortellino snapped. "'Cause I wasn't there. Did she send you emails about it?"

"No, verbal."

"You're traveling, you get close, you're having dinner, you feel good about her but clearly she isn't feeling the same for you?"

"Right, we're very friendly, but again, she said, I'm committed—made a commitment to Rusty."

As he asked questions, Cortellino had been moving his

chair even closer to table. He was now inches from Hemy, leaning in. Hemy moved back.

"You're a guy, I'm a guy, you pick up vibes," said Cortellino.

Hemy sputtered, "I talk about my children and what they're going through, and, you know, she's telling me there's pressures in the house because before she was the one that was in the house."

"This is good," Cortellino said. "This is important, man."

"And now, he's the one that's in the house and now she has to come to work. The initial agreement was that she'd be home at three thirty and she can't get home by three thirty."

"Right."

"Because sometimes there are meetings."

"She's venting with you. She feels comfortable with you."

"Yeah, I mean, she's venting with me. I'm venting with her. This is creating a lot of conflict. And again because our relationship was a friendship, and I'm the manager, I told her, I said—I gave her suggestions of how to make it work better, do things like leave earlier, take care of the kids, work later."

Hemy said he knew he couldn't take the relationship any farther "as long as she reports to me" but his feelings for her lingered. "She's a terrific lady."

"Awkward?" asked Cortellino.

"Once the boundaries are clear," said Hemy, "you carry on, you know?"

Cortellino asked if Andrea ever showed signs that she had the same feelings toward him.

"Well, I don't know," said Hemy. "Hard to say if it was wishful thinking on my part because of my situation, which it could be. I've been thinking about leaving my wife for a while so you might pick up on things that you normally wouldn't or you see things that aren't—I'm not a psychologist. I can't tell you whether it was my imagining that she felt the same way about me."

"Did you apologize?"

"Yes, it was difficult. I told her this: If you feel in any way at any time that our relationship is becoming unprofessional, you need to tell me right away and I will stop."

Cortellino asked if Andrea had mentioned any of this to Rusty.

"I don't think so," said Hemy.

"Did he call you?"

"No," insisted Hemy. "If she mentioned it to him, we would be in an awkward—that Tuesday night"—when Hemy went to their home to work with Andrea—"it wouldn't be, 'Hey, how's it going? What's going on? If there's anything I can do to help?'"

Barnes asked, "Send her cards, letters, flowers?"

"No," said Hemy.

"Gifts?"

"No."

"So let's get back to the eighteenth," said Cortellino. "I'm really concerned about that. You're telling me you're at work at five thirty, and stayed till eleven o'clock and that's when you took the van back, checked it in, and got your car out of the shop?"

"Yeah."

"Hemy, this is what we know," said Cortellino. "We got that van on video the day that Rusty was shot. I swear, the more I look at you, the more I see the person inside that van. I'm giving you every opportunity, man. I don't think things should have happened that way. You've got a heart, you've got a soul, man. You're not a criminal. Things could just go wrong. Things can go wrong in life."

Hemy sat impassively as Cortellino continued: "You're

in that van the day of the shooting and I'm just—we're trying to get you down to say it. And I'm going to say it for you. And then you're going to feel a lot better by it and that's why we're here. You're here because that van was there."

"Where?" Hemy appeared puzzled.

"It was over there, where Rusty got shot," Cortellino said. "Now, Hemy, look at me, don't doubt I'm telling you what happened, and that's what you got to say to yourself. You've got to admit to yourself what happened. Don't embarrass yourself by us going to GE and proving that you weren't there that morning. Don't and—don't raise your eyebrow at me. I'm telling you. You were there when Rusty got shot. Now, Hemy, you were there. I know you were, Hemy."

"How do you know that?" asked Hemy.

"'Cause it's on video. That van is on the video. The van was there. I've got it on video. And this is what you have to do—"

"No," Hemy said, shaking his head.

"You have to take the blinders off, son. You have to take the blinders off and have to look at the big picture. You start looking at yourself to help Andrea with this. Help her understand how this happened. Give us the reason why this happened. Why did it happen? Something triggered you in your mind for it to go like that. But why?"

Hemy said: "I don't have an answer for you."

Barnes now spoke again. "Listen, it's gotta be eating you up. He saw your face."

"What's that?"

"He saw your face. Did he recognize you? Was there shock on his face even though you were in disguise?"

Hemy didn't answer.

For the next couple of hours, Hemy dug in. He refused to answer their questions, dodged questions by answering with a question of his own, shaking his head, raising his eyebrow, calm in his intransigence. The detectives pounded at him with every tactic they could think of. They appealed to his humanity, urged him to ease the burden of bottling up a terrible truth, to stop embarrassing himself, to "man up." They suggested that Hemy was captivated by the "attractive" Andrea but "jealousy gets in the heart" and he killed out of envy for Rusty.

"Motive is because Rusty's got what you want," Cortellino said.

They appealed to his intelligence, implored him to recognize the unbelievable coincidence that the killer drove the exact same kind of van that he had rented. "What are the odds? What are the odds of that?" asked Cortellino.

Barnes showed Hemy the surveillance photo stills and then video of the van.

But Hemy wouldn't budge.

"I don't know what to tell you. I'm not there," said Hemy.

They told him he was too smart to talk like this, that they could easily check with GE security and his co-workers to destroy what little alibi he offered. Hemy responded, "If I'm such a smart man why would I do something so stupid." Cortellino suggested, "Because the heart overcomes the brain."

The interview devolved into a series of soliloquies by Cortellino and Barnes about truth, justice, family, love, passion, the unbearable load of guilt, and the unfairness of life.

Hemy just listened.

When the speeches didn't work, the detectives went old-school good cop/bad cop, with Cortellino being the friendly one saying he merely wanted Hemy to ease his conscience, while Barnes dished out bad cop show lines saying nobody was leaving this cramped room until Hemy spilled the truth. "Listen, friend, the jig is up," said Barnes, "you know. You're our guy."

This failing, the detectives spun elaborate metaphors, telling Hemy that his world had become a funnel and everything was going into it and Hemy was drawing down "like a damn toilet." Hemy again said nothing.

The only time Hemy seemed thrown off was when they brought up his wife. They asked if she knew about Andrea. When they threatened to talk to her, he said the only thing his wife knew was that he and Andrea had recently taken a business trip together to England.

"That's what she'll tell you," said Hemy, fidgeting. "Other than that there's nothing else for my wife to tell you."

As the session ground into the fourth hour, Hemy seemed to wear down the detectives. Nerves frayed. Barnes left the room at one point, then returned with a renewed anger.

"Well it's pretty simple to us," Barnes said.

"It is?" asked Hemy.

"Sure, he's gone, man," the detective said, referring to Rusty. "There's your chance."

"Commit murder?" Hemy said, exasperation creeping into his voice. "Are you kidding me?"

"The question is," Barnes said, "are you kidding me?"

Hemy waved his arms. "To devastate Andrea?"

"Do you think you're kidding us?" Barnes snapped.

"Why? Where? Where in my wildest dreams would I imagine that Andrea wouldn't be devastated by this?" Hemy asked.

Cortellino jumped in, suggesting, "Maybe she's in on it. Maybe we need to look at that."

Hemy looked away in disgust. He grabbed the water cup.

Cortellino pressed on. "Maybe she needs to be in here. Maybe we need to get her butt in here? Maybe she put you up to it? Maybe it's her plan? Maybe we do have the wrong man. Maybe it's her driving your van? That's a spin."

"Yeah," said Hemy sarcastically.

"You're all right with that?"

"With what?"

"Andrea being in the van? You lent her the van?"

"Yeah, right."

Finally, Hemy said he needed a break. He asked to go to the bathroom again. A disgusted Cortellino said, "Go pee and think about it. Go piss this out. You're confused, you're lost right now."

After Hemy returned, Barnes left the room, an apparent tactic to get Cortellino alone with Hemy.

"You're a very smart man," Cortellino told him.

"If I'm such a smart man why would I do something so stupid?" asked Hemy impetuously.

"Because the heart overcomes the brain," said Cortellino. Then he played good cop one more time, saying of Barnes, "He's more confident about it than I am. He's the evidence guy. I just deal with emotions. I'm not the one writing . . . He's a gopher. He's gonna dig it out."

It didn't work. Hemy seemed to become energized, engaging in verbal sparring. When Cortellino told him to come clean, to think about himself, Hemy replied, "Earlier you told me that I'm only thinking about myself and I have to think about others. Now you're telling me that I have to think about myself."

Barnes then walked back into the interview room. His voice was tough: "Here's a question for you: What do you think should be done to the person that shot Rusty?"

An incredulous Hemy answered: "What do I think should be done to the person that shot Rusty?"

"Yeah."

"What kind of question is that?"

"Damn straightforward."

"I know but—why are you—you're sitting here accusing me of doing that."

"And you're sitting over there neither confirming nor denying that you're the person that shot him," said Barnes. "So my question is: Are you prepared to tell me that you're not the guy?'Cause you haven't said, all afternoon, you have not said: *I did not do it.* Interesting."

Cortellino piled on. "Look me in the eye and tell me you didn't do it."

Hemy waved his arms around again. "Look, you, you, you guys are, are are—"

"I can't hear man. I can't," said Cortellino.

"You sit there and crowd me," said Hemy. "You, you come up with all this stuff. You—you're accusing me of something, and it was obvious from the beginning, because I knew you guys called me about the car, that you're somehow implicating me in this whole thing."

"Shut up just a second," Barnes said. "Is that your story? Are you here to tell us on a stack of Bibles that I did not shoot Rusty Sneiderman?"

Hemy paused, then mumbled to himself. Barnes leaned across the table. Cortellino was so close to Hemy, their legs nearly brushed.

Hemy spoke slowly, deliberately. "I was not there," he said. "I did not pull the trigger on the gun that shot Rusty Sneiderman."

After more than five hours in the little interview room, the detectives finally gave up. They seized the iPhone and iPad that Hemy was carrying and gave him one last chance to admit he murdered Rusty Sneiderman. They told him they would soon subpoena his cell phone records, which would place him at a cell phone tower near the preschool at the time Rusty was gunned down.

"How are you going to explain that away?" asked Cortellino.

"There's nothing to explain because it won't be there," said Hemy. "I wasn't there."

Hemy was escorted out of the interview room, hand-cuffed, and taken to the DeKalb County Jail. He had his fingerprints taken and posed for a mug shot before going to jail for the first time in his life.

CHAPTER 8

The same day that Hemy was being questioned by police, Andrea was also at the station, stewing. Feeling pushed aside, she had her own list of questions. Detectives hadn't spoken to her since her November 24 interview, more than a month earlier. She wanted to know if they were any closer to finding her husband's killer. She expressed frustration about being left in the dark.

After treating her gently at first, the detectives developed a bad feeling about her—not quite a suspicion, but a general sense that she was not telling everything she knew. If a fraction of what Hemy had said was true, Andrea seemed to have downplayed the extent of her relationship with him, omissions that the department officials felt cost them extra time and manpower by chasing dead ends. Her reactions to the search warrants had raised eyebrows. In fact, her behavior overall just didn't seem right. She had not acted in ways the public had come to expect from the widow of a murder victim in an open case. She issued no emotional pleas to find the killer, attended no candlelight vigils. At the station, she didn't get the answers she wanted and went home.

Within hours, police were at her door again. Chief Grogan personally went to Andrea's house. When he was let in, he told her, "We wanted to let you guys know that we made an arrest on the case."

"Are you serious?" Andrea asked. "I just talked to you today at two o'clock!"

"I understand," he said. "It happened after that."

"Since two o'clock?" she asked. Her voice grew more frantic. Her breathing quickened.

"Yeah, just a little while ago," Grogan said.

"Can you sit down?" she asked. "You're making me very nervous. Are you sure?"

"We've taken an arrest warrant."

"Are you sure?" she repeated.

"Sure," insisted Grogan.

She seemed to be panicking. "Are you sure?" she said again.

Yes, Grogan told her, very sure.

When he was done talking to her, it would occur to him that when initially informed of the arrest, she didn't ask who it was.

That same night, an announcement went out to the news media: Gather at the Dunwoody police station for a major development in the case. TV crews and photographers crammed into a conference room at the Dunwoody Police Station. The department's spokesman, Sergeant Mike Carlson, went to the podium. He was dressed down in civilian clothes.

"Good evening, everyone," he said as the room burst into camera flashes. "As you know, back on November 18, Rusty—Russell—Sneiderman was shot multiple times in the parking lot of 5493 Chamblee Dunwoody Road outside his child's daycare.

"I would like to announce that we have made an arrest in this case," he continued. "We have arrested forty-eight-year-old Hemy Neuman. He has been charged with murder and he is now being held at the DeKalb County Jail without bond. The investigation of this case is still ongoing. Additional information will be given at a later time. We are asking if you have any information about Mr. Neuman that you contact Detective Andrew Thompson."

Anyone expecting a hardened professional hit man out of *The Sopranos* would be disappointed. The face from the booking photo was a middle-aged man with neatly cut gray hair, bearing little resemblance to the swarthy bearded suspect from the police sketch. The *Atlanta Journal-Constitution* would describe him as "physically unassuming."

The suspect had no criminal record. "He is out of Buckhead," Carlson said, the address a surprise. If Rusty Sneiderman was an unlikely victim, then Hemy Neuman, from one of the best neighborhoods in Atlanta, seemed the most far-fetched of killers.

"We still have detectives that are actively working this case as we speak," Carlson concluded. "So for the integrity of the case, I'm not going to be able to answer any questions. We will be gathering information and when we do have information we will be releasing it."

While Carlson gave Neuman's residence as Buckhead, for reporters building biographies, the property records showed that he had a house in East Cobb, about five miles southeast of Dunwoody. East Cobb is essentially Dunwoody's demographic twin, another leafy, upscale neighborhood north of Atlanta where houses start at half a million dollars and soar upward. Reporters descended upon the thirty-two-hundred-square-foot home on Lasalle Drive with two stories, nine rooms, and three and a half baths. Taped to the front door was a handwritten note: "We will not be taking interviews at the moment. Please remain off of the property. Respectfully, thank you."

Neighbors said that Neuman lived there with his wife, listed on records as Ariela Neuman, and three children, two of them adults, one a teenager. "It's very shocking, totally not the kind you can imagine would do something like that at all," neighbor Dinesh Chaudhry told Channel 2 news. The last time anybody saw him, Hemy was barbecuing with his family. He had long and strong ties to the community. He helped with the Robotics Club at Cobb County's Walton High School and was active in the Jewish community. His Facebook page revealed he grew up in Israel, where he attended a school north of Tel Aviv. The school's website said the students came from abroad and Israel from disadvantaged families. His LinkedIn page showed that he had graduated from Georgia Tech. On Facebook, he wrote that he had spent the holidays traveling "with the girls in Florida," an apparent reference to his children. He last updated the page that previous Friday, wishing his friends a happy New Year.

His Facebook and LinkedIn pages also showed that he worked as an operations and quality manager at GE Energy in Marietta, just a few miles from his house. A spokesperson for General Electric told the media the company was fully cooperating with police and confirmed what many reporters had already started to figure out. Among the dozen or so people who directly reported to Hemy in the quality division within the Energy Group was Andrea Sneiderman, wife of the murdered Rusty Sneiderman.

Once again, the how-could-it-be shock rippled across the Atlanta suburbs. "A lingering question remains: How does a learned, accomplished man with a successful career, one who contributes to his community and has no prior record, find himself facing a murder charge?" asked 11Alive news. The *Atlanta Journal-Constitution* wrote, "Despite the arrest, questions still linger regarding why Sneiderman was killed and who was involved." It simply seemed impossible that somebody like Hemy Neuman could kill somebody like Russell Sneiderman.

But the revelation that Andrea worked for Hemy gave the local media something to chew on. Everyone now forgot the notion of a hit man targeting Rusty in a business dispute; the new theory centered on Andrea's job. The *Journal-Constitution* wondered "whether there had been any falling out between Sneiderman and her supervisor." But most people were just confused. Rusty's friend Paul Sims took one look at the picture of unassuming Hemy Neuman and drew a blank. "I've never heard of him before at all," Sims told Channel 2 news.

As for Rusty's family, there was a collective reluctance to say too much. "We talked to the police," his father Donald Sneiderman told the *Journal-Constitution*. "We just don't know enough, so we aren't going to comment right now." Rusty's brother, Steven, added: "There's still a lot of questions that we need answered. But we're grateful for the hard work of the Dunwoody Police Department and we look forward to seeing this case through to a conclusion." Unlike many others, they knew all about Hemy Neuman. Rusty had spoken of him. He had attended the funeral and shiva, giving a prayer and speaking both to Rusty's father and brother. And Andrea had said he had hit on her. None of this was known publicly yet; nor would people yet catch on to the simmering animosity between Rusty's family and Andrea.

* * *

On Wednesday, January 5, the day after his arrest, Hemy made his first court appearance. A patrol car drove him to the parking lot of the DeKalb County Courthouse in Decatur. Hemy wore an orange jail jumpsuit with DEKALB COUNTY JAIL stenciled on the back. With a beefy cop behind him and Detective Thompson in front of him, Hemy made a perp walk from the patrol car to the front door of the courthouse, surrounded by reporters and TV camera crews. He slumped over as he walked, not looking up, his posture no doubt bent by the shackles that wrapped around his waist and cuffed his hands in front of him.

"What do you have to say?" one reporter shouted at him. "Why did police arrest you? How do you know Mr. Sneiderman?"

"Do you have anything to say? Nothing at all?" asked another reporter.

Hemy took a seat at the far end of a wooden bench to listen to the judge confront him with his alleged misdeeds. He appeared forlorn in his jail wear and plastic jail sandals worn over white sweat socks. There were no family members, no friends, no co-workers to support him. Next to him sat another prisoner in the same orange jumpsuit.

The judge informed Hemy that he had been "charged with the offense of murder. What the defendant did with malice forethought . . . caused the death of Russell Sneiderman, a human being, by shooting the victim."

Hemy showed no emotion. He looked only at the judge, ignoring the crowd of journalists in the courtroom behind him, the media pool video camera to his right. He could have been in a management meeting hearing the findings of a quality-control report. He asked the judge a couple of questions in a calm, quiet voice. Among them was a request for a lawyer.

"Mr. Neuman, I'm appointing a public defender to represent you at your next hearing," said the judge. "That preliminary hearing," the judge continued, "will take place on February the eighth at nine o'clock in Courtroom A, which is across the hall. The detective will bring you to that that area and the public defender will be around to talk to you about your case."

The judge explained that if Hemy hired private counsel, those lawyers would need to notify the court and the public defender would back out. Hemy nodded and said yes quietly. A court staff person gave him a clipboard with forms on it. Hemy asked what he was signing. The judge told him it was a continuance form.

The brief hearing ended with Hemy being denied bail. He was led back into the parking lot as the cameramen swarmed. It was a cold, gray morning, the wind blowing in the microphones.

"Did you kill Rusty Sneiderman?" shouted a reporter.

Hemy kept his head down and kept walking. A cop placed him in the backseat of a black-and-white patrol car, which headed back to the jail.

At 1:30 p.m. that same day, Andrea Sneiderman was squeezed into the same cramped police interview room where Hemy was grilled, this time sitting across the table from the number two man at the Dunwoody Police Department. Deputy Chief David Sides, a veteran cop who had worked everything from patrol to sex crimes, spoke with an ominous drawl and exuded the cheerless demeanor of Dick Cheney, whom he resembled.

It was not their first meeting, but it would be the most intense.

"You and I have spent, I think, close to four hours together, and I've always been very forthright with you about what my goal is," he began. "My goal has always been to identify the suspect and prosecute him to the full extent of the law. And the only question I have is: Are you willing to help me do that?"

"Absolutely," answered Andrea in a small voice.

"We've made an arrest in the case, and I need you to help me," he said. "You have to tell me, what I have to have, I have to have the truth, nothing but the truth, all of it, unabridged, undiluted, pleasant or unpleasant."

"Right," said Andrea in a near-whisper, breathy and soft.

"If you're ready to do that, now is the time to talk. If you can't do that now, you need to tell me," he said. "Do you understand what I'm asking you?"

"I think—"

"Are you sure?"

"Yeah."

After Lieutenant Barnes entered the room and sat to Andrea's left, putting her in the corner area previously occupied by Hemy, Sides told her: "Let's establish a new foundation. The new foundation is that he sat in this room for about four hours yesterday and talked."

"Okay," said Andrea.

"The secondary foundation is I've had an investigator sitting at GE most of the day."

This seemed to throw Andrea. "Today?" she asked.

"Uh-hmmm," he said. "Based upon the foundation of what he told us yesterday and what the co-workers told us today, what is it you think they told us?"

"That my co-workers told you?"

"Um-hmm."

"I have absolutely no idea," she said.

"What do you think he told us?" asked Sides.

"Oh, I'm sure he told you that he thought I was in love with him, or something along those lines," she said, her hands placed on the table palms down. "He's crazy! I don't know. I don't know what he told you. That he was in love with me? That he was infatuated? That he stalked me? I don't know. You tell me. I don't know what he said. That he wanted to be my husband? That he went crazy? I'm hoping he said he went crazy—because he's crazy! I don't know what he would say."

"Why do you say that he's crazy?" asked Sides.

"Because you told me that he shot my husband. Why would someone shoot anybody else? Why would someone, no matter how they might feel about someone else, why would they kill them? Why? Why? Everyone at work loves him, they think he's the greatest thing ever, great boss, good mentor—how would we know that he's crazy?"

Andrea revealed that a week earlier, on December 28—a little over a month after the murder—Hemy sent her an iTunes gift song. It was Bruno Mars's love ballad "Just the Way You Are." Andrea said it made her "nauseated."

"Who sends a song?" she asked. "What was he hoping, that I would recover and fall in love with him? I don't have an answer to that. I really don't. I told Detective Andy—I told you right away that he had feelings for me. I told you. I mean, I didn't think it was anything worth telling anyone over. Yeah, he had feelings for me, he made that clear. Did that make him crazy? I don't know. I don't understand crazy people."

She stopped rambling and looked at the stone-faced cops. "Please, ask me a question. I don't know what you want."

After another lecture from Sides about the need for her to tell the truth, they asked her about the gift song and other emails she had received and sent. She told them that Hemy had brought her work laptop to her at the shiva and that she recently used it to submit an overdue expense reimbursement so her corporate American Express wouldn't get canceled. She saw the gift song on her BlackBerry while in Florida. Barnes asked to see the device, and she handed it to him.

"I like Hemy as a person," Andrea told him as he pressed the buttons on her BlackBerry. "There's no doubt about that, I thought he was my friend, I thought he—" She buried her head in hands. "We had dinners together, we traveled."

"We'll get into that in just a second," said Barnes. "Mind giving me your password?"

"My password is 'Rusty,'" she said.

"I'm going to ask you not to delete anything, okay," said Barnes, before asking Andrea once again about her business trips with Hemy. Barnes now asked most of the questions, assuming the role that Sergeant Gary Cortellino had with Hemy, with Sides sitting across the table watching Andrea and saying nothing.

Sometimes speaking in a whisper, Andrea went over her trips to Florida, Nevada, South Carolina, and the United Kingdom. She spoke of how he first expressed his feelings for her by Lake Tahoe. She told her friends about it but never reported Hemy to the company's human resources manager because she didn't think it was serious enough to jeopardize her job.

"And did you make any trips this year by yourself without him?" asked Barnes.

"I had training in Denver, auditor training."

"What month was that?"

"July also. It was like the week after Minden. I remember because my husband had to do two weeks by himself with the kids. I came home for the weekend. I then sort of had to leave again for this training class."

"Hemy was not in Denver?"

"No, not that I know of, but—"

Sides asked, "Did he ever express interest in a relationship after Lake Tahoe?"

"I mean, I guess, nothing that I directly point to," she said. "I guess he would say: I wish you would change your mind. That kind of comment."

Barnes asked about the day of the murder. "The first second you heard what happened, your women's intuition has got to be going off the radar?"

"That wasn't it at all," she said.

"What were you thinking?" Barnes asked.

"I didn't know Rusty was dead until I went to the hospital," she said. She explained that after Donna Formata at the school called her, "I asked her what was going on, I screamed into the phone, 'What was going on?' She said she just needed me to come. So I ran down the stairs, and I drove all the way. I called my mom, my dad, my brother and told them to meet me at Dunwoody Prep, that something happened to Rusty and I had no idea what was going on.

"I got to Dunwoody Prep, I pulled up and fell out of the car. All I see is yellow tape and a car. Rusty's car. I fell to the ground, somebody picked me up, some police person, and they walk me into Dunwoody Prep. I still didn't know what had happened, no one was telling me, no one was telling me what was going on. So they bring me into the office and Cortellino comes in and sits in front of me. I asked him what was going on? He says, 'Your husband's been hurt, we don't know what hospital he's at,' some bullshit lie. He then he says, he said, 'Is there anyone who would want to hurt your husband?' And I said, 'I have no idea.'"

"As the day goes on," asked Barnes, "and you're going through your mind, at any point did you suspect Hemy?"

"Never, never."

"You never thought Hemy would have done anything until yesterday?"

"No, it wasn't up until that email"—the iTunes gift song.

"And you got that email—it was on December the twenty-eighth?"

"Right. I didn't even read it until recently."

In the email Hemy also asked if she would be coming

to the office holiday party. For the first time Andrea now revealed that she had communicated with Hemy in the days before his arrest. "I told him I didn't want to hear from him," she said. Hemy responded that she "must be going through so much." Andrea told him she didn't want to go to the party. His email, she said, "just made me nauseated."

"Why wouldn't you have called us on the twenty-eighth and told us that he had sent had that? That's pretty bizarre."

"I don't know," said Andrea. "And you know what? I sat at my dining room on Friday after this happened, with Detective Andy, he asked me if anyone had feelings toward me. I gave him Hemy's name immediately."

Andrea became upset again, seemed on the verge of crying. "My in-laws are sitting right there at that same table. I wanted you to find something, because this—this is not my life."

There was a knock on the door and Barnes left the interview room. Sides went over previous questions for a couple of minutes before Barnes returned.

"Your mom thinks we're holding you hostage back here," he told Andrea. "Can you put her at ease? And then we can ask you a few more questions? We'd like to get done today, so I know this is not easy for you, but it is what it is, and you're the person who has the answers that we need. At least we have some more questions for you, try to understand why this happened. We need to talk to you."

Andrea left the room to speak with her mother, but she didn't return. She would never sit for another police interview again.

CHAPTER 9

Along Wildwood Parkway, amid the pricey neighborhoods where visitors have to check in at a guard shack, a driveway marked by a discreet sign cuts through the trees to a complex of sleek office buildings. These are the Marietta offices of GE Energy, and as Deputy Chief Sides had informed Andrea, detectives had arrived. With search warrants, detectives cleaned out Hemy's office drawers and seized his computer. They obtained the travel records of Hemy and Andrea, including their American Express card charges, plane reservations, and hotel and restaurant bills.

They also spoke to employees.

Alice Waters, an engineering manager, had worked in the Atlanta office since 2004, after transferring from the Schenectady, New York, office. She handled fifteen computer programs that automated various processes in her engineering group. On the same level as Andrea in a corporate ladder—Waters called her a "peer"—Waters served as a manager in another engineering group, also reporting to Hemy.

Two days before the murder, Waters saw Hemy at a ninety-minute status meeting. "Same as usual. Serious, getting into the work. I didn't notice anything unusual," she later said of the November 16 meeting. Ditto at a thirty-minute meeting on November 17. "He acted like he always had," she said. "He was serious, levelheaded, logical, just walked us through that we needed to go through. I didn't notice anything unusual."

Asked how Hemy interacted with Andrea, Waters said she noticed that they seemed to be closer to each other than with any other employees. At an Atlanta Braves game outing for work, for instance, they hung out with each other as the group waited to get into the ballpark. "The rest of us were milling around, having social conversations," Waters would later recall in court, repeating what she had told investigators. At meetings Hemy and Andrea usually sat next to each other. "The only thing I noticed is that they were very familiar with each other and I just assumed they had known each other before," she said.

Carmen Harting, a twenty-one-year GE veteran, was Hemy's secretary the last two years. She had observed her boss and Andrea driving together to work functions. Harting, who managed Hemy's calendar, noted, "They had a lot of lunches together." But neither woman said that they ever saw Hemy act affectionately—or inappropriately—toward Andrea. And Andrea never seemed uncomfortable around Hemy, and never expressed any complaints that reached them. The only hint of something brewing between them came that previous August, about three months before Rusty's murder, when at one meeting they suddenly and uncharacteristically didn't sit next to each other—they sat across from each other at the table. But that could have been due to any number of factors, the women said. The employees were constantly under deadline stress and even Hemy, despite his usual cool, had been known to occasionally snap at somebody.

Otherwise, Hemy was described as a model boss: organized, analytical, calm, logical. He rarely talked about his personal life. His staff heard him say at some point he had spent time as a child in Mexico and Israel, and he could speak Spanish.

One of the few people with whom Hemy was close was Al Harris, an audit program manager who worked for him and had an office next door. They talked at holiday parties, restaurant outings with the staff, the occasional office trip to an Atlanta Braves game. Hemy told Al his childhood was a "hard life," much of it spent in boarding schools. The previous fall Hemy revealed he was going through a divorce. In December, after the murder, Hemy spoke about having stomach problems that sent him to the hospital. Beyond that, Harris knew very little about the private Hemy Neuman.

But as employees thought hard, one thing about Hemy did stand out. On November 17, Hemy followed the thirty-minute meeting with Waters with a four-hour marathon meeting attended by, among others, Andrea. Starting at 10 a.m., the meeting's agenda called for Hemy to describe a new technical process and ways to audit that process. As usual, he went to a dry-erase board to draw diagrams, flowcharts, and process maps.

Jerry Morton, a quality program manager, noticed something strange. Hemy was diagramming a process that the employees already were doing. It was a mental lapse uncharacteristic of Hemy. Morton, who handled quality assurance for the engineering services division, pointed out the redundancy. Rather than responding, Hemy remained silent and looked over Morton's head, appearing lost in thought. Morton had never seen Hemy behave this way. Later on during the meeting, Hemy answered one of Morton's questions with another blank look. Morton assumed that something was on his mind.

The next day, Rusty was murdered.

Police retraced Hemy's steps in the hours before the shooting. Using his statement to Barnes and Cortellino as a road map, investigators went to Ed Voyles Honda on Windy Hill Road in Marietta, about two miles from the GE office. Greg Gibbons, the service director, confirmed that Hemy arrived on the afternoon of the seventeenth. Service records showed that Hemy's 2009 Odyssey van needed work on the computer software relating to the brakes. A recall notice had gone out and the warranty would cover the work. As Gibbons reviewed the service records for police, he saw a notation indicating that Hemy didn't want to stay at the shop while the van was worked on but would come back the next day. That Hemy didn't want to be a "waiter" struck Gibbons as unusual since the recall work would take only forty-five minutes. There was no provision for a free rental car.

Across the street, Christina Testa, branch manager of the Enterprise Rent-A-Car, told detectives that at 2:30 p.m. on November 17 she opened the door for Hemy. After introducing herself, she passed him off to another agent. Testa sees about twenty customers a day, but Hemy would stand out. He had reserved the car the day before, on November 16, but arrived half an hour early for his appointment. The compact car he had requested was still in transit from another branch. Hemy sat in one of the chairs to the side while the employee tracked down his car.

"He was very fidgety," Testa said, according to her written statement to a DeKalb County DA investigator. "You could just tell he was very uneasy like he was uneasy to go somewhere. So after a few minutes, and I'm like, oh crap. This guy's waiting in here and I don't want him to make a scene because he's been waiting. So he just sat there. He didn't really say anything. He was looking down a lot."

Testa told another employee, "We just need to get this guy out of here." They decided to offer him a free upgrade to a larger vehicle to get him on his way. Hemy accepted. He presented his driver's license and credit card and was handed the keys to a 2011 Kia Sedona minivan. The van was silver and had bar-code stickers on the front windshield and driver's-side window to identify the car.

The investigators found that the following day, November 18, 2010, Hemy did arrive early at GE as he had stated. This was confirmed by GE's security operations. Every GE employee gets a photo ID badge with an assigned number. The plastic badges give them access to the doors and elevators in the four buildings that make up what the company calls its campus: the main building with the number 4200 and three other buildings, the 3200 and 1300 buildings, and a building half a mile away at 2018 Powers Ferry Road. Every time the ID badge is used, a record is made with the time and location. In addition, cameras are focused on hallways and waiting rooms, entrances and the parking garage, and twenty-two security officers patrol the grounds. Guards monitor the front doors to the 4200 and 2018 buildings twenty-four hours a day, and patrols roam the rest of the campus. It is almost impossible to get in or out of any building, elevator, or parking garage at GE's Marietta offices without security knowing about it.

Footage from one of the eleven security cameras scattered throughout the four-level parking structure showed a silver Kia Sedona minivan entering shortly after 5:30 a.m. on November 18. Under subpoena, GE produced the records of all key-card activity, formatted as a computer-generated log stored on a server in a secure room and accessible only by security and authorized GE employees. A printout showed that Hemy Neuman swiped his security ID badge at the entrance to the main building at 5:37 a.m. Police went back through the records and found that Hemy's arrival time was uncharacteristically early—he normally got to work at between 7:45 a.m. and 8:15 a.m.

Thirty seconds after scanning into the front door, Hemy used his key card to activate the lobby-level elevator to the floor where his office was located. At 5:45 a.m. his computer was up and running. GE keeps records of when the password-accessible work computers are turned on and can keep track of the activity, from websites visited to emails sent and received. GE's in-house high-tech forensic examiner, Kathleen Gough, uses this data for a range of IT investigations, from sexual harassment to theft of company secrets.

Gough told investigators that while Hemy had turned on his computer shortly before 6 a.m., he didn't type on it. There were no records of emails, websites, or Word documents being opened. With his computer still on, Hemy left his office. A security camera trained on the basement hallway showed him leaving at 5:51 a.m., according to the time stamp on the video, apparently taking the stairs instead of the elevator. He had only been at work for twenty minutes.

Later that morning, an employee named Michael Farnam arrived at 7:30 a.m. and turned on his computer. A quality manager in the thermal engineering division, Farnam had been scheduled to attend a 9 a.m. meeting with Hemy. But his computer now showed an Outlook email from Hemy saying the meeting had been changed to 2:30 p.m. Farnam couldn't tell exactly when the email was sent, only that it came between 6 p.m. the night before when he left work and when he got to his desk that morning at 7:30 a.m.

That same morning another employee, Alan Schachtely, a software engineer and process engineer, was attending a training class. Schachtely had about the same rank at the company as Hemy—the two shared a boss—and he had known Hemy for about two years. Schachtely and Andrea supported the same organization that built the software for energy services. Their offices shared a wall and were located in a different building from where Hemy worked.

At 10:34 a.m. on November 18, Schachtely received a text on his BlackBerry from Andrea: "Call me asap pleas [sic]."

Not wanting to leave in the middle of the class, he wrote back, "5 min . . . ."

Andrea responded, "My husban [sic] was shot."

A stunned Schachtely wrote back, "Calling."

He walked out of the course and called her from the hallway. She asked him to call her manager to tell him her husband had been shot.

At 10:45 a.m., Schachtely sent Hemy a text:

"Hemy . . . . It's Alan Schachtely," he wrote, giving his full name because he didn't know Hemy well, having attended occasional meetings with him but never texting him before. "I need to make contact with you. Andrea has a family emergency that I need to make you aware of."

Hemy replied, "Call my cell."

Schachtely couldn't be certain, but believed he did talk to Hemy on the phone. Either way, Hemy got back to Schachtely, sending a text that said, "I just talked to her."

"Ok . . . Good," Schachtely replied. "You are in the know. Please let me know if there is anything I can do to help."

Later that morning, Schachtely told police, he spoke again with Andrea on the phone. She told him her husband had died.

Schachtely didn't know where Hemy was when he talked to him on the phone and texted him. They worked in different buildings. But Hemy's whereabouts twenty minutes later, at 11:06 a.m., when his debit card swiped a reader at a RaceTrac gas station on Delk Road in Marietta, was about two and a half miles from the office. Hemy purchased 2.43 gallons of gas for $6.41. He then turned up at the Enterprise agency, south of the gas station, and returned the van. The odometer showed that 123 miles had been placed on it since it was rented the afternoon before.

At 11:48 a.m., Hemy was back at GE. This time he didn't scan himself into his building using his key card but obtained a visitor pass to enter the nearby 2018 building—where Andrea worked. It's not uncommon for employees to get visitor badges if they lose or forget their regular ID badges; GE rules require the guard check a driver's license or passport to confirm the employee's identity. Visitor badge holders also have to sign a computer screen at a kiosk that is monitored by a security camera.

Security camera footage showed Hemy going through this process. The computer badge log showed that the visitor pass was swiped at 11:51 a.m. to access the second floor where Andrea's office was located. No cameras showed the private office space, so his activities weren't known. Whatever he did, it took about twenty minutes, for at 12:12 p.m. he obtained from the security guard a second visitor pass, this one at the front desk of the main building—his building. He scanned the card to get through the lobby and again access the elevator at 12:14 p.m. He would have had to produce an ID to the guard to get the badge. A video camera recorded him in the lobby.

At some unknown time he left the building—no cameras caught him—but twenty minutes later, at 12:36 p.m., he swiped his regular employee badge to reenter. At 1 p.m., Hemy was in his office on the phone when Alice Waters entered and overheard him say something to the effect of: "Let me know when you find out anything." He hung up and said nothing to her of the phone call.

She was there for their regular biweekly meeting in which Hemy catches up on her work. Ten minutes in, somebody came into his office—Waters didn't remember who—and Hemy excused himself to speak to this person outside her hearing range, returning about two minutes later appearing "a little disturbed."

"What's wrong?" she asked him.

Nothing, he told her.

"Something is bothering you," she said. "What is it?"

He looked at her and said, "Andrea's husband was shot and killed."

"Oh, my God," she said. "Oh, my God."

Hemy excused himself again, telling Waters to wait in his office while he contacted the human resources department to tell them what had happened. Reinier Van Ede, GE's human resources manager, welcomed Hemy into his office and started to make a joke. They worked on the same floor, their offices about fifty yards away. They saw each other frequently and got along.

Hemy stopped him.

"He came to me as HR manager," Van Ede later said, "letting me know that Andrea had to leave the office because her husband was shot." He described Hemy's demeanor as "appropriately concerned."

About ninety minutes later, Hemy appeared at his 2:30 p.m. meeting with Michael Farnam, the meeting that had been rescheduled overnight per the Outlook message. Nothing was said about Rusty or Andrea. "It was a normal meeting as far as I recall," Michael later said.

Taken as a whole, the security evidence and witness statements bolstered the police case against Hemy, contradicting his claim that he was in the office during the time of the shooting. His alibi was shattered.

CHAPTER 10

"Good morning," DeKalb County district attorney Robert James greeted reporters at his office. "During the course of the last four weeks, my office began to work with the Dunwoody Police Department to investigate the death of Mr. Russell Sneiderman."

Robert James was young, handsome, and ambitious. Raised in Tennessee, James is the son of NFL star Robert James Sr., a three-time Pro Bowl defensive end for the Buffalo Bills in the late 1960s and early 1970s who after football became a minister and assistant high school principal. His mother Barbara James also was an educator. After graduating from Middle Tennessee State, where he played basketball and was president of the African-American Student Association, Robert Jr. moved to Atlanta to study law at Georgia State. Stints as Rockdale County assistant district attorney and DeKalb County solicitor-general, the office that prosecutes misdemeanors, earned him a spot on *Georgia Trend Magazine*'s "40 Under 40" list. In 2010, he ran for DA in a special election to complete the remaining three and a half years of the term of Gwendolyn Keyes Fleming, who resigned when President Obama appointed her to a top post in the Environmental Protection Agency. The thirty-nine-year-old James trounced attorney Constance Heard with 64 percent of the vote.

Three days after James took office, Rusty Sneiderman was murdered. The new DA seized the moment. James not only provided investigators, but also controlled the flow of public information. After the police department announced Hemy's arrest, Chief Grogan wanted to hold a second news conference on January 6, two days later, but James nixed it. "At that point we were deep into an active investigation," James later told the *Dunwoody Crier.* "You want to control the integrity of whatever information comes out and goes in. If certain things get out, it makes it difficult for us to conduct our investigation. We really wanted to make sure that no one would talk to the media and the only way to do that was to close ranks and take it over at an earlier-than-normal phase."

If Grogan felt slighted, he kept it to himself. Others in Dunwoody weren't so quiet. "Information Blackout in Sneiderman Murder," complained the *Crier* in a headline, which reported on a tense Dunwoody Homeowners' Association meeting following Hemy's arrest. About two hundred people packed Dunwoody United Methodist Church, anxious to hear from Grogan what was going on with the murder case. "I'm going to talk about our community outreach programs," the chief told them. "I know what you all want to know, but I can't comment on that issue." The pressure reached City Hall. Councilman

Denny Shortal sent an email to constituents: "Many of you have asked why there isn't more information released to the public concerning our progress in these investigations. Folks, investigating a crime, especially a capital crime, is not a public-affair event. In fact, it is just not good practice to release information to the public on the progress of investigations."

It was shades of the bad old days of DeKalb County rule for many residents. For the next month, Dunwoody remained subjected to what the *Crier* called the "party line of no comment," all part of James's strategy to keep the case from buckling under the weight of growing media interest and public pressure for answers. James later admitted in the *Crier* interview that his tactics were "challenging, given that it was so early in the administration." But he insisted he had no choice.

Now, on Tuesday, February 8, James was front and center before the TV cameras with the first official statement in weeks.

"Since Mr. Sneiderman's death in November of last year, the Dunwoody Police and my investigators have worked tirelessly to bring justice to the loved ones of Mr. Russell Sneiderman and the citizens of DeKalb County," he said. "Today, at 9 a.m., the DeKalb County Grand Jury returned a two-count indictment of Hemy Neuman. The indictment is currently being filed with the DeKalb County Clerk of Superior Court. Neuman was indicted by the Grand Jury for one count of malice murder and one count of possession of a firearm during a commission of a felony.

"Our collective goal," he continued, "is to continue to seek justice and preserve the public safety of our community, not only for the Sneiderman family but for anyone who has lost a loved one because of violent crime."

The announcement came as a surprise. Most had expected a preliminary hearing, where James's office would present a bare-bones case against Hemy to secure a charge. The hearing could have answered some of the burning questions regarding why Hemy Neuman had allegedly murdered Rusty Sneiderman. By taking the case to a grand jury, James kept the details under wraps. Grand jury proceedings are conducted in secrecy, even from defense attorneys, and charges are virtually assured in all cases.

"We will not try this case in the media nor will we discuss the evidence that will be presented at trial," James explained. "Our job is to the present the facts, the truth and to seek justice." He underscored that the policy of secrecy would continue. "I cannot comment on what may or may not happen in the future as far as our evidence," he said, but added, "If I were not confident I would not have presented the case to the grand jury this morning."

The next step, he said, was an arraignment for Hemy, where a judge would formally present the charges to him, allow him to enter a plea, and set a trial date. "Again," James said, "to ensure the integrity of this case, I will be unable to answer any questions from the media as it pertains to this case."

Not only were the media and public left in the dark, Hemy would also have to wait to find out what evidence prosecutors had against him. Soon after his arrest, his mother, Rebecca Cohen, and her boyfriend reached out to a family friend who was a lawyer. That lawyer referred them to Robert Rubin and Doug Peters, who have a three-partner practice in Decatur, not far from the Stone Mountain Judicial Circuit Superior Court building where Hemy's case was being handled.

In January, the two attorneys squeezed into a cubicle in the visitor area at the DeKalb County Jail and through Plexiglas spoke with Hemy Neuman. "In every case, when you meet someone whose life is in jeopardy and they're looking for someone to put their trust in to save their life, you hope to build a rapport," Rubin said later. "We had an immediate rapport with Hemy Neuman. It was more of a personal connection. He felt comfortable talking to us. We felt good about him. We liked him. He was a very likable guy."

Both attorneys have long practiced in the Atlanta area. Raised in Ohio, Rubin moved to Atlanta in the late 1970s to complete his undergraduate studies and law school at Emory University, northeast of downtown and close to Decatur. After working as a public defender in Fulton County, Georgia, and in the Georgia Attorney General's Office prosecuting doctors appearing before the state medical board, he went into private practice while also teaching criminal litigation as an adjunct professor at his alma mater.

His three decades in Atlanta have given him a trace of a local accent, though he doesn't come close to his partner. With his bow ties, pocket hankies, and smooth drawl, Douglas Peters affects the very picture of a gentleman southern lawyer. Born and raised within a few miles of his law offices, Peters attended the University of Georgia for his bachelor's and law degrees, served as an assistant district attorney in Clayton County, Georgia, and as a municipal court judge in the city of Lithonia, twenty-five miles west of Atlanta, before hanging out his shingle in Decatur.

The two lawyers had their share of high-profile cases dealing with the darkest aspects of the human condition. Rubin represented one of the defendants in the Final Exit Network case, four members of an alleged assisted-suicide group being prosecuted for their roles in a man's 2008 suicide. Peters has developed an expertise in representing people accused of child abuse and child molestation, including women in shaken baby syndrome cases.

"When we first sat in that attorney's booth, the first time

we heard Hemy give us his account of what had happened—
I'll never forget that—we both knew, Bob and I, that things
were not adding up," said Peters. "We felt he was out of
touch with reality in terms of what he described to us about
the offense. Bob and I are not psychiatrists or psychologists. But from the first time we met him, it was not ratio-
nal how he described it."

They needed more information. While awaiting the
prosecution's discovery—the police reports, interview tran-
scripts, lists of physical evidence—the attorneys hoped to
learn more from a preliminary hearing.

"We were anxious to have an opportunity to have an
individual judge evaluate the presentation of the case,"
Peters told reporters after James announced the grand
jury indictment. "Unfortunately, that is not going to be the
case." Until they started getting discovery materials, Rubin
added, "We don't know what the District Attorney knows."
Until then, Hemy would remain behind bars without bail.
"He's obviously distraught," said Rubin, "for his family
and the Sneiderman family."

With little known to the public about Hemy or his alleged motivation, the lawyers sought to fill in the gaps.
"The arrest of Mr. Neuman is also a tragedy," Rubin told
reporters. "There are a lot of people affected by Mr.
Neuman's arrest: his family, his kids, his friends and co-
workers are also affected by this. He's very emotional,
very distraught, very worried about his family and worried
about the Sneiderman family."

The lawyers also dropped some tantalizing hints that
there was more to the case than what had been released
publicly. "We do believe there's somebody else the police
should be looking for," said Rubin. "However, we don't
have the resources of the state to do that kind of investigation." He didn't say whom they should be looking for, but
the media connected the dots. The next day the *Journal-*

Constitution noted that "the extent of the relationship between Neuman . . . and Andrea Sneiderman has not been disclosed," adding with a journalistic wink that "they worked together often."

The day of the grand jury indictment brought another player in the case to the forefront. Since Hemy's arrest his wife, Ariela Neuman, had stayed out of the public eye, all the attention focused on Andrea. Now for the first time her side of the story would filter out. Ariela, too, had hired an attorney, Esther Panitch, a Miami-raised, magna cum laude graduate from the University of Miami's law school with a local civil and criminal practice. Comfortable in front of the microphones, quick with sound bites, and fond of colorful camera-friendly attire, Panitch would become a constant presence throughout the Sneiderman case (as well as a legal analyst on HLN in other cases) and a force to be reckoned with for both the prosecution and the defense attorneys.

She made her debut by saying Ariela was "stunned by the allegations and the indictment which came down today," and revealed that at the time of the murder, the Neumans were separated, having split in October after twenty-two years of marriage. When asked by a TV reporter if Ariela wanted to pass on any thoughts to Rusty's family, Panitch said, "Mrs. Neuman and her children feel a great deal of compassion for the Sneiderman children." Her answer pointedly left out Andrea Sneiderman.

It would be the beginning of an increasingly loud drumbeat: What was Andrea's role? She still was not talking to the media, but her lawyer did release a statement:

"The murder of my husband, Rusty Sneiderman, has been devastating to me and our families. I was thankful and relieved when the police made an arrest but I was shocked to learn that the man charged with the murder was my former boss, a person who we thought was a friend of our family.

"I have been assured by the DeKalb County District Attorney's Office that Mr. Neuman is Rusty's killer and that they will do everything in their power to bring him to justice. My family and I are cooperating in any way we can to assist them in their efforts."

CHAPTER 11

On a nondescript building along a busy highway a red neon sign flashes OPEN. Over the door is painted an American flag, and next to it a sign advertises a shooting club. Parnell's Firearms and Range in quaint Woodstock, Georgia, sells a full array of pistols, long guns, ammunition, scopes, reloading supplies, all sorts of gun accessories. The shelves include goods from Remington, Ruger, Browning, Benelli, Weatherby, and US Repeating Arms. The shop also buys new and used antique and collectible guns and provides appraisals. Once you buy a weapon, you can shoot it right away without having to leave the grounds at the indoor shooting range.

On Halloween Day, 2010, at 2:47 p.m., a call went from Hemy Neuman's 770 area code Apple iPhone to Parnell's.

The evidence came from hundreds of pages of cell phone

records produced under subpoena. Detectives who initially thought they were looking for a savvy master criminal instead found in Hemy a man who did virtually nothing to cover his tracks. The trail included not only phone calls made and received, but also Hemy's whereabouts when he placed the calls—based on the nearest cell phone tower from which the call was "pinged." The subpoenas also produced a record of virtually everything he did on his laptop and iPad, the history retrievable—in many cases even if it was erased or deleted—with forensic software that finds things hidden amid the memory bramble. David A. Freyman of the Georgia Bureau of Investigation created an image of the data on Hemy's iPad, extracting both the stored history information plus anything that hadn't been written over by the device. Among the findings: On October 15, 2010, Hemy created a bookmark labeled "gun." Over the next two weeks the term *range* was repeatedly searched.

When Hemy called Parnell's on October 31, phone records placed him near a cell tower in Dalton, Georgia, in the foothills of the Blue Ridge Mountains, about eighty miles away from Dunwoody up Interstate 75, which bisects the Perimeter and shoots north. This placed him near the Northwest Georgia Trade & Convention Center, a complex of meeting rooms and large banquet halls. The center hosts everything from high school proms and weddings to the Georgia Rampage indoor football games. On this weekend, the center hosted the traveling Eastman Gun Show. As "Proud supporters of your Second Amendment rights since 1981," the show bills itself as a one-stop shop for "a good deal on the firearm, ammo, holster, scope, clip or magazine, knife or whatever you are looking for," with sales consummated on the spot. "You may purchase a gun, ammunition and other accessories at the shows and take them home the same day."

On that Halloween Day 2010, a Sunday, one of the convention hall's sixteen security cameras captured Hemy Neuman walking through the admissions area. What he did next wasn't known as no more footage of him inside the gun mart could be found, and there was no paper trail if he had purchased a weapon. Georgia has among the nation's most lax gun laws. Residents don't have to register firearms; in fact, the state prohibits registration. A concealed weapons permit is relatively easy to obtain. The state does forbid so-called straw purchases: Somebody can't coerce a dealer to sell to somebody other than the actual buyer. And it's illegal to sell a pistol or revolver to a minor. Certain weapons—including some (but not all) sawed-off shotguns, machine guns, and bazookas—are also illegal to possess without proper federal licenses. The federal government calls for a criminal background check for people buying guns from dealers, but not in private-party sales, as at gun shows like the one Hemy visited.

One way or another, the day after going to the gun show, a Monday, Hemy Neuman had a gun. He made his way to Woodstock in a semi-rural area near Allatoona Lake. Woodstock relies on day-trip visitors from Atlanta strolling the brick-paved 1870s-era downtown with antiques stores, gift shops, and tearooms. The outskirts are dominated by fast-food restaurants catering to freeway traffic heading to Chattanooga, Tennessee, and beyond.

Take a right just past the Taco Bell onto Main Street— which is more like a highway—and Parnell's Range sits on the right. At 6:30 p.m. on November 1, 2010, Hemy walked in. John Turner, a retiree and part-time employee and gun enthusiast whose salary is supplemented by free range time and targets, waited on him. Turner handed Hemy the insurance liability forms required to use one of the store's six shooting lanes. While state law frowns on paperwork concerning guns, the same is not true of gun ranges, which must worry about getting sued if somebody gets hurt. Hemy signed a form attesting that he had read and understood the safety rules written above. He also printed his name and added the date and time, and for one dollar purchased a target: a two-foot-by-four-foot silhouette of a man with rings providing points for accuracy: the closer to the heart, the higher the score. This is the most popular target at the store, far outselling the conventional bull's-eye. Hemy's form reflected that he used the target lane from 6:35 p.m. to 7:05 p.m.

When investigators interviewed Turner they found that there was no record of the kind of gun Hemy shot. The store keeps track of the manufacturer, model, and caliber of guns loaned for the range. But people who bring their own weapons don't have to fill in that information. The store did, however, have piles of used shell casings going back months. Some of them could have come from the gun Hemy shot at the range and could be compared to the shells found at the murder scene.

Investigators filled up fourteen five-gallon buckets of brass and hauled it to ballistics man Kelly Fite. Among the state's leading ballistics experts, Fite had logged thirty-one years as a firearms supervisor with the Georgia Bureau of Investigation before going out on his own in 1999 as a private consultant. One by one, the Parnell's casings went under stereomicroscope magnifications of five to thirty times. Fite looked at the telltale ejector marks—where a gun's mechanism grabs onto a shell after firing and kicks it out of a chamber. Like fingerprints, no two ejector marks are alike, so they can be used for identification in court. Even for an examiner accustomed to tedious work, Fite found this project particularly challenging. He said that there are about one hundred casings per pound, with three hundred pounds in the buckets, working out to thirty thousand casings that went under his microscope. In the end, the effort proved fruitless. Not one matched the murder-scene casings.

Around the same time, Mark Potter, an investigator on loan from the DeKalb County District Attorney's Office, was combing through Hemy's cell phone records when he came across a name that he didn't recognize: Jan DaSilva. A check against the files found no match to a GE employee or a family member. Potter called the number on the records and a man answered. After hearing what the man had to say, the detective set up a meeting at his workplace.

The Buckhead Diner on Piedmont Road Northeast is the quintessential ITP restaurant, with enough black-and-white tile, chrome, and neon to evoke a classic America diner but prices and ambience in keeping with Buckhead's expectations. The restaurant promises a "fun menu" and "taste of nostalgia" to go with "snappy service, upscale atmosphere and retro style [that] gives this Atlanta icon a funky flair all its own." The restaurant's website includes a "celebrity spotlight" of black-and-white pictures of guests including Kevin Bacon, Alyson Hannigan and Kathy Griffin, and Eugene Levy.

On Feruary 22, 2011, Potter met Jan DaSilva outside the Buckhead Diner. A former petty officer in the navy where he was a mechanic on F/A-18 Super Hornet fighter jets, DaSilva left the service and now parked cars as a valet. Potter placed on the trunk of a car a photo lineup—six pictures of different men—and asked him if he recognized anybody. Without hesitation DaSilva picked out photo number 4—Hemy Neuman.

The detective asked DaSilva how he knew the man and how DaSilva's phone number came to be in Hemy's cell phone records.

"I sold him my gun," he said.

It was a Bersa Thunder 40, a big and powerful

handgun—over seven inches long and weighing nearly two pounds. A semiautomatic that can carry up to thirteen rounds, it comes in a black or nickel finish and gets generally glowing reviews from gun owners. Christiangunowner.com gushes that the Bersa Thunder is "worthy consideration for anyone wanting a full sized shooter." A commenter on thefiringline.com says, "I love this gun. I can shoot it quite well. The weight makes recoil very manageable, and the .40 cal is, in my opinion, the perfect pistol caliber." A common drawback is that it may be too much gun for people with smaller hands.

It shoots .40-caliber bullets, the same kind that killed Rusty Sneiderman.

DaSilva originally obtained the gun on April 8, 2010, from Nick's Gun and Range on Canton Road in Marietta. He filled out the federally required form from the Bureau of Alcohol, Tobacco and Firearms, passed the criminal background check, and was handed the weapon along with two magazines that carry ten rounds of ammunition each. After six months, however, his interest in firearms was eclipsed by a new passion: skydiving. Needing extra money to pay for his certification to become a skydiving instructor, DaSilva listed the Bersa on a gun sales website called gunlistings.org for $375 in October 2010.

He received just one email reply on his Yahoo account. A prospective buyer contacted him and asked if the gun was still available. DaSilva said it was and they arranged a date and time to meet, but DaSilva missed the appointment because he had gone skydiving. He sent an apologetic email and asked the potential buyer if he was still interested. They set up a second appointment for October 31, this time at another restaurant where DaSilva also worked as a valet.

Owned by the same company that operates the Buckhead Diner, the Atlanta Fish Market on Pharr Road NE

promises a "relaxing retreat from the hustle and bustle of
Buckhead" with fish flown in daily and a "menu printed
twice daily." As DaSilva waited in the parking lot, he got
a call on his cell phone call from the man saying he was
nearly there. Minutes later a Honda Odyssey minivan
pulled up into the big driveway and came to a stop at the
valet hut next to DaSilva. After the man introduced himself as Hemy Neuman, they chatted briefly and found some
things in common. Hemy said he had been born and raised
in Puerto Rico as DaSilva had, immigrating to the United
States when he was eighteen. The two now spoke in Spanish. Hemy said he'd graduated from Georgia Tech and had
a daughter there; Jan said his uncle went to the university.

DaSilva then opened a box to show him the Bersa. He
explained how the gun worked, gave him a cleaning kit and
two kinds of Winchester bullets: about a hundred solid-
brass rounds used for target practice and another fifty hollow points designed for self-protection, the hollow points
spreading out in a body upon impact, causing maximum
harm. Hemy gave him $380 from a wad of $20 bills he had
just gotten from an ATM and Jan returned $5 change.
Hemy drove off with his gun.

DaSilva thought this was the end of it, but one evening
about two weeks later Hemy Neuman appeared at the
Buckhead Diner while DaSilva was parking cars. DaSilva
didn't know how Hemy got there, seeing no car. Hemy apparently walked up to him. Speaking English this time,
Hemy asked if DaSilva remembered him. DaSilva said yes,
of course. Hemy reminded him anyway that he was the
man who had bought the gun and asked if he could talk to
him. DaSilva reluctantly agreed, wondering how Hemy had
found him at his other job. Without being asked, Hemy said
the other valets at the Atlanta Fish Market had directed him
to the Buckhead Diner.

Hemy went on to tell DaSilva that "something bad happened with the gun," DaSilva later said. DaSilva asked if the gun had malfunctioned and worried that Hemy wanted his money back. Hemy wouldn't say what went wrong, only that he had to get rid of the gun. DaSilva asked if he had sold it, and Hemy replied that he had disposed of it where nobody would find it.

Then out of the blue Hemy said, "Don't ever have a mistress."

DaSilva didn't know what to say, so he just said, "Yes."

Hemy told a convoluted story about a mistress causing trouble with a family and that this family knew Hemy had the gun—somebody had seen him flash it—and members of the family got scared. So Hemy tossed the gun into Lake Lanier, a resort with boating, sandy beaches, banquet halls, a boardwalk, and a water park fifty miles northeast of Atlanta.

DaSilva listened, unsure how to react. Hemy explained that some people might try to contact DaSilva asking if he'd sold Hemy the gun or if he'd ever met him. If that happened, Hemy advised, DaSilva should just say that the pair knew each other through mutual friends at Georgia Tech and that DaSilva was trying to get them jobs at GE where Hemy worked. DaSilva agreed to lie for him but felt uneasy. Hemy offered him a bunch of twenty-dollar bills from his pocket, but DaSilva said he declined. Hemy asked if he was sure he didn't want the money; DaSilva told him yes and added that he really needed to get back to work. Hemy walked away.

Rattled by the conversation, DaSilva that day approached an Atlanta police officer. He asked the officer if a person could get in trouble for selling a gun that was later used in a crime. According to DaSilva, the officer told him that if the gun had been sold legally, the seller need not be worried. Feeling assured the sale was legal, DaSilva said nothing more about it until he was contacted by Potter.

Hoping to obtain a shell casing for comparison, the investigator asked DaSilva if he had ever fired the weapon in the six months he owned it and kept any of the shells. DaSilva said he shot it about five hundred times at a range but had not kept the casings.

But he did know where he might be able to find one. When DaSilva purchased the gun, it came with a shell from a test fire. Excited about his first gun purchase, he gave that shell to his girlfriend, Aurora Juarez—also a gun enthusiast. It was "like a gift," he later said, "nothing special."

At Potter's request, DaSilva called Aurora, who was at home and said she'd talk to him. The detective went to her house, flashed his badge, and asked her if she had kept the shell.

"I keep everything," she said.

It had been in her room. Potter took the shell casing to Fite's laboratory in an envelope. Through the stereomicroscope he compared the casing with one found at the crime scene, looking at their respective ejection marks.

Fite, who had testified twenty-seven hundred times in cases for both the defense and prosecution, was prepared to go to court to give his expert opinion that Rusty Sneiderman was gunned down with the $375 Bersa Thunder 40 that Hemy Neuman bought from Jan DaSilva.

CHAPTER 12

In late July 2010, Hemy Neuman left for a business trip to Colorado, telling his wife, Ariela, he was meeting an HR representative. She would later find that the trip went on the family credit card and not Hemy's corporate American Express. She was aghast that Hemy, who had put the cash-strapped family on a budget, found the money to dash off to Colorado for a few days. Pressed on his expenses, he admitted to Ariela that he had in fact purchased two bottles of wine during the meetings. Only later did Ariela discover what she called the true identity of the "HR representative." So, too, did detectives.

Tracing Hemy's travels for GE proved easy. Everything was meticulously documented in GE's travel files, from dates and locations to the names of restaurants, hotels, and items purchased. GE Energy had a liberal travel and expense policy, leaving the details to the discretion of the boss. Hemy could decide how frequently and how extravagantly employees could travel on the company dime, and with whom he would travel. In the seven months before Rusty's murder, his companion was usually Andrea.

Going through her expense records as well, investigators found the trips that she had spoken of in her police interviews. Her May 24, 2010, excursion to Florida shortly after she was hired was there. So was her July 13–14 trip to Minden, Nevada, where she said Hemy revealed he had feelings for her—the fleeting moment she said the two had quickly put behind them.

Investigators also found the June 21 overnight trip to Norfolk, Virginia, that Andrea and Hemy took. The receipts showed they dined at the Sirena Cuchina Italian restaurant downtown, with Hemy's expense form showing a bill of $154.34, including a $50 bottle of wine. They also found the July 18 trip that Andrea took to Longmont, Colorado, north of Denver, where she stayed at the Hampton Inn, a Hilton property that gave her travel points.

Andrea told police that she traveled there solo for auditor training. But interviews with hotel staff revealed a different story.

Before Andrea arrived, the phone rang at the front desk. Hampton Inn day shift clerk Ruth Ingraham answered. It was 11:30 a.m. and a man was calling to say that his wife, whom he identified as Andrea Sneiderman, would be checking in that night after arriving on a 7 p.m. flight. He said they were newlyweds and that she had come to the hotel on business. He said they had never been apart since getting married and he worried that she would be very lonely.

"And he wanted me to purchase flowers, chocolates, and

a nice card to write a note in to be put into her room," Ingraham later said in court, repeating what she had told local police recruited to assist Dunwoody detectives. "And he said he would be flying out during the week as a surprise and that he would repay me."

A new employee at the hotel, Ingraham didn't know what to do. "I said it's very romantic, but I just don't know what the rules are," she later recalled.

The man wouldn't take no for an answer. Becoming "very insistent," she said, he tried to talk her into buying the flowers and chocolates, but she refused. He finally gave up, but did ask if she would leave a message for Andrea when she arrived. Ingraham agreed. As he dictated, Ruth scribbled into the front desk logbook: "Andrea, for the sweetest and most beautiful woman in the world. Peaceful sleep knowing that you are always in my dreams. Love, Hemy." For the clerk, he left his full name, Hemy Neuman, and a phone number with Atlanta's 404 area code. When night clerk Brady Blackburn took over the front desk and read the log, he added his own notation: "WTF am I supposed to do with this?"

The insistent Hemy had become the talk of the Hampton Inn staff. At a company picnic the next day, Ingraham asked her boss, the hotel owner, what to do about the request to buy flowers and chocolates. He told her she didn't have to buy the items. That night after the picnic, Hemy called again, this time telling Blackburn that his new wife Andrea would be lonely traveling without him. "He impressed upon me what a great travesty, what a problem that she was going to be apart from him," Blackburn later recalled.

When Hemy asked Blackburn to buy the flowers and chocolates, the clerk suggested that he contact a florist himself to arrange a delivery to the room. But the man said

the florists were closed and asked if the clerk could somewhere find flowers and leave them in the woman's room,
and then be reimbursed with a personal check when the
man arrived a few days later.

Blackburn laughed. He told the man that would be impossible, that he couldn't afford anything like that. The man
asked why. The clerk told him it was none of his business
and the request was outside of hotel policy. Through the
conversation, the man struck a strangely familiar tone,
telling the clerk, "You're my friend." When Blackburn
repeated that he wouldn't do it, the man was "disappointed,
dejected, but he didn't fight me on it," he later said.

When Andrea Sneiderman checked in later that night,
Blackburn told her she had a message. He didn't read it
verbatim, instead paraphrasing it: "Andrea, Hemy says
he loves you."

Andrea blushed and looked down, according to Blackburn.

Andrea got a room with two queen beds. But contrary to what she told police, she would not be alone in
Longmont. Three days later, on Wednesday, July 21, 2010,
Hemy took Frontier Airlines Flight 305 from Atlanta to
Denver, arriving at 8:20 p.m., charging the airfare on his
own credit card and not the corporate American Express, records showed. That morning, Andrea asked a
clerk named Lindsay Clayton to move her to a room with
a single bed. Andrea also said the room would have two
guests instead of one.

And she requested a late checkout for Thursday, her last
day at the hotel.

According to flight records, Andrea and Hemy returned
to Atlanta on July 23 on the same Frontier Airlines flight,
leaving at 11:48 p.m. from Denver. Andrea had arranged
for a seat next to his, with GE covering Andrea's expenses
and Hemy paying his own way.

* * *

The day before the Longmont trip, Hemy had sent Andrea an email about a natural wonder called Ruby Falls in the Lookout Mountains near Chattanooga, Tennessee.

"It's a waterfall in a cave and wishing I shared that tranquility with you," he wrote on July 17. "Wishing you were here."

Andrea responded, "Ditto."

This was the first of hundreds of emails and text messages between them, obtained via subpoena, covering the months leading up to the murder and adding another layer of information about their travels and relationship. Two days later, on July 19, after Hemy had pestered the Hampton Inn staff to leave flowers and chocolates for Andrea, he sent a photo of roses.

"Those are gorgeous, seriously," Andrea replied. "I have an appreciation for perfectly open roses, not sure what else to say but thank you. Unbelievably thoughtful of you." She told him it was "so thoughtful and sweet. I knew you might try something like this." In a message, Hemy alluded to his calls to the hotel staff, telling Andrea that a clerk called him "the last great romantic."

"Romantic for sure," Andrea replied. "Talk to you in a few."

When they had both returned to Atlanta two days later, Hemy messaged her that he was "exhausted" after the trip but that, "You're in my every thought."

Andrea replied, "Try to get some rest. Please enjoy the day."

Like Andrea, Hemy had not told police about going to Longmont, and when investigators later spoke with Hemy's wife, she recounted how he had claimed it was a business excursion but ended up paying for it himself. Then, just two weeks later, on August 12, Hemy met Rusty. This was the lunch meeting that both Hemy and Andrea had told police about in which Hemy sought help getting a new job. If Hemy and Andrea were secretly having an affair, Hemy clearly hid it well. An email from Rusty (copying Andrea) showed that the men got along famously.

Hemy,
Thank you for making time to get together for lunch today. I thoroughly enjoyed it and I can see why Andrea is enjoying working with you.

During our conversation, you mentioned something about GE that reminded me of my favorite case in business school. It's about a GE executive who leaves GE, buys a business and sells it a few years later for a significant profit. When you have a minute, you may want to check out his story.

Please let me know when you have time to continue our conversation. I am looking forward to it.

Talk to you soon,
Rusty.

Rusty then emailed business associates:

My friend, Hemy Neuman, is currently an executive with GE Energy and he is interested in learning more about future career options with growing private equity backed companies. Would you or someone on your team be willing to advise him on what additional skills, experiences, etc. he should try to obtain at GE to make himself more marketable to growing PE backed companies in the future? For reference, a copy of his resume is attached.

Meeting Andrea's husband did nothing to dampen Hemy's interest in Andrea. Four days later, on August 16,

Hemy sent her a highly personal message. Under the subject line "Balance," he offered advice on juggling work and home responsibilities. Mentioning nothing about GE Energy, Hemy's message reflected an intimate knowledge of Andrea's apparent struggles.

"There is no panacea for balance. You are overwhelmed because you are trying to find answers and get it all together," he told her. "It will come. The small things you do to try to achieve that balance. So it starts today. You will reach your balance by doing these two things and you must do them." He went on to recommend that she "leave at 3:30 p.m., pick up Sophia, go buy stuff with her, let her settle in at home and then start working at 5-ish," then advised that she "let Rusty pick up Ian at 5:30 p.m. During the 3:30 to 5:45 p.m. [period] think of nothing else but Sophia. Nothing else matters at that time."

Andrea followed up by text-messaging Hemy a picture of herself and her daughter, Sophia. This prompted Hemy to write her: "I just saw your text messages. I am so happy for you and Sophia. You can't imagine. Thank you for sharing with me. I feel like I was there, standing by the doorway, looking adoringly with a huge proud smile on my face. It made my week." It was signed "Hemy" with a happy face.

Andrea then sent him more pictures: an album of ninety-eight photographs taken at Sophia's birthday party.

"You and the kids are amazing," Hemy wrote back. "Thanks for sharing that with me." The photos showed Sophia helping make her elaborate four-foot-tall cake. "Looks like you had fun," Hemy wrote, "though a twinge of stress there for a minute." A couple days later he emailed her coupons for a *Sesame Street* show and the play *Peter Pan*.

On Thursday, August 26, Andrea departed for her fifth business trip in four months. She would later say that she bid good-bye to Rusty, dropped off the children at school, and met Hemy, who drove them 135 miles to Greenville, South Carolina, where GE operates a sprawling plant. Hemy made the two-hour Greenville run frequently, though he usually treated this as a day trip. Travel records showed that Hemy and Andrea stopped for lunch at the Macaroni Grill in the Mall of Georgia in Buford, then went to a Publix Super Market to purchase a bottle of wine. The receipt identified it as a Shiraz from FishEye vineyards. Arriving in Greenville late in the afternoon, they checked into adjoining rooms, the records showed, before having dinner together at Cazbah, a tapas restaurant and wine bar. The bill came to $84.56—including a $31 bottle of wine. The name on the wine label said, "Bitch." The next morning, they had a meeting, lunched for $29.65 at a P. F. Chang's in Greenville, then hit the road for Atlanta.

Unlike the Longmont trip, the hotel clerks had nothing to offer police. The email traffic between Andrea and Hemy was a different matter. Whatever happened in Greenville, it left them both reeling.

"I caused you so much pain when all I wanted was to give you so much," Hemy wrote on August 27, 2010, the day they returned. "I know it doesn't help, but I am sorry. I shouldn't have come over. You are so beautiful and such a great person. I discovered the mature, responsible Mama Andrea. Don't respond."

The emails didn't disclose the reason for his apology. Whatever it was, it triggered days of soul searching for Andrea. "I really don't know what to say at this point. I am angry. Your apology is heartfelt but it does not make the ongoing pain go away that I now have to repent and live with the rest of my life. Not sure what I was thinking. I'm also feeling that we may have ruined it. Not sure. I'm not trying to be hurtful. I'm just trying to be honest. I'm not sure how to live with this."

"This is the last one from me," Hemy wrote back. "I know it won't help, but please never forget how much I love you."

"I know," replied Andrea, "but so do other people. I betrayed them all. I'm not sure how to deal with that for now—but my burden, not yours."

Another day passed before Hemy—despite telling her he was done talking about the matter—sent her a late-night email: "One last thought: besides the birth of Tom and Lee, that was the most beautiful experience of my life."

The next morning, at 7:46 a.m., Andrea wrote back, her tone sharp.

"I appreciate that, but please understand what I am feeling. I am having constant feelings of anger towards you, me, everything," she said. "Yes, mixed with other feelings as well. But selfish feelings I am trying to suppress at every moment. Thursday night was one of best I had in a long time. It was such a great evening as a whole and now I feel sad I will never have that again. So many other things to say but not appropriate for email, most result in me getting angry."

In his response, Hemy implored her to forget her anger and focus on something else.

"Marry me," he wrote. "You're thinking I'm crazy and you've made your intentions clear. But before you respond, spend a night thinking about it. It won't solve anything but you know I will give you, Sophia and Ian the world. Together we can make it all work. Marry me."

In a long email, Hemy told Andrea that her feelings of betrayal and anger are "not about you" and that feeling that was "a copout." He then recalled their trip to Minden, Nevada, when they had dinner at Lake Tahoe, and the time they spent together in Colorado.

"It's about how you felt when we looked at the stars in Tahoe, when we woke up Friday morning in Denver and we walked out of the restaurant on Thursday when you took my hand and nestled your head on my shoulder. Blaming it all on Friday morning doesn't cut it. I keep trying to suppress thinking what it would be like to make Friday dinner together, to share a mah jong [sic] night with friends, or watch a movie in bed, that I know how to make you and Sophia happy even though I have never met her. You can't stop thinking about it but you're so locked in that it would not fail that it tears you apart. It's a betrayal not to those that love you but to yourself and it happened way before Friday morning . . . I know now more than any other time, that it is you I want to share everything with and you are pained because it is also what you want but can't have. Think about it. Be with me forever."

Andrea wrote back, "I feel terrible that I have not supported you in your situation"—an apparent reference to his marital problems. "I want to do that but you know how conflicting the whole thing is. But I still want to do it. If you want to talk this week, and I'm available, please do call me. I will try to call you on my way home today, around 4 p.m. Andrea."

Hemy responded, "Please don't be, dealing with it, as difficult as it may be. Just knowing you are there for me is enough. Thank you for being my friend. And as your friend, I won't do that to you because it just pains you." Hemy said he would be out of the office on a business trip that afternoon. "I'll be on the flight when you are freed up. Go home, relax on the way. Think of me and smile."

Andrea told him that if his flight was delayed, "You will have no choice but to talk to me"—she added a smiley-face emoticon. "Not a lot of relaxing going on these days. I am trying to get there. I need a routine. Is that even ever possible?" She signed it "Me" with another smiley face.

* * *

A week later, on September 1, Andrea had lunch with her close friend Shayna Citron at a Fuddruckers hamburger restaurant near the GE complex. It was their first lengthy discussion in some time, their busy lives with children, husbands, and jobs leaving increasingly little time for some of the things they used to do. Close friends for eight years, they had met at book club, and over the years they went together to baby showers, playdates, birthday parties, and weekends at the Sneidermans' lake house. That previous May, Citron and her husband attended Andrea's dance recital—"She's a very good dancer and always has been," said Citron later—and afterward the two couples went out for dinner. Andrea gushed about her new job at GE but lamented it intruded on her dance practice. Watching Andrea interact with Rusty, Citron detected a change. "It was at that dinner that I saw for the first time that they were going through a rough time," Citron said. "They seemed awkward and uncomfortable together, which I had never seen before." Three months later, at a fifth-birthday party for Sophia, where the little girls got manicures and played in a jump house, Andrea "revealed for the very first time . . . that she and Rusty were having problems." When they finally got together for the long lunch in September, Citron said, "I realized these issues were more serious than I once knew." Halfway through the meal, she asked what was going on. "She said something like, 'Rusty and I are having major problems,'" recalled Citron. "It all stemmed around work, travel, picking up the kids, who was doing what. She started to mention grumblings around the house about all this time she is spending at work, that she is not making the same amount of money as Rusty had been when he was working." When Andrea came home at night, the children would run and cling to her, which troubled Rusty. It was clear the children missed her—and Andrea desperately missed them. Citron asked Andrea if she was happy with the job. "She said, 'Yes, I am. This is the first time that what I'm doing, I'm important. I like the people I'm working with.'" Andrea felt she was making a difference and that her co-workers all told her she was doing an amazing job.

"Then she also told me that [her boss] told her that he was in love with her ," said Citron. Momentarily stunned, Citron asked Andrea how she felt about her boss. "She said that if maybe she had not been married she'd be interested in him." Citron asked if he was good looking. "She responded saying, yeah, he's got dark features. He looks professional." When Citron asked if Andrea was thinking of getting a divorce, "She said to me that she would never divorce Rusty."

Andrea then asked for advice on dealing with her boss, particularly when they traveled together. Citron, who also traveled for her work, said that she, too, had been hit on. "It's sort of the nature of the beast," Citron remembered telling her. "It does happen. You have to stay strong and stick to your guns, and the one thing I told her, for sure, without a doubt: Do not stay on the same floor in a hotel with someone that is hitting on you. Because I knew that if she were to get off an elevator and walk to her room and that person was there doing the same, it might become very uncomfortable if he would be walking her to her room. That might lend itself to an opportunity that married women shouldn't be involved in."

Andrea didn't want to tell anybody at GE about her boss. She feared she would lose the best job she'd ever had. "She told me some things that she had never told me before," recalled Citron. "She started talking about how everything in their married lives had always been about Rusty, whatever job he had, whatever problems were going on in his job." It went back to when Rusty went to business school—Andrea worked to help pay his tuition—and after graduation Andrea agreed to follow him to Atlanta for a job opportunity.

It was supposed to be a one-hour lunch but turned into two hours. When it was over, a rattled Citron went to her parents' house, lay on the sofa staring at the ceiling fan, and told her mother, who also knew the Sneidermans, that "Andrea has checked out of her marriage." She later discussed it with her husband also.

Citron saw Andrea next at lunch a couple of weeks later at another restaurant near GE—she thought it was a Hoolihan's or a Houston's—to celebrate Citron's birthday. A third friend joined them. Andrea was getting ready to go to London for business and talked excitedly about the trip, the castle she planned to see. Andrea asked if it was appropriate to go to a dance club with a co-worker, and Citron told her, "It just depends on how you're dancing." Regular dancing should be fine. "If it was risqué," said Citron, "that would not be okay."

The next month, after Andrea had returned from the UK trip, the families gathered at Citron's parents' house for an annual Halloween costume party. Andrea and Sophia dressed alike as sock-hop girls with poodle skirts and ponytails. "Andrea had a bright pink ribbon in her hair," recalled Citron. "She looked amazing. She looked the happiest I had seen her in a long time, absolutely radiant and glowing." Rusty came dressed as Fred from Scooby-Doo and Ian had on a Scooby-Doo costume. "Rusty was wiped out," said Citron, "his eyes, everything." She and her husband came as Fred and Wilma Flintsone and they tried to make silly small talk with Rusty about how both the husbands were dressed as Freds. Rusty wouldn't have any of it. That's when it occurred to Citron and her husband that this was the first year that Rusty and Andrea had not come dressed as a king and queen—instead of coordinating their costumes with each other they had coordinated with their children. "I remember my husband saying, 'What happened to the king and queen?' and Rusty said, 'I had to dress this way to save my marriage.'"

Andrea expressed the same problems with another friend, Tammi Parker, that she felt it was unfair that Rusty was angry. Andrea said she only went back to work full-time because Rusty had quit his job at Discovery Point to pursue his business dreams, and that this was not Andrea's choice. She told Parker she had grown tired of discussing the issue with Rusty. Weekends left the only time for Andrea to see not only Rusty and the children but also her friends. So when Rusty insisted that the family spend a weekend at their lake house—his "retreat," as Andrea called it—Andrea struggled to muster the strength. Rusty was also pressuring her to socialize more often.

"I'm not sure I have much of a choice but to go to the lake, which is what he wants," Andrea wrote to Tammi in September, shortly after returning from the UK trip. "I have been told I need to give him that for now and schmoozing with friends is not a top priority for the health of my marriage." She then warned Tammi, "Please do not forward this one. I know you understand it is a rough patch right now for me. I guess I knew it was coming when I took the job but not this bad." She told Tammi she'd try to get together with her later in the month, "but I cannot push it because it only ends in a fight and I am tired of fighting."

Around the same time, Hemy also confided in friends. Late in the summer of 2010, Hemy met with Melanie White, a Realtor for Coldwell Banker. Melanie had known the Neuman family since May 2006 when she sold them their home in East Cobb. As with other clients, she kept in contact with them. About twice a year she spoke with

Hemy by phone, usually small talk, asking him if he knew of anybody who needed a Realtor.

In one such phone call, Hemy requested a meeting in person. He told her that he was in trouble financially and wanted to discuss a short sale of his house. Two years into the recession, the real estate market was declining in Atlanta along with the rest of the country. Meeting at the Sunflower Café in Sandy Springs, they began by talking about what they usually did—his children, his work, the house. She then explained the parameters of a short sale, how banks will consider it once the borrower misses three mortgage payments. Hemy told her that he may qualify. He said he and his wife had chronic money problems, and more. He said he had moved out the night before and was staying in a Marriott hotel in Marietta near his office.

"What's the problem?" asked White, who would recount the conversation for authorities.

Hemy told her they'd always had problems but now he "just couldn't take it anymore. He told her that his wife never really had a job and that now the family needed her to work to keep up with the bills, including college tuition for his twins.

White asked him if there was somebody else in his life. He told her that there was one person, a woman at work who was married with two small children. He refused to give her name because she was Jewish and White likely knew her or knew somebody who did. When Hemy asked White for her advice, she told him, "Go back to your wife, go back to your kids, leave the other person alone. She's married."

If Hemy said anything in return, White didn't remember it. Mostly, she said, he met her advice with silence. They left their meeting by agreeing to get together again to follow up on the short sale. Hemy noted that his wife was close friends with another Realtor in their subdivision but that if he had to sell the house he'd do everything he could to give the listing to White.

They met again that same month, September, in the food court of the Perimeter Mall, the Nordstrom-anchored shopping mall in Dunwoody. Telling her that he valued her opinion, Hemy said he and his wife had gone to marriage counseling—it was not going well—and talked about his continuing money troubles. Then he told her about an upcoming business trip to the United Kingdom in which he'd be traveling with the woman he'd mentioned before.

When White heard the dates, she was dismayed. Yom Kippur fell that year on the same Saturday that Hemy was to board a plane for Scotland. "I felt that was odd given that we're all Jewish and that's like the holiest day of the year," she later said. She felt that rather than going to Europe with a potential lover, Hemy should be spending a day of atonement in temple, fasting and repenting for the sins of the previous year.

If Hemy had any pangs of religious guilt, he didn't show it. He told her he was "excited" about the trip.

Andrea, too, was looking forward to it. This was to be her biggest work trip yet—and she made no secret of her own excitement. She recruited Rusty to help her with the itinerary. Both meticulous planners, they created a spreadsheet and entered the places Andrea wanted to see: the castle in Edinburgh, Scotland, and a West End show or two. She found out *Dirty Dancing*, *Chicago*, *Billy Elliot*, and *Grease* were all playing. Andrea also wanted to see the campus of Cambridge University and fancy London restaurants.

Andrea also went over the itinerary with Hemy. When Hemy suggested they go to a dance club, Andrea said that sounded like a "fantastic idea" but worried about fitting in. "I have always wanted to go to a club in London, although I am sure I am nowhere near cool enough," she wrote. "My clothes are certainly not trendy enough." She added a smiley face.

Departing September 18, they took the same flights and stayed in the same hotels, first in Scotland and then in London, meeting with GE employees at the company's operations there. Andrea never did go to a dance club—she later said that would "not be appropriate"—but did see many of the sights.

But like the Greenville trip, drama accompanied them. It had begun before they left with Hemy asking if Andrea still felt comfortable traveling with him.

"I will continue to be the best boss you ever have or ever will," he wrote a few days before. "I don't have to go to England. But if you think that it is good that I go for work reasons then I will."

Something then happened overseas, according to a cryptic email from Andrea to Hemy after they returned on September 25: "Honest is good and maybe I'm not being honest enough. Not sure, but I do not want it to ruin the trip overall and you know that. Desire versus reality as you know is a world I'm trying to ignore because I have to. So sorry, not fair to you, I know. I have other thoughts but not the time right now."

Hemy forwarded this and other emails to Melanie White, who saved them and later provided them to police. Hemy had a quick turnaround—he left on another business trip on September 27, this time to Houston, and emailed White from the road. In one early-morning message on September 28, he recounted for White that the UK trip ended with a good-bye scene at the airport in which Andrea gave him a kiss.

"I guess I should put this in context for you," Hemy told White. "We left the flight with a kiss knowing that I was traveling [to Houston] and I told her we really shouldn't communicate over the next one to two weeks. She wholeheartedly agreed."

By now, White knew Andrea's name, though she didn't know Andrea personally or her family. Hemy recounted how Andrea told him "that I'm the only one she can talk to about us and Rusty, that everyone else will be so disappointed. She tells people snippets, controlling the whole story. She also says that it won't change the outcome, that she is staying no matter what. So any advice is pointless.

"Anyway," Hemy continued, "on Sunday she sent me a text and then we went back and forth a few times regarding how the kids are great, etc. I did give the advice that she must concentrate on them. Today, as much as it killed me I did not contact her."

It was Andrea who reached out to him. "She pinged me that she wanted to talk to me about some work thing," he said. "Again, some chat and text when she agreed she would call me at 1 p.m. while I was waiting for my flight. She called and we spent 15 to 20 minutes talking about the kids and the presents we got them. She paid but we chose them together. I told her briefly that we never talked about my situation and that it was quite messy. I told her that I couldn't have sex with someone I didn't love and that it was killing me to pretend I was somebody I wasn't." They chatted more about work. She had to cancel a meeting they were to attend because she had a training session. Hemy wrote back to Andrea with a sad face. She wrote back "ditto." They continued to text each other through the night.

Hemy told White, "I don't want to lose her."

White was mortified.

"Hemy," she wrote him, "it continues to sound like she is lifting you up and knocking you down because she herself displays emotions that are up and down. Always in the end, she continues to tell you she is not leaving her marriage. I am not sure if she is trying to convince you or herself. In my opinion, a person does not have an affair, whether emotional or physical or both unless they have a portion of their heart and foot in/out the door."

White told him that Andrea sounded "remorseful and confused" and that her emotions are jumping between wanting to be with him and the getting "angry at herself for thinking that way" and pushing him away. "It is a see-saw of emotions and will continue to be that way," warned White. "Hold on. You must be patient and take care of yourself and your family. You're going to have a lot come down on you once you positively announce your marriage is over and there is no way to get it back."

Again, Hemy didn't say whether he'd take her advice. He wrote nothing in response over email and remained impassive when they spoke about the same issues later by phone.

While in Houston, Hemy met with a longtime colleague, Orna Hanison. A native of England, Hanison had worked with Hemy in Atlanta and became what she'd later call a "fairly good friend" over the years, the two often talking about their children. She also would become friendly with Hemy's wife, Riela, who in late summer or early fall of 2010, as their marriage was crumbling, asked Hanison to try to talk some sense into Hemy and persuade him to take counseling more seriously.

Now a human resources manager in the oil and gas division in GE's Houston operations, Hanison met Hemy for dinner the night of September 28, 2010, the same day he had emailed White. They talked business at first, with Hemy expressing frustration about being passed over for a promotion and saying he wanted to test the job market. Hanison offered advice on interviewing skills. The conversation then turned to Hemy's marriage. Hanison later recalled, "They didn't love [each other] anymore, and that she had spent a lot of money and got them into a lot of debt."

Hemy said he was pondering a divorce and that he was having an affair. "I told him I thought he was having a midlife crisis," Hanison said, "and he should go home and go to counseling, and do what he could to save his marriage."

Hemy, she said, responded with a laugh.

Hemy revealed little to her about the woman. He wouldn't give her name but did say she was younger, had two small children, and was Jewish. When Hanison asked if she worked at GE, he said no. As an HR manager, Orna knew that sleeping with a direct subordinate violated company policy and an internal investigation could lead to a demotion or firing.

Hanison repeated that he should go to counseling and that he should be able to face his wife and children and tell them he'd done everything he could to save the marriage. As he had with White, Hemy didn't respond.

The next day, Ariela Neuman called Hanison for an update on the dinner. Hanison told her said she had urged him to go into counseling, but Hanison couldn't bring herself to reveal that Hemy admitted to an affair. Since Ariela never asked directly, Hanison never offered. "She and I were not the closest of friends," Orna later said, "so I felt I would probably do more harm than good."

After going over his personal issues with Melanie White and Orna Hanison, Hemy made a major life decision. On Sunday, October 3, while still in Houston, he sent an email to his wife, children, and fifteen relatives and friends including White.

"Dear Reli/Lee/Tom/Addie/Family/Friends," he began. "I am writing this to everyone so as to prevent any confusion or misunderstanding. I know this hurts . . . I am sorry to everyone. I do love all of you very much." He then addressed each person individually, starting with his wife. "Reli," he wrote, "This morning I got up to yet another discussion about our future. Do you deserve to have an honest discussion . . . yes. But the truth is that I needed time to sort out my feelings, to understand, after all we went through, how I can make it happen." He had come to the conclusion that while he tried to be more open about his feelings with her in the last month and had tried to be more affectionate—massaging her and holding her, kissing her and cooking for her—it still wasn't enough for her, or him. Although he still considered her a "beautiful wonderful person," and despite their "22 mostly wonderful years" together with three children, "this relationship is destructive." The fault, he said, lay with him. Writing in staccato form with his thoughts separated by ellipses, he said, "I'm fucked up . . . probably . . . do I need help . . . probably." Another trip to the therapist, he believed, would do no good. The children will be affected, he know, but he had to end it. "You have been a wonderful wife . . . no longer for me, unfortunately not anymore."

To his children, he wrote, "Lee/Tom/Addie, I wish it was different. I wish you didn't hate me right now. But you do." Hemy insisted that he tried to make the marriage work but that the last "2.5 weeks" convinced him that to carry on would only result in him "hating myself, hating my life." He noted that he had gone out into the garden and prepared it for the winter. "That's who I am . . . I take care of those I love and I do not absolve myself of any responsibility," he wrote. "Not to you. Not to your mother. Ever. I love you. I will always be there for you."

Finally, in a section addressed to "Family/Friends," Hemy acknowledged that they must feel "extremely disappointed" at the collapse of something that "all seemed so perfect" but said it was a facade. "I keep it all in . . . I have my poker face." He urged them to support his wife and that he would be speaking to them all shortly. He signed the email, "I love you all, Hemy."

The next day, October 4, Hemy returned to Atlanta—and moved out. He'd eventually end up in the apartment of family friend Ruthy in Buckhead.

The public airing of their private troubles in the email left Ariela embarrassed, stunned, and, she'd soon find, in a financial bind. This was in stark contrast with Hemy, who seemed relieved. About two weeks later, he had after-work drinks with an old friend at the Crown and Prince, a pub around the corner from GE Energy. James Vono, a fourteen-year GE employee, general manager of global operations for field services, in charge of the organization that fixes power plants around the country, used to supervise Hemy. From 2007 to 2010, they'd see each other a couple of times a week, emailed each other frequently, and collaborated on projects. Vono held Hemy in high esteem for his logical thinking and organization. They occasionally socialized, a couple of times after work and at office holiday parties.

Vono would later estimate they went to the pub on October 17. About to leave his position at GE, Vono told Hemy that he might be interested in the job. But Hemy had other matters on his mind. Usually reticent to talk about his personal life, Hemy now shared that he was going through a divorce, had moved out of the house, and was struggling to put two of his kids through Georgia Tech. Somber as he ticked off his problems, Hemy perked up when he mentioned he had met a woman and that they "were together," Vono later said. Hemy said the woman was married with children, but considering leaving her husband. Hemy shared that he was in love with her and that they had amazing sex—"like magic," in his words. She made him feel young again, like he was back in high school.

Hemy did not give her name and Vono didn't ask, figuring if Hemy wanted to say it he would. (Although he worked at GE, Vono didn't know Andrea Sneiderman—he'd later say that if he had met her in the office, he didn't remember her.) The conversation left Vono uneasy. Though friends for a long time, Hemy had never confided in him like this.

Within days, the newly separated Hemy hit the road again with Andrea for a second trip to Greenville. On the way to Andrea's house to pick her up, Hemy called Melanie White. "He was really excited," she recalled, adding that the hotel reservation called for adjoining rooms. They checked in to the Hampton Inn on Saturday, October 21, 2010. The reservation originally called for two rooms anywhere in the hotel; it was changed to two adjoining rooms, according to travel records.

After check-in, Andrea and Hemy went down the street to Pulse, a nightclub/lounge. Open Tuesday to Saturday, Pulse offers live music, dancing, drinks, and sometimes a full dinner. Christine Olivera was tending bar when they walked in at about 8:30 p.m. October is past the busy season and nobody else was in the bar except for the DJ playing tunes. The couple had Olivera's undivided attention on this slow night, and she'd remember everything clearly.

"I recall the music was playing," she said later in court. "Mr. Neuman seemed very happy to be there. They ordered their drinks. He had a discussion with me about how happy he was and how nice the bar was."

Andrea gave off a different vibe. She "seemed a little upset" and went to the bathroom a couple of times, Olivera recalled. It was during one of these trips to the ladies' room that Olivera asked Hemy if everything was okay with his lady friend and if they needed anything. Hemy said that Andrea was "dealing with a real jerk at home." That's why,

Hemy said, she needed to be someplace like Pulse, to get away from her troubles. Over the next hour, Andrea seemed to perk up, and Hemy's mood soared.

"He asked if the band or the DJ played every night, said that the ambience was very nice," Olivera recalled. "He kept thanking me for the service, and saying that she really needed this, again repeated that she was dealing with a jerk and going through some personal stuff and that she wanted to go out and take her mind off things."

The two of them went on the dance floor, with Andrea spinning to salsa music. Andrea seemed to be dancing specifically for Hemy, giving him a little show, Olivera said. At one point, he pulled her toward him and they began "groping each other," she recalled. "He had his hands on her rear end, she was hugging him," she said, remembering that at one point she had to look away. They kissed about three times. Quick lip-to-lip kisses—"pop kissing," she called it, "not like making out." It happened while they were dancing.

After about an hour they started to leave, closing Hemy's bar tab of $25.35, which he would expense to GE. Hemy asked about upcoming events at the bar and Olivera told him about the Halloween dress-up party at the club. She overheard Hemy telling Andrea that they should try to come back for that. They left "very happy," the bartender said, their arms around each other.

Over the course of the evening, Hemy and Andrea had a drink or two each, but didn't seem drunk. "They were fine, they left the bar fine," Olivera said. "Responsibly, I could let them leave, they were walking to the hotel that they had mentioned." Her lingering impression was that it was "like a first date." Hemy's demeanor suggested he was thinking: *Wow, I got her.* Said Olivera, "He was very excited to be with her."

While in Greenville, Hemy called Melanie White with

an update. He told her that he and Andrea had walked by a lake, had a drink, a nice dinner, and went upstairs to the hotel, ending up in the same room, where, Hemy said, "She gave in."

Afterward, though, "Andrea was very distraught," said White. "From what Hemy told me, she was very upset with herself and she wanted to sever personal ties with Hemy and just keep it business." Hemy had a different reaction. According to White, "He could not leave that alone."

After this, for the four weeks leading up to Rusty's murder, detectives found no more messages of evidentiary value between Andrea and Hemy. But they remained in touch, both at the office and by phone.

Chad Fitzgerald, an FBI analyst, examined the phone records with specific attention to calls Hemy and Andrea made at critical junctures of the case. Much of what he uncovered detectives could already have surmised. On July 1, 2010, for instance, Hemy and Andrea's phones both connected with a cell phone tower at the airport in Norfolk, Virginia, while they both traveled there. Later in July, phone records placed both of their phones at the Denver airport—they were calling each other—suggesting that he and Andrea traveled from the airport to Longmont together. And their phones pinged the same cell phone towers in Greenville, South Carolina, when they traveled there in late August.

Other calls, however, raised questions. On October 15, shortly after Hemy split with his wife and moved out, he placed twelve calls and texts that pinged a tower in Marietta near a business on Austel Road called Wild West Gun Traders. Among these was a sixteen-minute call at 1:45 p.m. to Andrea's phone. A little over two weeks later, the same day that Hemy was in Dalton for the gun show on October 31, he sent a text to Andrea's phone at 11:34 a.m. The contents of the message were lost; all that could be determined was that the text was relayed by the same tower used by the convention center hosting the gun show. Less than two hours later, he called Parnell's Firearms and Range, where he arrived the next day with a gun and ammunition. On another day, Hemy called two costume shops—in between he called Andrea.

Finally, the FBI analyst checked Andrea and Hemy's calls for November 18, 2010. Less than half an hour after Rusty's murder, at 9 a.m., Hemy made a flurry of calls. Timed between 9:27 a.m. and 10:50 a.m., the fifteen calls pinged a tower far away from GE Energy. Of these, nine were to Andrea's phone. All of them went unanswered or apparently went to voice mail until 10:30 a.m., when a call between Hemy's phone and Andreas's lasted forty-two seconds.

It was at about this same time that Andrea also spoke to Rusty's father, Donald Sneiderman, and texted her co-worker Alan Schachtely, telling them that Rusty had been shot. Reviewing her statements to police, she claimed that at that time nobody had told her what happened to Rusty.

Had Hemy told her what he had done? Or had Andrea known all along?

After the murder there were no more emails or phone calls between them that caught police's attention. Those who saw Hemy at the funeral and shiva said, even in hindsight after his arrest, that they saw nothing unexpected. Al Harris, the audit program manager at GE who had been hired by Hemy, would later describe his boss at the shiva as remorseful, sorrowful, concerned about Andrea and everybody else. "He looked sincerely sorry for what happened," said Harris later in court, repeating what he told investigators after Hemy's arrest. "He hugged Andrea for a long time and said so sorry." Later in November or early December, Hemy reached out to a childhood friend of

Rusty's who had been at the shiva. In an email later obtained by WSB-TV, Hemy described Rusty's death as "so tragic and unfortunate" and said it was "hard to find the words." Hemy summed up his feelings this way: "Too much shock."

Orna Hanison saw Hemy Neuman the week of Thanksgiving, about three or four days after the murder. Hanison had been transferred from Houston back to the Marietta office with a different job title, and Hemy popped by her new office. He gave her a hug, welcomed her back, and said it was great to see her again.

"We must do lunch," Hemy said, she recalled.

Hanison remembered Hemy as being pleasant. He laughed about his new living arrangements—he had by now moved out of his house—rooming with an older woman in Buckhead, he told her. He jokingly called her his "girlfriend."

And just days before his arrest, when Hemy had already been contacted by Sergeant Cortellino about the rental car, he showed no signs of stress. He called Hanison on December 3, to wish her a happy New Year, a message he also posted on his Facebook page. Hanison would describe his demeanor as "upbeat" and "normal."

As for Andrea, she stayed away from work and mostly away from Hemy after the murder. In late December, she traveled to Florida with her parents to go to the synagogue where she was married for what would have been her tenth wedding anniversary. It was then that Hemy sent her the iTunes love song from Bruno Mars.

Then Andrea and and her friend Shayna Citron discussed the police sketch of the killer that had at the time been recently released. According to Citron, Andrea said the longer she looked at the drawing the more she "recognized the eyes." They looked like Hemy's.

It was an observation Andrea didn't share with police.

CHAPTER 13

In early March 2011, the news media revealed detectives'
increasing suspicions of Andrea. "Investigation revealed
that there was continuous communication between Andrea
Schneiderman [sic] and the defendant before and after the
homicide," said a search warrant affidavit leaked to the
press. According to the affidavit, investigators were seeking "information (historical) call detail records, and digital evidence of communication between the defendant and
Andrea Schneiderman [sic] and any accomplices or witnesses, known or unknown to law enforcement . . . that
would indicate planning, premeditation or collaboration to
commit murder and/or any indication of participation in
the murder of the victim." The affidavit said while this
communication was "not necessarily illicit" it "may reveal
motive to murder him."

Other news reports revealed that Andrea's husband knew Hemy and that the pair had lunch at least once to discuss future business ventures. Then 11Alive news reported on an email Hemy sent Andrea around 2 a.m. on August 8, 2010—three months before the murder—titled: "Raising Good Kids Can Be Easy." It listed what Hemy called his ten "principals [sic] for raising good kids," and quoted Hemy with this signoff: "Andrea, that's it for now, and I'm getting tired. Good night, Mon Ami and thanks for the inspiration."

The heat was building on Andrea. Her attorney Seth Kirschenbaum told reporters, "We understand that this is part of the investigative process and we continue to cooperate with the DA's office." He stressed that the warrant didn't indicate Andrea was actually involved in the murder, but he did confirm a number of earlier press reports, based on leaks, that Hemy and Andrea had traveled together on business trips to the UK and Colorado, the UK trip including plans for a castle tour, dinner cruise, and possibly a West End musical.

On March 7, Hemy's wife had had enough. Just days after the first TV reports about the search warrant affidavit, Ariela filed for legal separation. The filing claimed cruel treatment and sought alimony and child support for the youngest of their three children, a seventeen-year-old daughter. It also alleged adultery. "We believe there was an extramarital relationship between Hemy Neuman and Andrea Sneiderman," said her attorney Esther Panitch.

With a trial date looming, the onslaught of publicity posed a grave threat to Hemy's hopes of finding an impartial jury. His attorney Doug Peters asked everybody involved in the case to stop making comments that "could unfairly prejudice one side or the other," but Ariela's camp had no inclination to let up. As part of the separation filing, Ariela's lawyer asked the court for a subpoena for "any

and all documents, records . . . or other tangible evidence
of communications" between Andrea and Hemy from May
2010 to the present. Panitch also wanted to question both
Hemy and Andrea, separately and under oath, in deposi-
tions. Hemy resisted, and so did the district attorney, the
two adversaries in the murder case joining forces for the
time being against Hemy's estranged wife. On March 10,
the DA made it official, asking the court for a protective
order to shield it from handing over anything to Ariela.
"The state objects to the production of the information
sought by the plaintiff for two basic reasons: (1) that
the information sought by plaintiff could be discovered
through other means and (2) that the information could
be released to the media," wrote Chief Assistant DA Don
Geary.

The DA's motion, however, did acknowledge that
the "state does possess material and information which
responds to the plaintiff's subpoena to produce." In the
second week of March prosecutors turned over to Hemy's attorneys three thousand pages of documents as part
of discovery. An inventory of the evidence, leaked to the
media, included a sign-in sheet from Hemy on November
1, 2010, showing that he practiced shooting at Pannell's
Firearms in Woodstock; evidence of purchase of a
.40-caliber Bersa pistol in April 2010—police had not re-
covered the weapon but had a ballistics report from the
scene; reports from interviews with at least thirty people,
including GE co-workers; details on how detectives tracked
down the silver minivan; and twenty-one various supple-
mental reports. Among the evidence, according to the inventory, were "material and information" which "prove a
romantic and/or physical relationship between the defendant and Andrea Sneiderman."

Of these bankers' boxes full of documents, none went
to Hemy's estranged wife. Panitch filed another motion,

this one seeking "correspondence, memoranda, business notes, personal notes, greeting cards, gifts, gift recipient cards, internet use, web site registrations, web site postings, electronic and/or cellular communications" pertaining to Hemy. Also requested were "documentation," "itineraries," and "receipts" for trips taken by Andrea since May 2010 "whether as part of employment or for personal travel."

With Hemy in jail and no longer working, Ariela had no choice but to press the issue, said Panitch. Returning to work as a teacher's assistant, Ariela made a fraction of what Hemy had brought home, and now the family had fallen behind on the mortgage on their five-hundred-thousand-dollar home and feared foreclosure. Two of the children were in college, and tuition payments were coming due. Ariela claimed that while Hemy was locked up, she couldn't even get access to the bank accounts to pay the bills. "Mr. Neuman was the primary breadwinner in the home," Panitch told reporters. "He has access to funds which he has not given his wife access to."

As the separation battle heated up and the prosecution's murder investigation fell into place, Hemy made his second court appearance. Guards escorted him into the courtroom on April 4 to formally enter a plea to the charges in the indictment. Hemy had not been seen since his initial court appearance the day after his arrest. Wearing a dark suit instead of the jail uniform, he appeared thinner and grayer than four months earlier. He smiled at his attorney Doug Peters, who was wearing his traditional bow tie.

"We enter our plea of not guilty to those charges," Peters said.

Hemy's wife and children were not there, nor were any friends or co-workers. As always, Andrea didn't attend.

At the hearing, District Attorney Robert James announced he was ready to go to trial but Peters asked for more time. "We're very determined to study very carefully what the district attorney's evidence shows," the attorney said. James didn't oppose the request. "I think some additional time would be reasonable in this case, given this is not your average murder case, I would just ask for a limited amount of time." The judge set a trial date of October 17.

After the hearing, Esther Panitch continued to pound at Hemy. In remarks to reporters, she portrayed him as a deadbeat dad and nonsupportive estranged husband while his wife suffered financially and emotionally as she struggled to keep the family together. "Imagine waking up and having the police come to the door and say your spouse is accused of murder when they've never had a history of any criminal activity. It's devastating," Panitch said. "She is doing as well as can be expected under these horrific, awful circumstances." Hemy, she said, had not even seen his children since his arrest.

In his own statements to reporters, Peters acknowledged that Hemy had not seen his children but claimed they had corresponded. Calling Hemy a "very committed, loving father" who had "always had" his children's interests "utmost in his mind," Peters said, "He's been a great father. He's had an entire life of providing for his children. He's doing all he can now to remain being a good father." A matrimonial attorney, Joseph Winters, had been added to Hemy's legal team but declined to comment, saying the publicity "only adds to everyone's pain."

Two months later, in May, lawyers for Hemy and Ariela appeared in a different court. What normally would be a routine meeting in the divorce action turned contentious as Panitch accused Hemy of tying up tens of thousands of dollars from his retirement accounts. Winters shot back, "This is a waste of time, money, and assets for everyone concerned." He claimed that what money Hemy had left all went to his family. Panitch said that was not true. "He is a liar. He wrote an email saying, 'I have a poker face. I lie'"—a reference to Hemy's email announcing their separation. "His word means nothing." Claiming Hemy had hidden his money, Panitch said, "I need to be able to find the assets."

When Panitch again sought a subpoena of the entire investigative file, Andrea's attorney Seth Kirschenbaum stood up to object. "No one on this earth wants [Neuman] convicted more than my client," he said. He accused Ariela and Panitch of being "motivated by vindictiveness" and blasted Ariela's ongoing efforts to depose Andrea. Kirschenbaum accused Ariela and her attorney of tactics "designed to embarrass and humiliate" Andrea. This prompted Panitch to suggest that Hemy's lawyers were joining forces with Andrea's to stymie the divorce proceeding and to save Andrea's hide.

Fulton County Superior Court judge Margaret Dorsey had finally heard enough. Saying that she too was "a little bit concerned" about what impact Ariela's requests would have on the murder trial, the judge put Andrea's deposition on hold. The case file would remain only for the eyes of the DA and Hemy's lawyers.

The rhetoric proved to be the last gasps for all sides. Days later, lawyers reached a deal in which Ariela would have access to the family's financial records and what was left of their dwindling assets. According to court papers, the family had fallen behind on the mortgage and Hemy had to borrow three hundred thousand dollars from his mother, the funds presumably going to his legal bills because none was given to his wife and children. Hemy's lawyer griped that Ariela merely accepted "the same offer we made several months ago," but Ariela was satisfied. "She's relieved this part of this is finally over," Panitch said. "She looks forward to having the assets turned over so she and her children can continue to live."

The deal also gave Ariela leverage against Hemy if he didn't deliver. By not formally filing for divorce, only separation, she remained his legal wife, leaving the decision in her hands whether or not to testify against her husband, Atlanta law saying that a wife could not be compelled to do so. Said Panitch, "It's a question of when it's best for her."

Overlapping the marital dispute was a scrimmage in criminal court over publicity and evidence. On Tuesday, May 17, 2011, Dick Williams of the *Dunwoody Crier* found himself thrust into the middle of the Sneiderman murder story when he was called to testify at a pretrial hearing by Hemy's attorneys. His own paper would later report that Williams was "somewhat startled and confused" by his subpoena, though the defense's intention became clear. Hemy's lawyers were seeking to show that the vast publicity in the case had prejudiced Hemy's chances for a fair trial and that the judge needed to impose a gag order and continue sealing documents. Although many court papers had been filed under seal, the case had been an information sieve to the detriment of Hemy. Only Hemy's statements during his questioning had remained under wraps, and his lawyers wanted to make sure that they stayed that way. The Atlanta media, including the lawyers for Cox Media, which owns the *Atlanta Journal-Constitution* and WSB-TV, objected. They wanted the judge to unseal previously sealed court papers, including pretrial motions, which often are made public.

Williams was called to show how saturated the region had become with news about the Sneiderman killing. In his testimony, the publisher noted that for the *Crier* the case was in fact close to home, literally, as the shooting occurred across the street from the newspaper offices. Williams himself went to the scene shortly after it happened. "Since then we have assigned one reporter to cover this case until it is wrapped up," he said. He told his staff that the case was the "highest-priority story going forward." The *Dunwoody Crier* alone had published fourteen articles in the paper and online, a huge amount for a weekly.

"Based on emails, phone calls, and my experience in the business, this is a case that has caught the public fancy," Williams said under questioning from defense attorney Robert Rubin. "The fact is that my discussions at lunch and my own staff can't get enough information about it . . . that is how many news judgments are made." The case had received widespread coverage from much larger outlets, but the *Crier* wouldn't back down. "I don't want to get beat," he said.

Those larger outlets were at the hearing in force. So many lawyers showed up to represent the Cox media outlets that District Attorney Robert James gave up his counsel table to them and quietly sat in the back of the courtroom. The judge put off a decision, keeping the investigative documents sealed for now. It was for Hemy's team a small victory, and one they'd have little time to savor, for more trouble was coming Hemy's way.

CHAPTER 14

The hearing began on August 15, two months before the trial was to begin, and it would concern the admissibility of some of the most damaging evidence against Hemy.

The stakes were high for both sides. Rusty's father and brother, who flew in from Cleveland, sat in the audience section of the courtroom. They had not seen Hemy since the shiva at Rusty's home after the funeral when he was just another face in the crowd. "We wanted to be here for Rusty," said Steven Sneiderman. Andrea did not attend, represented again by her lawyer.

Waiting in the wings to testify was Ariela Neuman.

Hemy's lawyers sought to throw out almost everything police had collected under a search warrant from Hemy's house and office, including his computer, as well as records for his cell phone and email accounts. The searches, the defense claimed, produced evidence tainted by "defective warrants, issued based upon affidavits that failed to establish probable cause or that provided stale information." Hemy's lawyers also wanted Judge Gregory Adams to bar most of what Hemy said during his police interview on the grounds he was not properly informed of his rights. And the defense wanted to control the verbiage at trial, seeking to bar the DA from saying things like "murder" and "malice murder," and "possession of a firearm during the commission of a crime."

The hearing put the Dunwoody Police Department under the microscope. Called to testify, Detective Andrew Thompson acknowledged that the Sneiderman killing was his first murder case and had to answer for what some had argued was deferential treatment of Andrea. Thompson revealed publicly for the first time that he didn't talk to her until the day after the shooting and that "she did mention that Hemy was her supervisor at that point, and that he did make an advancement toward her," he said. Addressing why the department didn't go after Hemy sooner, Thompson said Andrea "seriously minimized the encounter and said that was a onetime incident. Nothing ever came of that." Therefore, he said, "That information about Hemy was not shared. We were being driven toward other avenues of investigation by the family . . . by Andrea's parents, by Andrea herself."

Sergeant Gary Cortellino also testified, telling the judge that investigators had "yet to compare notes" before talking to Hemy and that only later did they obtain the search warrants for phone records and texts and emails between Hemy and Andrea.

"So when you decided to arrest Mr. Neuman, you had the same information essentially as you had when you began this videotaped interview?" asked defense attorney Bob Rubin.

"Right," said Cortellino.

That made Hemy's interrogation—and all the information gleaned from it—the basis for most of what evidence later was collected. The defense attacked the tactics of Cortellino and Barnes, suggesting they ran roughshod over Hemy's constitutional rights. Cortellino said that Hemy only waived his Miranda rights about an hour into the interview and even then after a back-and-forth between him and the detectives over the subject of an attorney.

"He asked me, he said, 'Do I need a lawyer?' and I told him, 'I don't know, do you need one?'" said Cortellino (the recording and transcript of the interview had not yet been released publicly).

"Mr. Neuman says, 'I'm not waiving my rights,' correct?" asked Rubin.

"I'm not waiving my rights, but I do want to talk," corrected Cortellino.

"At that point, did you stop questioning him?" asked Rubin.

"When he said that I didn't know exactly what he meant," said Cortellino, who then went on to continue questioning him. "I had no inkling of his role in any of this. So there was no need to Miranda as far as I'm concerned because he wasn't a suspect. He was just somebody that was in the circle knowing the family."

Of course, the detectives had more than an inkling—they had Hemy's name on a rental form for the van most likely used in the murder, and they knew that Hemy was Andrea's boss. In his questions to the detective, DA Robert James ticked off the many things that went right in the interview, noting that Hemy never was in custody, legally speaking, before he was Mirandized. He also said that Hemy voluntarily rode with detectives to the police station—he was not arrested or handcuffed. Nor was he ever denied the chance when he got to the interview room to call a lawyer or even get up and leave, even though he had a good excuse to because of the doctor's appointment.

James noted, "At no time did Neuman say I need for this to end," and argued that a "reasonable person would not feel he was in custody and was going to be in jail that night." In the end, James said, a DVD of the interview would speak for itself, showing that Hemy "did indeed waive his rights" and that the information provided was "freely given and not given in custody."

After a week-and-a-half break, the suppression hearing resumed August 24. The focus now was on the search of Hemy's house the day he was arrested. For this, the DA had a star witness.

Ariela Neuman had shoulder-length blond hair with bangs and glasses and wore a white blouse with a necklace. She took the stand and gave her name for the record. Asked what her relationship was to the defendant, she answered, "I am his wife."

The first time the public saw Hemy's estranged wife made for a dramatic day in court. The *Atlanta Journal-Constitution* observed, "Neuman seemed taken aback by the presence of his wife of 22 years." Channel 2's reporter said Neuman "appeared surprised." The *Dunwoody Crier* said Ariela "avoided eye contact" during her brief testimony. The only thing that would have heightened the tension was a face-off with Andrea Sneiderman, but she once again did not come to court.

Answering questions from Chief Assistant District Attorney Don Geary, Ariela said that at the time of his arrest Hemy had not been living with her for months but had access to the house. "He came back and forth," she said. "He had the keys. He had the [garage door opener] to come into the house, and he was there, definitely." When police initially arrived, they told her that her husband had been arrested—it was the first time she'd heard about that—and that they wanted to search the house.

"I gave them permission to take everything they want," she testified. Police stood by awaiting a warrant. Only when it arrived, she said, did the officers take the home computer and two storage drives, even though her husband was no longer living there.

Her testimony was a blow to Hemy—his attorneys had claimed she was coerced by police into the search. "She chose to help because she's always cooperated with law enforcement," said her attorney Esther Panitch. "She has always claimed there was an affair. And at the beginning she couldn't believe that her husband would be tied to a murder." The case had placed Ariela "in a very unfortunate position," said Panitch. "We are hopeful that she will not need to appear again as she tries to move forward with her life in the wake of this devastating trauma related to the outcome of an affair between her husband and Andrea Sneiderman."

On September 8, Judge Adams issued a written ruling. "The defendant voluntarily accompanied officers to the Dunwoody Police Department," the judge wrote. "The defendant spoke to and gave a video recorded statement to officers of the Dunwoody Police Department. During the defendant's statement there was no coercive police or government activity [and] during defendant's statement there were no improper threats or promises." The tactics by Cortellino and Barnes, from haranguing Hemy to crowding him in the small interview room, passed legal muster, the judge found. What's more, the judge said, "During defendant's statement the defendant did not exercise his Constitutional right to remain silent nor did defendant make an unambiguous or unequivocal request for counsel, and . . . the defendant was not in custody until informed that he was under arrest at the completion of the recorded statement." Signing the rights waiver, even so far into the interview, meant just what it said it would: Everything Hemy said could be used against him.

The judge refused to dismiss the search warrants and refused to toss out Hemy's statements to police, before and after his Miranda warning. The DA scored a slam-dunk victory. All of the evidence amassed against Hemy Neuman could be used at trial.

What's more, as part of the ruling, the search warrants were released to the media, laying it all out for every potential juror to see: the van rental; the purchase of a Bersa handgun for $375—the same day Hemy withdrew $400 from an ATM; the gun seller picking Hemy out of a lineup; the iPhone and iPad records; and more allegations about Hemy's relationship with Andrea.

"Investigation revealed that the defendant and Andrea Sneiderman were spending an inordinate amount of time together, and frequently made overnight trips away from the Atlanta area," the search warrant said. "It is probable that the defendant may have made some statement and/or admission to Andrea Sneiderman regarding his involvement in the murder of the victim, which may have been conveyed by electronic communication."

Soon more revelations would reach the media, including details of the email Hemy had sent to Andrea with the Bruno Mars gift song after the murder. Then another search warrant affidavit stated in the strongest terms yet the official theory for why Rusty was murdered: "Law enforcement has cause to believe that an extramarital affair between the defendant and . . . Andrea Sneiderman in large part provided motive to murder Russell Sneiderman."

Suffering a major pretrial defeat and the daily drumbeat of negative publicity, Hemy's lawyers caucused. With a mountain of evidence against their client, a traditional reasonable-doubt defense was an option. But they had another choice, one born out of developments behind the scenes that the public—and prosecutors—didn't yet know about that opened the door for a bold legal gambit. It was legal strategy rooted in an obscure nineteenth-century event, one that has frequently failed and now promised to subject Hemy to nationwide ridicule. But it appeared to be his last best hope.

"We don't pick the defense," his attorney Doug Peters later said. "The defense picks us."

Andrea Sneiderman's combative, sarcastic and at times evasive perfor-mance on the witness stand in Hemy Neuman's trial in February 2012 may have contributed to her being charged with murder, though the charges were later dropped. She later claimed she was unprepared for the tough questioning by the prosecutor. *(Courtesy: Associated Press)*

After his arrest in January 2011, Hemy Neuman's mugshot only deepened the mystery: How could this mild-mannered-look-ing executive be a cold-blooded killer? *(Courtesy: Dunwoody Police Department)*

In a defense mocked by prosecutors and the media, Hemy Neuman contended he was insane at the time he gunned down Rusty Sneiderman, driven by messages from an angel who sounded like Olivia Newton John and looked like Barry White. *(Courtesy: Associated Press)*

Donald Sneiderman buckled under the emotional strain of his son's murder, but provided devastating testimony against Andrea, whom he suspected of orchestrating Rusty's killing. *(Courtesy: Associated Press)*

Young and ambitious, District Attorney Robert James Jr. (standing in front of his chief deputy, Don Geary) gained international publicity prosecuting Hemy Neuman only to stumble as his murder case against Andrea Sneiderman began to crumble. *(Courtesy: Associated Press)*

After months of attacks by her in-laws and withering pressure from authorities, Andrea Sneiderman is arrested in August 2013. She would complain of heavy-handed police tactics including use of a SWAT team. *(Courtesy: Associated Press)*

Hemy Neuman now looked like the mental patient he was after the murder trial, as he continued to insist that Andrea had nothing to do with Rusty's killing. *(Courtesy: Georgia Department of Corrections)*

NEUMAN, HEMY ZVI

GDC ID: 1000778905

PHYSICAL DESCRIPTION

YOB:	1962
RACE:	WHITE
GENDER:	MALE
HEIGHT:	5'07"
WEIGHT:	150
EYE COLOR:	BROWN
HAIR COLOR:	UNKNOWN

Nestled in a grove not far from the region's biggest shopping mall, the Dunwoody Police Department could be mistaken for a financial office. *(Courtesy: Michael Fleeman)*

Working off the description of a witness who saw the killer escape, a police sketch artist created the image of the suspect. Andrea never told police her suspicions the picture reminded her of her boss at General Electric. *(Courtesy: Dunwoody Police Department)*

###

Andrea Sneiderman's dream house – five bedrooms, four bathrooms with a gourmet kitchen and a deck – was the site of her first fateful police interview in which she said her boss Hemy Neuman had made romantic advances – a tip detectives didn't follow. *(Courtesy: Michael Fleeman)*

After working part-time from home for years while setting aside her career for husband Rusty, Andrea plunged into the corporate world in April 2010 and, prosecutors alleged, started an affair with her boss, Hemy Neuman. *(Courtesy: Michael Fleeman)*

On October 31, 2010, Hemy called Parnell's Firearms and Shooting Range two hours after leaving a gun show in Dalton. The next day, he showed up with a gun and ammunition. *(Michael Fleeman)*

On the morning of November 18, 2010, people waiting in line at the post office heard gunfire across the parking lot from the direction of Dunwoody Prep preschool; they raced over to find a man bloodied and dying while inside teachers huddled with students. *(Michael Fleeman)*

Hemy Neuman's attorneys, Robert Rubin and Douglas Peters, argued that he didn't know right from wrong at the time he fatally shot Rusty Sneiderman. *(Peters, Rubin & Sheffield)*

At the DeKalb County Courthouse in February of 2012, Hemy Neuman went on trial in the murder of Rusty Sneiderman. *(Michael Fleeman)*

CHAPTER 15

Daniel McNaughtan was a 19th-century Scottish wood-turner who had grown to hate the ruling Tories and Prime Minister Sir Robert Peel. On what historian Richard Moran described as a "raw January afternoon" in 1843, Mc-Naughtan walked up to a carriage he believed to be carrying Peel along Downing Street in London and, according to the *Times of London*, "put the muzzle of the pistol into the back of the unsuspecting gentleman. He then fired."

It turned out the gentleman was not Peel but his private secretary Edmund Drummond. There is some dispute about whether McNaughtan meant to kill Drummond or if it was a case of mistaken identity; the newspapers of the day were not yet able to print photographs, so the appearances of government officials weren't well known. The gravely wounded Drummond stumbled to his brother's

Charing Cross banking house and, despite receiving the best medical care of the time, died five days later. Mc-Naughtan was quickly apprehended and charged with first-degree murder.

In a sensational trial in the Central Criminal Court of London, McNaughtan's lawyers called nine medical experts to prove he was driven by a "fierce and fearful delusion" that caused him to believe the government was persecuting him. He suffered from what would be called "such a defect of reason, from a disease of the mind" that at the time he pulled the trigger he did not know that what he was doing was wrong.

In a shocking decision, the court agreed. It found Mc-Naughtan not guilty and spared him the gallows. Public outrage followed. The *Times of London* said the doctors who testified on his behalf had hijacked the trial. "The judge in his treatment of the madmen yields to the decision of the physician, and the physician in his treatment becomes the judge," the *Times* wrote. The *Standard* griped about "mad doctors" who delivered testimony that was "crude" and "absurd." Even Queen Victoria weighed in, calling for judges to take a firmer control of the courtroom. "The law may not be perfect, but how is it that whenever a case for its application arises, it proves to be of no avail?" she wrote to Peel, complaining that the "ablest lawyers of the day . . . allow and advise the Jury to pronounce the verdict of Not Guilty on account of Insanity—whilst everybody is morally convinced that both the malefactors were perfectly conscious and aware of what they did!"

One hundred and seventy some years later, on September 10, 2011, Hemy Neuman's lawyers Doug Peters and Robert Rubin held a news conference. It was held on the porch of their offices in front of a sign reading PETERS, RUBIN AND SHEFFIELD, TRIAL LAWYERS with a picture of a scale. Peters told reporters, "Mr. Neuman had a mental illness, because of that mental illness, at the time of the shooting, he just was unable to understand the difference between right and wrong."

He was referencing what had become to be known as the McNaughtan Rules on criminal responsibility adopted after the Scotsman's case and dominating Anglo-Saxon law ever since. Most American states, including Georgia, still use this as an insanity test either by itself or in conjunction with another test, the best known being diminished capacity. Hemy planned to plead not guilty by reason of insanity.

"This is our notice to the court that what this trial is about is not what happened, but why it happened. It is our notice that this is about the people who are involved and how this transpired," Peters said. "This case is not about whether or not he pulled the trigger. He is the one who did the shooting. The question is, and what is provided by Georgia law, is What was his mental capacity at the time?"

Hemy's lawyers didn't reveal what they believed Hemy's mental illness to be. He was currently being "evaluated by the best and they feel very, very confident in their diagnosis in the case which of course will be revealed," said Peters. "Mr. Neuman, through us, has always maintained that he is innocent, that he is not responsible for this crime. A crime requires criminal intent, there was never criminal intent in this case . . . We have confidence that there will be a jury that can be seated here in DeKalb County that will give us a fair trial."

The insanity plea announcement didn't go over any better in 2011 than it had in the 1840s. Leading the charge was Ariela's attorney Esther Panitch, who said Ariela was "devastated" to find out her estranged husband admitted to killing Rusty, but couldn't accept the reasoning.

"She always believed the evidence from the district

attorney, but to hear it come from the defense really brought it home," said Panitch. "I don't think anyone wants to believe their spouse is capable so there's always some scintilla of hope that they couldn't have done this and this wipes out this hope." She noted Ariela saw "no sign of mental illness" and suggested the tactic was a ruse. "He acted like a man who was cheating on his wife and tried to lie about it," she said, adding, "The inability to fight the overwhelming desire to be with your lover is not a legal reason for insanity." She also questioned why it took nearly ten months after his arrest to decide that he was insane. "I suspect there has been so much overwhelming evidence of his guilt that this might be the only thing that they feel they have."

Andrea's attorney Seth Kirschenbaum released a statement saying, "We are relieved that Mr. Neuman has admitted that he killed Rusty Sneiderman. This was a cold-blooded, premeditated murder, however. Hopefully, the prosecution is prepared to rebut his insanity defense."

DA Robert James seemed as surprised as anyone. Nothing in the investigation to this point had turned up a trace of mental illness. On the contrary, the witnesses all used words like *calm* and *methodical* and *organized* to describe Hemy. His restraint under pressure during the interrogation was such that he never raised his voice, never broke down, never grew angry, leaving the detectives frustrated. After the murder he acted as he always had. There were occasional times he broke his reserve—the breakup email with his wife was the most dramatic example. Otherwise friends and co-workers described him, if anything, as boring.

The same held true after his arrest. When Hemy was processed into the DeKalb County Jail, just another of the thousands of inmates who go through each year, he underwent a routine psychiatric evaluation. Dr. William Jerome

Brickhouse, the jail's director of mental health, said Hemy also got a follow-up examination based on some of the findings of the screening the next day, on January 6, 2011. Working off a checklist, Brickhouse asked Hemy about a range of topics, from how many children he had (three) to whether he had suffered any hallucinations (he said none). Hemy had said that two weeks earlier he had "contemplated" suicide by drowning himself in the ocean while he was visiting Florida but that he didn't go through with it because of his love for his children and his Jewish beliefs that it would be a sin. Brickhouse determined that Hemy was safe for regular incarceration, that he was not suicidal or homicidal—not a risk to himself or others—and found no signs of a serious mental disorder.

By March, Hemy appeared to be adjusting to jail life. He was held in a two-person cell in an area—the jail calls them pods—with thirty-two inmates and reported no problems. "We talked about the living situation, his accommodations," Brickhouse said. "Had he been threatened? Assaulted? He said he was fine." With his Spanish skills, Hemy had become something of a mediator between the Hispanic and black inmates in his pod. "He said he was comfortable and had no request to be relocated," said Brickhouse.

The prosecution went to the judge seeking "information, documents and recordings relevant to defendant's claim of insanity." Hemy had been visited by mental health professionals hired by the defense, and the prosecution wanted to know what Hemy told them—and how they came to their conclusions. The prosecution also wanted its own experts to examine Hemy. The defense countered that Hemy didn't have to do this as it could infringe upon his rights against self-incrimination. The law "does not require a defendant to cooperate with the court's expert and provides no sanctions against a defendant who refuses to so cooperate," according to a defense motion. "In this case, the defendant retains his Fifth Amendment rights, and does not intend to waive those rights beyond what is required to give the state a fair opportunity to present its own expert testimony. Accordingly, there will be no examination and report generated by a court-appointed psychologist or psychiatrist."

The judge disagreed, handing the defense yet another defeat. Hemy's case file would be open to the prosecution. The story of Hemy's insanity defense unfolded.

It began in March 2011, three months after Hemy's arrest. At the time, things were looking bad for the defense. In addition to the media leaks from the search warrant affidavits and the battle with Hemy's estranged wife, the ballistics examiner had just determined that the "souvenir" shell casing provided by Jan DaSilva's girlfriend matched the shells at the murder scene, linking the gun scientifically to Hemy. Attorney Robert Rubin called Dr. Julie Rand-Dorney, a forensic psychiatrist. As an instructor at Emory University and the lead physician for the forensic unit at Georgia Regional Hospital in DeKalb County, Rand-Dorney was a highly sought expert in criminal cases, testifying for the prosecution sixty-one times, the defense twenty-eight times. Rubin asked her to conduct a screening to determine if Hemy showed signs of psychological issues that would be relevant to a defense, and, if so, whether he was faking those signs.

She began by taking a personal history from Hemy. It turned out that Hemy's reserve hid a lifetime of pain. In an account to Rand-Dorney, with details added when he spoke to other mental health experts later—and echoed in court in the testimony by his sister, Monique—Hemy described a life of fear, isolation, and physical pain, the seeds of which were rooted in the Holocaust.

His father, Marc Neuman, was among 130 family members taken to the Auschwitz Nazi death camp. This included Hemy's great-grandparents, grandparents, six uncles, and various cousins and other relatives. Of them, only twelve survived, including Marc and his brother—Hemy's uncle. After the war, Marc Neuman made his way to Mexico. He was a small man, barely five feet tall, but apparently had his charms, for he married the stunningly beautiful and very young Rebecca Cohen, seventeen years old to his thirty-six. They had a boy—Hemy's older brother—followed by Hemy and, eighteen months later, his sister, Monique.

The concentration camp never stopped haunting his father, seared into his psyche like the number tattoo on his forearm, Hemy claims. Hemy and his sister said Marc Neuman was a detached father and husband, the marriage strained by constant arguing. Hemy was born in Mexico but grew up in Puerto Rico after the family moved there when he was young. His father had jewelry shops selling to tourists, but went bankrupt at least twice.

Hemy spent little time with his mother; she was a socialite who would be out on the town or traveling to see relatives in Venezuela and Mexico, Hemy's sister would later say in court. With their mother largely absent and the father consumed with business troubles or his personal demons, Hemy and his sister fended for themselves. They would say that they felt no attachment to their parents and spent most of their time together. When their father was around, it became even worse. In an account under oath from Hemy's sister, Marc Neuman would come in around 6 p.m. from work, the children never knowing what his mood would be. When their mother was around, she, too, was tense. The smallest things would set him off. If the children's hands were dirty, he'd erupt. Their mother would make sure the children washed before he came home. He'd scream if he couldn't find his nail clippers where he usually left them, according to Hemy's sister.

The first thing Marc Neuman would do was drink one or two scotches, Hemy's sister would say in court. Then whoever was home would sit for dinner. If Hemy's mother was there, the first of the night's arguments would start at the dinner table. The shouting would lead to violence, according to Hemy and his sister. Hemy's father would slap the children with an open hand, they claimed. He once shoved a vegetable spoon into the nose of Hemy's sister, she said. He would scream at his wife, but she wouldn't budge. He couldn't control her, and that made him even angrier, Hemy would tell therapists. Hemy's sister, Monique, recalled coming home one day with shaved ice, and for some reason this set off her father. He yanked a picture off the wall and hit her with it. She could remember being hit so much her buttocks were the color of eggplant. Then the storm would pass and Marc Neuman would become a doting father.

Hemy said he bore the brunt of the abuse. With his older brother away at college, Hemy was the only boy in the house. His father would hit him with his hands and swat him with a belt, Hemy told therapists. The violence was unpredictable and impossible to understand, according to Hemy and his sister. One night, Hemy's sister said in court, the children were playing a game of Mastermind—Hemy, his sister, and some cousins—when Hemy got up for ice cream. Their father was lounging on a La-Z-Boy. Hemy stumbled and the ice cream went flying, enraging his father. According to Hemy's sister, their father slapped Hemy repeatedly. His sister burst into tears, fearing it would never stop.

If his mother was there, she would implore Marc Neuman to stop hitting Hemy. This only seemed to make his father want to hit Hemy more, Hemy and his sister claimed.

In time, Monique said, she devised ways to get out of the beatings. Sometimes crying worked. Other times, she'd blame Hemy for something going wrong—and Hemy would take another beating. Once, his sister recalled, she blurted out the word "bitch" while they were driving. Her father asked her where she'd learned the word. It was actually from a cousin, but she told her father it was Hemy. Their father pulled over to the side of the road, leaned Hemy up against the car, and beat him.

When it was over, Hemy looked at his sister and said, "Thanks a lot." But Hemy never resented his sister for this; he was a protective older brother and often took the blame to spare her.

"I was the sandwich. I was in the middle," Hemy would explain to a therapist. "My sister would do something stupid and then blame me for it. She was my father's little princess. He would come home and hear it and give me a beating. I was just getting it from all sides. I might as well just stay away. Just leave me alone."

Their mother missed most of this. She'd be with friends, playing bridge or gambling at a casino, according to Hemy's sister. Their father became enraged when he didn't know where she was or realized that she wouldn't take orders from him, Hemy and his sister said. The children didn't seem to blame her for being away. They would, too, if they could.

When they came home from school, if their mother was there, she would be sleeping off a big night before. Their father didn't want her awakened. It was her beauty sleep and he wanted to protect her beauty, he would say, according to Hemy's sister. The family always had a maid, who would let the children in, feed them, watch them. But the kids always felt as if they raised themselves.

Despite it all, Hemy did well in school. He was the bright one in the family. Things seemed to come easily to him.

When Hemy turned thirteen, his already difficult life was plunged into upheaval. "Pack, you're going to Israel," his father told him one day.

Hemy was being sent to a boarding school. He had never been to Israel and didn't speak Hebrew. His mother apparently knew nothing of this and was out of the picture at the time, separated from their father. His father drove him to the airport, dropped him off, wished him good luck, and gave him a piece of paper with the father's phone number and the name of the boarding school. The plane arrived in Israel at 11:30 p.m. The person who was supposed to pick him up at the airport never materialized. Young Hemy hailed a taxi, which took him to the school, but the gates were closed that late.

Hemy would later describe his feelings as "scared shit-less." A guard came up but Hemy couldn't speak to him. The man was short and scary—like the Hunchback of Notre Dame, Hemy would recall—but he opened the gates and let him in. It was now past midnight. Hemy spent the first few weeks not in the classroom but in the infirmary in a sickly haze, his temperature soaring to 104 degrees. A nurse asked him where his parents were so they could pick him up. Hemy said they were in Puerto Rico and wouldn't be coming. He said he had relatives in Israel but didn't know where they were or how to contact them. As Rosh Hashanah approached, the nurse asked where he would spend the holidays. Hemy said he didn't know. So the nurse brought him to her home. She placed him in what Hemy later described as a shack that lacked heat in January. He felt orphaned and abandoned and plunged into what would later be determined to be depression.

After boarding school, Hemy went to the United States to study at Georgia Tech. There he would be a solid student. But in 1981, his sophomore year, the dark feelings returned. He lacked energy, had no motivation, didn't want to go to class, didn't want to study. All he wanted to do was sleep. When he was awake, he felt in a fog, unable to focus. His GPA fell and for the first time he didn't make the dean's list. That summer the depression lingered, even though he joined his sister in Miami.

Their parents had divorced by then and their mother remarried. Their father also would remarry and move into an apartment with his new wife. The divorce did them well. Their father's rage subsided—he was a different man without their mother around. Every day, Monique would thank God that her parents had divorced. The nineteen-year-old Hemy stayed with his mother and stepfather and his sister at their town house. The new husband bought Hemy a new Mustang, but that couldn't pull him out of the depression. For weeks all he did was sit on the sofa and watch HBO.

After graduating from Georgia Tech and returning to work in Israel, he married Ariela. He had a good job and they started a family, welcoming the twins. Then in 1998, Hemy surprised everybody. During a trip to South Florida to visit his family, he impulsively bought a house in Boca Raton and moved his family there. He quit his job and was unemployed when they arrived. They lived off the proceeds of selling their house in Israel. He put the twins in a private Jewish school. His energy level soared; he couldn't sleep. He toyed with becoming a pilot. He never found employment. The money ran out and tensions ran high at home between him and Ariela, family history repeating itself, though their fights were always verbal.

They moved back to Israel, where Hemy worked for a few years before returning to the United States for his job at GE. The steady, high-paying employment didn't seem to make matters better at home. When his sister visited in 2008, she could feel the tension. Money problems had been mounting. The family could barely afford a housekeeper and yet when Monique arrived she saw her brother installing a garden with a waterfall. Ariela had a new diamond ring. Hemy seemed manic. They threw an elaborate birthday bash for the twins. Hemy was the life of the party, something he never had been before. He paid for his sister to visit, another thing he hadn't done in the past.

At work, Hemy described himself as a "terror." The company asked him to erase a sixty-five-million-dollar budget deficit and he did it. Yet at home the spending spun out of control. Between March and August 2008 the Neumans burned through seventy-one thousand dollars. They paid college tuition and bought an air-conditioning system for the home. He cashed out a hundred-thousand-dollar pension with the idea of paying off seventy-seven thousand in credit card debt. Instead, by year's end, the credit balance hovered at seventy-four thousand dollars.

Hemy's moods would swing wildly, up for one stretch, down the next. His sister had flashbacks of her father. During a visit for the twins' college graduation, a party for which he spent twenty-five hundred dollars, Hemy exploded at his mother for no reason while they were taking pictures of the children. His mother reeled. Everybody felt uncomfortable and embarrassed.

By 2010, his marriage was in trouble. He claimed that he had tried to work on it, coming home and greeting his wife with a hug. But she would only cross her arms, he said. He felt alone again, like when he was sent off to boarding school. He felt as if he was slipping at work. A big project he had developed ended up going to another employee. He felt his energy ebb; all he wanted to do was sleep.

The only thing that kept him going were his children—and a new woman entering his life.

Asked by Dr. Rand-Dorney how he felt about Andrea, Hemy recounted a biblical story. He had been reading the Bible and the Torah more frequently of late and said the first and second books of Samuel spoke to him. In the passages, David, the first king of the Jews, saw a beautiful and beguiling woman named Bathsheba bathing in the open on a nearby rooftop. Hemy said this reminded him of his August trip to Greenville, South Carolina, when he fantasized about Andrea and, according to the therapist's notes, "thinks he saw her naked" coming "out of the shower toweling herself."

"She was a beautiful person," he told Dr. Rand-Dorney. "I thought of her as Bathsheba."

Hemy took it a step farther. He became fixated not just on Andrea, but on her children. He told Rand-Dorney that he "went back and forth" on whether he believed Sophia and Ian actually belonged to him and not Rusty. Becoming confused at times, he started to think the children were in danger. He told the psychiatrist, "I feel like I need to protect them."

After speaking with Hemy for several hours at the jail, Dr. Rand-Dorney found symptoms of a psychotic disorder and the possibility that he was driven by obsessive thoughts. He developed toward Andrea what mental health professionals call "erotomanic delusions" but wavered on whether he actually had sex with her or just thought he did. "As that relationship evolved, he became more and more consumed by it but depressed at the same time," Rand-Dorney later said. "At points he said he had sex with this woman, and then I'd ask, and he'd say, 'I don't know if it's true.'"

Rand-Dorney's screening found signs of paranoia, psychosis, and delusions, but more testing would be needed for a solid diagnosis. Another expert, Dr. Peter Thomas, a licensed psychologist and former president of the Georgia Psychological Association, was recruited. Although he had decades of experience, he had never been involved in a criminal case before. His work had mainly focused on child and family counseling. When his colleague Julie

Rand-Dorney asked for his assistance, he agreed to advise the defense as long he did not have to testify.

On May 11, 2011, he met with Hemy at the jail for a clinical interview and psychological testing. As with Rand-Dorney, the work was preliminary, the tests intended to find potential issues, not to come up with a diagnosis. Thomas's first impression was that Hemy spoke in a way that was "very naïve yet sophisticated," with statements that came off as both "confusing" and "bizarre." Hemy seemed to be driven by a mission that other people didn't understand. In the ink blot test—the famous Rorschach test—Hemy kept seeing in the blotches a "demon" trying to engulf him with its evil. When discussing his relationship with Andrea, he couldn't say for certain whether they had been sexually intimate. Thomas thought Hemy might have "psychotic behaviors" and recommended more evaluation. "I wasn't sure if he knew what was real and what wasn't," Thomas said.

After this limited assessment, the defense moved on to another expert for a detailed examination. Two months later, in August 2011, when the pretrial hearings were not going well for Hemy, his lawyers placed a call to Dr. Adriana Flores, one of the top forensic psychologists in Georgia. She had conducted a dozen evaluations previously; her opinion was so valued that DA Robert James also had contacted her in September but he was too late. She visited Hemy in jail on September 8, 2011, for the first of three sessions. Her work would consume one hundred hours, requiring her to read through binders of reports and conduct additional interviews with people close to Hemy, including his parents and sister. Flores wanted to talk to Andrea, but she refused.

Hemy once again recalled his difficult childhood, his abrupt relocation to a boarding school, and the horrible time in the cold shack, only this time he added details.

"One day in the shack he experienced a demon," Flores later said. "He was feeling really, really horrible, asking God what he did to deserve this, why have I been forsaken." He described the demon as over six feet tall in a heavy cloak. "He said he felt anguish, deep pain," said Flores. "At that moment he did not want to live and he prayed to God to take him." The demon was there to take Hemy away, but he didn't go.

Hemy said the demon would periodically return, the next time in 1981 when Hemy was a sophomore at Georgia Tech and suffering the depression that left him unable to do schoolwork and constantly craving sleep. Hemy did not see the vision again for years, absent during his manic years when he moved to Florida, then back to Israel, then to Atlanta, where he was a fiend at work and ran up bills at home.

Then in February 2010, it reappeared. At the time, the financial and marital strains had sent Hemy into another depression. "He was feeling like a failure, a wreck, very low energy, oversleeping, wanted to sleep life away," Dr. Flores would later say. During a day trip for business to Greenville, the demon emerged in Hemy's car. It seemed to wrap itself around him in an evil embrace and spoke to Hemy: "Come to me, I won't ever abandon you."

The feelings of pain and abandonment overwhelmed Hemy. Up ahead on the road was a concrete barrier. Hemy considered slamming the car into it, then changed his mind. He couldn't do that to his children. He continued on to Greenville and the work of GE Energy.

It was shortly thereafter, in March 2010, that he received the résumé from Andrea Sneiderman. He hired her and they began traveling together, Hemy feeling an immediate connection. They chatted easily and commiserated and drew ever closer, bonding over their shared personal problems at home. She was, Hemy told Dr. Flores, the first person he could ever really talk to, and he held back nothing, his childhood stories about his abusive father and the boarding school flooding out of him for the first time. During the trip to Minden, Nevada, they had what he called an intimate dinner in Lake Tahoe, where he read her a poem and told her she was beautiful. He said they kissed, a chaste kiss but one he'd never forget.

A few weeks later, when Andrea went to the training session in Longmont, Colorado, Hemy initially stayed behind, he said. But then a spectral vision appeared. This time it took a female form, sort of an angel. Materializing while Hemy was attending a dinner party with his wife, the angel told him that Ian and Sophia Sneiderman were his children and that he needed to let Andrea know.

It was on this night that Hemy frantically called the hotel in Longmont and tried to get the staff to buy flowers and chocolates for Andrea. He then spent his own money to fly there. Andrea met him at the airport, he told Flores, and joined him for dinner. Hemy told Andrea, "If you search the world over there is no better father for Sophia and Ian than me." He related Andrea as replying, "That may be, but I made a commitment to Rusty and I'm not breaking up."

For Hemy, what he saw as a growing relationship with Andrea brought both joy and sorrow. While in Longmont, he said, he could feel her putting up an emotional wall. They returned to the hotel and shared a bed, but Andrea did not want to have sex, he claimed. He tried to cuddle but she resisted. The next day she was angry and he bought her flowers. But over dinner her mood changed. They shared a bottle of wine and spent the night in the same bed, the morning spent cuddling. She stroked his chest. He would describe it as the most incredible moment of his life. Then she would change again. She sent him the email expressing confusion and regret.

The next time a vision came was after Hemy saw Rusty during a visit to the Sneiderman house in August 2010. While driving home, a female angel appeared in the car. According to Hemy, she told him that Andrea's children were at risk from Rusty. "He's going to hurt them," the angel warned. "And you have to protect them. You can't let this happen again."

A tremendous pain overcame Hemy.

"As he's driving he thought: I have to kill him," said Flores. "And he said that from that point on he said: 'I got my marching orders. I was a faithful soldier doing what I had to do.'" He never second-guessed the orders or analyzed them. His only thought was: *How do I do it?*

He considered poison. He thought about running Rusty over. Then he decided on a gun. It would be a "fire and forget mission," homing in on the target and then proceeding without looking back, according to Hemy, all to protect the children. It was around this time that Andrea had sent Hemy the photos from Sophia's birthday party. The fact that Rusty wasn't in any of them reinforced Hemy's belief that Rusty posed a threat to the children.

Entering another manic phase, Hemy made the Greenville trip with Andrea on August 26. In his retelling to the psychologist, they had adjoining rooms and fed each other during a dinner of tapas and wine. Returning to the hotel with another bottle of wine, they cozied up in bed and watched *The Goodbye Girl* on the computer, both in their pajamas, kissing and cuddling. His memory now faded. They may have had sex, but he couldn't be sure. All he knew was that afterward she was upset, the feelings she later expressed in her emails when she told him she felt horrible and would have to live with this the rest of her life.

For weeks there was emotional push and pull, and Hemy wavered on whether to go to the UK with her, eventually deciding to, only to face more mixed emotions from Andrea. When they made their second trip to Greenville, the pattern continued, one minute Andrea expressing regret, the next dancing with him at the Pulse nightclub. Their communications would become more frequent and intense, emails and texts and phone calls, Hemy's obsessions building, his plans to commit murder coming into focus.

The first attempt came on the morning of November 10, 2010. The homeless man lurking around the gas meter at the Sneiderman house was in fact Hemy wearing a disguise, lying in wait to shoot Rusty. But then Rusty called 911 and Hemy had to flee into the woods, which he knew about because he'd visited their home previously.

Eight days later, Hemy set out again to kill Rusty. He bought a different disguise, rented the Kia Sedona minivan, followed Rusty into the preschool parking lot, and this time shot him dead. Hemy took full and complete responsibility; Andrea knew nothing about it, he told Dr. Flores. If anything, he worried what Andrea would say if she found out the killer was Hemy. The fake beard was not intended to fool Rusty, he told Dr. Flores, but so Andrea wouldn't know who killed Rusty. Hemy didn't want her angry at him.

Dr. Flores diagnosed Hemy as suffering a bipolar 1 disorder with psychosis manifested by delusions. The mania and depression spoke to the bipolar disorder, as did Hemy's "hypersexuality" at the time. The angel telling him to protect Andrea's children indicated delusions. How much of his relationship with Andrea also was a delusion was harder to determine, Flores said. She found enough independent evidence to suggest they had at least an emotional affair, but how far it went physically couldn't be determined.

Dr. Flores believed that Andrea played a strong part in Hemy's emotional problems, giving him "cues" that reinforced his delusions and created his perceived attachment to her. Andrea, according to Dr. Flores, was "manipulating him into believing what she believed and thinking what she thought." Andrea's inconsistent rewards and punishments perversely created a strong emotional bond. No matter how much she distanced herself from him, Hemy could count on Andrea coming back, Dr. Flores said. Whether Andrea did this wittingly or unwittingly was unclear, though Dr. Flores would insist, "The only person who could've known he was delusional . . . was Andrea Sneiderman, because the delusions were about her."

His mental illness was so severe, she concluded, that he was not criminally responsible for Rusty's murder and that at the time he pulled the trigger he did not know the difference between right and wrong. "Everything," she said, "points to him being criminally insane."

There was always the possibility that Hemy was faking all this, inventing the demon and angel only so that he would appear insane and wiggle out of a murder rap. So much of Dr. Flores's findings hinged on what Hemy told her—if he was lying, her conclusions would be wrong. Dr. Flores conducted a battery of tests to determine if Hemy was faking mental illness—"malingering" in psychological parlance. She concluded that Hemy was telling the truth. His mental illness, she said, was so severe that typically somebody in his condition would be committed to a mental health facility.

A second defense expert, Dr. Tracey Marks, a psychiatrist, would also meet with Hemy, in September 2011, and come to the same conclusion. "Mr. Neuman, at the time of the alleged offense, was unable to distinguish right and wrong" due to his bipolar disorder, she'd later say. In fact, months after the murder, Hemy was still delusional about Rusty's murder. "He really believes this stuff . . . and has such little insight into the gravity of this stuff," Marks would say. "People who have no insight don't get it, and he doesn't get it."

The prosecution predictably cast a skeptical eye. For one thing, the timing seemed suspicious. For the better part of a year, he had been a model prisoner—no fights or complaints, no reported problems with other inmates. That suddenly changed in October 2011. Just days after his attorneys' press conference announcing the defense strategy and shortly after Hemy met with Dr. Marks, Hemy sent a request to speak with Dr. Brickhouse. Unavailable at the time, Brickhouse had the on-call clinician follow up. Hemy reported that he had grown concerned for his safety. A new group of inmates had moved into his pod, among them two men who "were contemplating throwing him down the stairs," said Brickhouse. "They took exception to the fact he was Jewish and made reference to the fact that Jewish people did not accept Christ."

The jail moved Hemy to protective custody, an area with a smaller pod—twelve inmates—and single-inmate cells. A day later, on October 12, Hemy sent a "sick slip" with another plea to talk to Brickhouse, this one marked "urgent." After conferring with the clinician, Brickhouse met with Hemy, who related the threats. He said he now felt physically safe but had come to feel suicidal. Asked if he had made any plans to act on this, he said that he had five razors he had been keeping for some time in case. "At that time," Brickhouse later said, "he shared that he had committed the murder he was charged with, something he did not mention in January. He also shared that he changed the nature of his legal defense," an apparent reference to his plans to plead not guilty by reason of insanity although Brickhouse didn't know the details at the time.

Brickhouse wasn't entirely convinced Hemy wanted to kill himself, but he told Hemy that ethically he would have to take action. As a precaution a guard searched his cell, finding and seizing the razors, and the jail transferred him to a section called 3A, the mental health ward, with twenty-seven beds staffed twenty-four hours a day by nurses and security. Under observation by nurses making rounds every fifteen minutes, Hemy spent his time reading and praying. He showered and shaved and seemed to have no trouble sleeping. He suffered what would be labeled "situational depression," not unusual for someone suddenly stripped of their liberties and locked up, but Brickhouse saw no signs of a more serious psychosis. After about two and a half months, Brickhouse spoke to Hemy. They discussed the timing of his transfer—whether it should happen before or after the Jewish holidays and Christmas. The decision was made to do it after the new year, in January 2012. "His mental state was completely unremarkable during that period of time," Brickhouse later said. "There was never any documented evidence of any delusions, there was never any documented mental health requests. His behavior was exemplary."

To see if there was any evidence that Hemy was faking his problems—and to build ammunition to rebut a defense insanity case—prosecutors hired their own expert. Dr. Pamela Crawford was a former US Air Force psychologist who retired as a major. Licensed as a psychologist in South Carolina, Dr. Crawford did not have a license in Georgia where the trial would be held. She also was not currently board-certified, having allowed her certification to lapse three years earlier. This, along with the fact that she would charge the state about sixty thousand dollars for her work, would make her vulnerable at trial. But her review was extensive, including two interviews with Hemy.

More important, unlike the other experts, Crawford conducted her interviews on video.

They met on November 4 and 5, 2011, after the four

defense mental health professionals had already talked to him. They covered the same issues, from his childhood through the hiring of Andrea Sneiderman, but Crawford delved deeper into Hemy's claims of seeing the visions. Crawford asked first about the demon that appeared at the boarding school, at college, and then in the car.

"How far away from you is he typically?" Crawford asked.

"Probably arm's length," said Hemy. "I mean, he's big."

"How big?"

"Not as high as the ceiling but almost. Like towering over me."

Crawford asked what the demon sounded like. "It's a voice outside your head? Is it a low or high voice?"

"It's a deep voice. I've never been asked before—almost like Barry White."

The female angel that appeared at the dinner party was also big, tall enough to reach the ceiling, he said. She had a wide face and a flowing light-pastel-blue robe. Hemy could both hear her and feel her, like an embrace.

"What does the voice sound like?"

"I compared his to Barry White," he said of the demon. "She's got a light voice." Hemy tried to think of whom the angel reminded him of. "What's her name? Oh, goodness, I can just hear her. The Australian who played in *Grease*, what's her name?"

"Olivia Newton-John?"

"Yes, like that kind of soft."

"Does she have an accent?"

"No."

"Not Australian like Olivia?"

"No."

Crawford asked Hemy if he thought the visions were real.

"When he comes, I think he is real."

"Do you think he is real now? What do you think he is?"

"Now I'm talking to you and sort of analyzing," Hemy said, "probably not."

"What do you think it is?"

"I don't know, my own fears, insecurities I have coming manifesting themselves in a physical way. I don't know."

Asked who else knew about his visions, Hemy said that he never told anybody until after he was arrested.

"You said you tell Andrea about things," said Crawford. "Tell her about the demon?"

"No."

"Do you remember consciously not telling her about it?"

"I don't know that we ever got—once again, it's not a very pleasant experience."

The first person he told, he said, was his lawyer Robert Rubin.

"What made you talk to him about it?" asked Crawford. "What made it significant to you?"

"We couldn't figure this out. For the life of us we couldn't figure it out," said Hemy, "and then it hit me because we talked about the angel."

At best, an insanity defense is a major gamble, and history was not on Hemy's side. Daniel McNaughtan may have avoided execution, but he did not escape punishment. He wound up in Bethlem Hospital, the infamous asylum for the mentally ill—from which the word *bedlam* comes—then transferred to another hospital for the criminally insane. He died in 1865 among the lunatics, remembered only as a legal abstraction.

There was, however, one wild card in the defense strategy. While Hemy would admit that he killed Rusty Sneiderman, both the prosecution and the defense came to believe he was driven by more than spectral visions and voices.

Andrea Sneiderman, the object of his passion and infatuation, was with him every step of the way, texting, emailing, talking, and phoning.

How much blame for her husband's death could be laid at her feet? And what did she have to say now?

The wait for answers would not be long.

CHAPTER 16

Superior Court judge Gregory A. Adams doesn't just take the bench. He makes an entrance. He bursts into his fifth-floor courtroom through a door just to the right of the bench, then slams the door behind him. The clock drives his courtroom; his favorite phrase is "at this point in time." Minutes matter to him. Court starts promptly at 9 a.m. Ten-minute breaks last exactly ten minutes. His voice cuts through all others, loud but never shouting, and he gives lawyers what could be called a friendly glare. Even what are normally quieter moments in court make a racket. When the lawyers gather at the bench for a private sidebar discussion, Adams activates a switch that fills the courtroom with an abrasive static noise so nobody can hear what they're saying. A former prosecutor for DeKalb County, he's amassed awards and titles, from past president of the DeKalb Bar Association to an honor from the Boy Scouts of America. There's even a building named after him: the Gregory A. Adams Juvenile Justice Center.

On the morning of Tuesday, February 21, 2012, Judge Adams presided over opening statements in the case of *Georgia v. Hemy Zvi Neuman*, charged with murder and the use of a gun in a felony. From an initial pool of 250 people called to the courthouse in Decatur, a jury of nine women and three men was selected. As is often the case, this courtroom was smaller in life than it appeared on television, with four rows of wooden benches in the audience section where family members were seated. It was a tense group, invisible lines between Rusty's family—his parents, his brother, and his brother's wife—on one side and Andrea and her supporters, including her mother and friends, on the other. Rusty's family had become convinced that Andrea was involved in the murder even though she hadn't been charged. The news media came out in force. National network correspondents delivering reports for the *Today* show and *Good Morning America* joined the local television and newspaper reporters, who live-blogged and tweeted from the courtroom. HLN carried portions of the trial live.

Hemy Neuman sat at the defense table between Robert Rubin and Doug Peters—Peters in his customary bow tie. Hemy dressed business casual in a zip-up navy sweater jacket over a blue dress shirt, with no tie, his white T-shirt poking through. The man who'd be called "the defendant" for the next several weeks appeared quiet, impassive, as if he were just another observer. DA Robert James took his seat at the prosecution table and watched as Chief Assistant District Attorney Don Geary stood and gave the opening statement for the state. In his presentation, Geary spoke of the one person not in the courtroom, Rusty Sneiderman. Retracing the bloody events of November 18,

2010, step by detailed step, Geary described how Hemy followed Rusty to the preschool parking lot, waited while Rusty dropped off Ian, then shot him. "As Rusty falls, the defendant's not satisfied. He walks up and, in near contact, he puts [the gun] to Rusty's neck and fires again," Geary told the jury. "Then this man who didn't know the difference between right and wrong goes to his van and drives off quickly."

The opening statement played to the emotions while also attacking the insanity defense, but as powerful a presentation as he delivered, Geary could not hold the jury's full attention. For behind him in the audience section was Andrea in a gray sweater with a Star of David necklace. She was sobbing uncontrollably. She drew heaving breaths as her mother comforted her. It was the first time many people had seen Andrea, a powerful impression few would forget—and not the last one she'd leave at the trial.

Next, Doug Peters gave the defense opening. "This case is about two good men," he said, calling Rusty Sneiderman "a great father to his two children" and Hemy Neuman a "great father to three." But on that morning in November "the lives of those men and their families were shattered, broken in pieces on the ground, never to be put back together again," Peters said. "Why? Everyone in this courtroom and this community is looking for the answer." He told jurors to look no farther than the victim's wife. Hemy had an affair with her, Peters said, and by the end he became convinced he had to kill Rusty to save Andrea's children, prodded into murderous action by visions of an angel and a demon. "Now, that's a dad gum story," Peters acknowledged, but insisted it was one he could prove.

The lawyers done, Adams cleared the courtroom for a break, during which prosecutors revealed they would call Andrea first. It was a surprise, not least for her. She had not spoken to police in months, her relations with authorities souring as they continued to suggest she played a role in Rusty's murder. Her lawyer, Seth Kirschenbaum, requested a hearing. Ever mindful of the ticking clock, Adams welcomed Kirschenbaum to the podium with a most unwelcome stare. The judge bluntly reminded the lawyer that he had no standing in this criminal trial since Andrea was a party to the case and that technically Adams didn't have to listen to a word he said. But as a "courtesy," the judge would let him speak, briefly.

"The purpose of the motion," began Kirschenbaum, "is brought on by the fact that Peters made it clear in his opening statement that he plans to put Andrea Sneiderman on trial and shift the blame for this crime from his client to my client. The way he's going to do it is to completely focus on the more salacious aspects of this case whether or not they are true."

The motion, he said, was to bar the television camera from the courtroom while Andrea testified. "I'm not asking you to clear this courtroom, but what I am asking you is to protect Andrea Sneiderman, to protect her children, and to protect the morals of all people who may hear this case that you order that Andrea Sneiderman's testimony not be televised," he said. "Why? Because it's going to focus on alleged improper conduct or acts of the sexes. Not only to protect Sneiderman, society, to protect her children."

"Mr. Kirschenbaum," the judge said, "as a courtesy I did recognize you. All right, as of this time, you may be seated."

No more would be said on the matter. The camera stayed on.

"Bring in my jury, please!" the judge boomed. As they filed in, Adams prodded them, "Come on in, you may be seated in any seat, no assigned seats, come on in, ladies and gentlemen, make yourself comfortable." The judge then barked, "Call your first witness!"

Geary said, "The state calls Andrea Sneiderman."

"Come on up!" the judge said in a voice suggesting he wouldn't be disappointed if she jogged to the witness chair. "You'll be sworn in!"

Andrea had her hair just past shoulder-length and wore glasses that were narrow and severe. Her expression was grim. She raised her right hand and heard the bailiff give the oath. She swallowed hard before saying yes. After spelling her name for the court reporter, she pulled her chair up and swallowed and shook her head as if she had a crick in her neck.

"Ma'am," said Geary, "did you know Rusty Sneiderman?"

"Yes," she said, smiling.

"How did you know Rusty?"

"He is my husband."

In a slow, deliberate, and business-like fashion, Geary elicited the basic personal details from Andrea—her date of marriage, number of children, their employment histories, including her hiring at GE Energy. She spoke about the family's finances, how they saved money and lived within their means, amassing an eight-hundred-thousand-dollar bank balance despite Rusty's periods between jobs, with two houses, their primary residence half paid off.

"You wouldn't consider yourself broke, would you?"

"No," she said.

Geary then ventured into Andrea's relationship with Hemy Neuman, a relationship that she acknowledged developed over the many hours they spent traveling for GE, when talk would drift from business to the personal. The prosecutor's tone remained calm and respectful, ever mindful that the jury may empathize with the grieving widow.

"In the course of the time that I knew him," Andrea began, "he discussed in the beginning how he was very happy with his children, had some financial problems but happy in his marriage. Then it progressed on to: I'm not happy in my marriage and my wife, that we are not getting along. She's confrontational."

Hemy told her about his early years, going to the boarding school in Israel, only he called it an "extremely positive influence," Andrea testified, with Hemy telling her he became a leader and made many friends.

"Ever tell you about encountering a demon?" asked Geary, his first of many jabs at the defense theory.

"No," she said.

Instead, she talked to Hemy about "everything from hobbies I had, to my children's interests, to Rusty's business ventures, to previous jobs I had had. Everything you would talk about with something you're developing a friendship with."

"Did you consider him a friend at that time?"

"Yes."

"How would you describe him prior to November 18?"

"Extremely friendly individual, caring—pretending to be a caring individual," she added, "seemed to have a very close relationship with all the members of his team . . . willing to take on any obstacle. That, at the time, seemed like an admirable quality for somebody in a corporation like GE. It can be tough to navigate a company like that. He seemed to have that figured out."

"Prior to November 18, 2010, did the defendant tell you ever that he was having hallucinations?"

"No."

"Did it ever appear to you that he was having hallucinations?"

"No, he appeared to be an extremely normal individual."

"Did you ever hear anything about him having hallucinations?"

"No."

"Did the defendant ever tell you that he saw or talked to a demon?"

"No."

"Did the defendant ever tell you that he saw or talked to an angel figure?"

"No."

"Did you ever see the defendant, prior to November 18, 2010, act illogical or irrational?"

"Never."

"Did you ever see the defendant act manically depressed such that he couldn't function?"

"No."

"Did you ever see him confused?"

"No."

"Did you ever see him act bipolar or have extreme mood changes?"

"Never."

"Was he pretty stable, pretty solid?"

"Extremely stable person."

"Did the defendant ever tell you how many children he had?"

"Yes."

"How many children did he tell you he had?"

"Three."

"Did he ever tell you he thought he had five?"

"No."

"Did he ever tell you that he thought your children were his children?"

She answered with an emphatic, "No."

At the defense table, Hemy sat and watched. Sometimes he would look up at her through his glasses, sometimes looking down, his expression neutral, as if he were attending a slightly boring business meeting, attentive but not fully involved.

Andrea seemed nervous. She wrung her hands in her lap and twitched. She spoke so softly at times that the judge had her repeat answers.

"Did the defendant ever express his feelings to you?" asked Geary.

"Yes," she said, and recalled the business trip to Minden, Nevada. "Before dinner, we were outside the restaurant, and he pulled out his phone and read a poem. The insinuation of the poem to me was that he had deeper feelings for me than just friends. We immediately sat down. I remember the first question out of my mouth was: 'Are you happy in your marriage?' "

"What did he express to you?"

"I don't remember what the poem said. The poem insinuated that he thought I was beautiful, which to me meant that he had more romantic feelings for me than just being friends."

"Is that the only time prior to November 18, 2010, that he expressed that to you?"

"It's the only time that he expressed it in that way. There were other times where in passing, or in a fleeting moment, or in what seemed like a very silly email, he would seem to be expressing feelings for me. None of those feelings were ever returned and I made myself completely clear where I stood."

"Do you have any idea what would make, what you believe, why the defendant would have these feelings for you? Do you know why he might have them?"

Andrea paused for a long time before answering. "Ummm," she began, "I think I'm a pretty nice person. If you ask any of my friends, I get very involved in their life. I care about them. I get to know them. I try to help them. I did nothing but try to help Hemy Neuman. I suggested to him to seek counseling for him and his marriage, suggested that he not move out of his home, and I would do that for any friend. I think he viewed me as someone that had some sort of expert knowledge, answers."

"Did you ever tell Rusty about the poem or the defendant's feelings towards you?"

"No."

"Why not?"

"I really thought that I could handle it," she said. "I knew if I told Rusty that I would quit my job and it was the only source of income we had at the time. I thought I had everything under control. At the time it seemed benign in a sense, no reason to tell him, only to make him emotional and worried about my career and about me."

"Did you ever report the defendant's conduct to anybody at GE?"

"No."

"Why not?"

The question brought a change to Andrea. Her voice took on a firm tone, like she was lecturing the prosecutor.

"I would have been fired," she said. "I think that it's fairly clear in writing how those things are handled, but I think that any woman that works in a corporation, that has just started her career over again, almost for the second time, knows if you were to report something like that, and you only worked at the company for two or three months, your chance of success at that company are pretty limited."

Geary then brought her through her business trips with Hemy, starting with a trip to Norfolk.

"Do you remember that trip sharing a bottle of wine?"

Andrea appeared thrown off by the question. "I think almost every time I sat down to a business dinner I had a bottle of wine—shared a bottle of wine."

He presented her with a receipt for a fifty-dollar bottle of wine.

Andrea leaned forward and stared at Geary. "I never picked the wine that we drank."

"Question for you," he asked. "Why would you share a bottle of wine at dinner far away from home, without your family there, with a man that just expressed those feelings to you?"

"I worked in consulting and have had many jobs since then at which drinking a bottle of wine while you're out of town is very commonplace," she shot back. "And drinking a bottle of wine did not enter my mind, my psyche that that was relevant to. Sorry, when I told him I wasn't interested, he seemed like everything was fine. So at the time . . . he understood and respected my decision and I felt very comfortable that he could continue a normal friendship regardless how he expressed his feelings to me."

Shown more receipts and then emails, she gave variations on the same answer. She either didn't remember things or downplayed the significance of them. Geary played a video of Andrea talking to Deputy Chief David Sides the day after Hemy's arrest in which she was asked if Hemy had been with her in Colorado with her and she stammered, "No, I do not—I know that—I'm trying to think."

"Do you remember now?" Geary asked her.

"I don't know," she said. "If that's what I said, then that's what I said."

It was, Geary suggested, not the kind of trip she'd forget, with the email from Hemy with a picture of roses, and her reply about that being "thoughtful" and a "sweet gesture."

Asked if that was her email, she answered, "Yep." It was a word she'd use increasingly often, her answers becoming more terse. Then with strain in her voice she said, "I don't remember every email that I've written."

Geary showed her additional emails, from Hemy to her, from her to Hemy: more trips, more hotels, more wine. Andrea replied to Geary as if he were a child, condescension in her voice. She shrugged her shoulders and she glared. She didn't remember everything Hemy told her and she didn't remember what she told him back. How could she? It was so long ago. Then she'd say, If the emails say it, then it must have happened—but not the way it looks. The change in rooms in Longmont? She didn't like the room she was in. It had nothing to do with wanting a single bed.

She was shown receipts from their first trip to Greenville, an eighty-four-dollar dinner with a thirty-one-dollar wine called "Bitch." There was an overnight, followed by emails filled with guilt and remorse and anger—emails Andrea read aloud in court as they were projected on a screen for the jurors and audience to see.

"What happened in Greenville, ma'am?"

"We were holding each other's hands," she said, "and that's it. It may sound worse than it is, but to me that was a betrayal."

"So you're repenting in the email, at least, from holding his hand?"

"Yup."

She took a deep breath, and the questioning continued.

She didn't remember him telling her he loved her. She considered his email about wanting to marry her "ridiculous." Most of things he said or wrote she never kept track of or paid much attention to, they were just a handful out of thousands of emails that were otherwise benign. He was being "silly," she said, "mannish." Then he'd go back to being her friend and she wouldn't worry about it. She never told GE, she never told Rusty. She felt comfortable enough with Hemy that she went to the UK with him.

"I do want to just note that we did not go to the dance club," she said in reference to the email about her saying she had taken dancing lessons for years. "In fact, we did not do any of the things that are insinuated that we did on that itinerary because there were definitely points during this manipulation that I was under, which is exactly what it was, that I realized that every activity we were doing, every situation that he put me in, was a convenient situation to get what he wanted, to get me in a position that he wanted, to get me to spend time with him. And when we were in England, I realized that none of that was appropriate and so we did not do any of that."

Repeatedly she insisted the emails weren't an accurate picture of what was happening. Shown messages to her friend Tammi about apparent strains in her marriage, she suggested she misquoted herself in her own email.

"Yep, I told her it only ends in a fight, I'm tired of fighting," Andrea testified. "I used the word fighting. I think that word is being misused in the email."

For the rest of the afternoon in court, she responded with sarcastic relies of "yep" and "yup" and "nope." She treated each email as a revelation, a dim memory to her that meant nothing at the time and even less now.

Geary turned to Andrea's second trip to Greenville with Hemy and asked her if she went to a restaurant called Pulse.

"It's a dance club not a restaurant," she corrected.

"Do you remember going there?" he asked.

"We went to dinner at a restaurant, an actual restaurant, and then afterwards, we were walking along. He said, 'Let's check out this place. I found this place online.' It was a place just to have [a] drink. That was my impression at the time."

"Did you go there?"

"Yep."

"What did you do there?"

"We had some drinks at the bar. Maybe one, two."

"Did you dance?

"I went onto the dance floor myself," she said. "As I explained, I've been a trained dancer for some time, being able to dance to me is like a release, I'm very much in my own space when I do that. I got up and I was dancing alone on the dance floor."

"Did you dance with the defendant?"

"He came to join the dance floor. Did not join me on the dance floor initially, and he was also dancing, and then there was a time where he reached out his hand and as the defense has said twirled me around, and that's it."

"Were there other contacts?"

"There was not."

"Besides dancing, like partner dancing?"

"Nope."

"Did you kiss him or did he kiss you?"

"No. I—I—no," she said. Then added, "I guess you have people that have said that that did occur."

"Do you have any idea why someone would believe you were kissing him?"

She shrugged. "No, I don't."

"Okay."

Without prompting, she added, "In this case when you are talking about alleged affairs and someone else's husband being murdered I think people tend to think they saw a lot of things."

"Well, let me ask you that," said Geary. "This is a gentleman up to that point in time who asked you to marry him at least twice that we're aware of, correct?"

She began to sniffle. "Correct."

"And has expressed his love for you in just emails numerous times, correct?"

"Correct."

"And you're going to a dance club drinking with him, correct?"

"I didn't go to the dance club as a drinking activity, and nor did I know at the time that it was a dance club until we got in there. But yes I was there."

"And you stayed?"

"Yep, I stayed."

"Did you have adjoining rooms in that trip in Greenville?"

"Uh, yep."

"Did you and he spend time in each other's room or in one of the rooms, together?"

"When we got to the hotel, I remember sitting briefly on the balcony of my room, but that was that, there was no other additional time, if that's what you are asking."

Geary asked, "Did the defendant ever tell you he was going to a gun show in Dalton?"

"No."

"On October 31 of 2010, did the defendant text you while he was at the gun show in Dalton telling you that he was there?"

"No," Andrea said, exasperation and disbelief in her voice. "Telling me that he was at a gun show?"

"Yes, ma'am."

"I do not remember him texting me that."

"Now is this like the other emails, that it could have happened, you just don't remember?"

"No, I'm pretty sure I would remember a gun show."

"You didn't remember 'I love you' but you'd remember a gun show?"

"I didn't say that I didn't remember, I just didn't remember all these emails from two years ago. Similarly I don't think I could remember the content of texts from two years ago."

Geary then asked her about the morning Rusty called 911 to report a man on the side of the house. She recounted how Rusty had called her at work to tell her what happened.

"And as soon as Rusty ended that call or you ended that call, who did you call?"

"I have no idea. I was at work, so I was presumably doing work things."

"Any idea why you would immediately call the defendant after talking to Rusty?"

"I'm sure it was—no—I'm sure it was work-related," she said. "It does seem coincidental. But I'm sure that there was something else going on that I had to call him about. I talk to him frequently about work matters. And I had a meeting with Hemy that day and I told Hemy exactly what happened on the side of my house."

"Why would you do that?"

"I told the person that worked for me, I told Hemy and told like six other people also what happened on the side of the house because it was bizarre and scary. And he stared at me and looked at me and it was him the whole time."

"Did you know that then?

"No, how could I know that? He was sitting there like an absolute normal individual. He came to work. He was at work. For all I know he was at work the entire time. We don't work in the same building, I don't know where he was at that time. Rusty didn't recognize him. How would Rusty recognize him? He was wearing a disguise. He described him as a Mexican worker."

Her testy answers turned to anger as Geary asked how Hemy would know how to approach their house through a sidewalk hidden in the woods.

"Someone had to tell him about that," he said.

"Someone had to tell him?" she answered angrily.

"How else would he find out?"

She snapped at him, "He had been stalking my house for months."

"How did you find that out?"

"I think we all know that by now."

"So that's a guess on your part?"

She leaned back. "It is speculation on my part, yes."

Andrea continued to simmer, lashing out again when he questioned her about Hemy coming to her house two days before the murder while Rusty was there and the children were upstairs asleep.

"I keep going back to this, but I just want to clarify: You had a man over to your house with your children—"

She interrupted him sharply, "I had no choice but to continue my career and my job and—"

The judge now jumped in with a warning. "Miss Sneiderman, the lawyer has a right to ask the question. You can give a response. But let him finish the question. He's going to allow you to finish your answer."

"Thank you, Judge," Geary said. "This is the same man who repeatedly said he loved you, he repeatedly asked you to marry him, who came to your house with your children in their beds to work on a project?"

Andrea said, "Yep."

"At your house?"

"Yep."

"And at this time did Rusty know about the advances of the defendant?"

"Nope."

By now she'd been on the stand most of the day, her nerves appearing frayed, when Geary asked her how she found out about the shooting.

"That morning, did you get a phone call from the day-care?"

"Yep."

"What did they tell you?"

"Really didn't tell me anything," she said, her voice now dropping. "They said there has been an accident."

"I'm sorry, speak up a little please."

In a whisper, she said, "They said there had been an accident, that Ian is fine. But there had been an accident."

"And the accident specifically was directed to Rusty, or did they tell you?"

"They didn't really tell me," she said, speaking louder, "and then I screamed into the phone asking what was going on, and they just said you need to come here and so I dropped the phone and ran out of my office."

"Did you, prior to dropping the phone, did they clarify it was Rusty or they didn't tell you?"

"I don't remember. I presumed it was Rusty. I don't know whether they actually said. Maybe they said it had something to do with Rusty. I don't remember."

He asked again, "Did they at any time tell you what had happened to Rusty?"

She responded with an emphatic "Nope."

After receiving the call from Donna at the preschool, Andrea recalled running to the parking lot and driving to the preschool, making several calls along the way.

"Do you remember who you called?"

She sighed. "My parents, my brother, Rusty's parents," she said.

"Rusty's parents—do you remember who you talked to?"

"Yep, I talked to Rusty's dad." She pointed him out in the audience section.

"Don Sneiderman?"

"Yep. I said something's happened to Rusty. I have no idea what, and that's all I said, and I was belligerent on the phone."

"At that time did you know what had happened to Rusty."

Andrea leaned forward again. "No," she said, her voice full of restrained rage. "I didn't know what had happened to Rusty until I got to the emergency room. No one told me what happened to Rusty."

"Who else did you call when you were on your way to the daycare?"

"I don't remember, but evidently I tried to call Hemy," she said, pointing to him, "probably to tell him that I had left the office, that something had happened, which was a very normal thing for me to have done, to tell my boss that I had left my office and something had happened to my husband."

"Do you remember what his cell number was at the time?"

She cracked a smile. "No I don't."

She couldn't remember how many times she called Hemy or whether she left him a voice-mail message. "I barely could have my foot on the gas pedal and go fast enough," she said.

"How many times did you call Rusty?"

"Call Rusty?" Andrea seemed taken aback by the question.

"Rusty," Geary said.

"Zero times."

"Why didn't you call Rusty?"

"Because they just told me something had happened to Rusty," she replied. "What are the chances that he's going to be answering his cell phone?"

Geary offered, "They didn't tell you what happened to Rusty."

"Is there a question?" she asked.

"Yeah, just curious why didn't you call Rusty?"

"Is that the question?"

The judge had tired of the sparring and told the prosecutor to ask another question.

"You arrived at the daycare, how long did you stay there?"

Andrea couldn't remember, saying it was a chaotic experience, her emotions running wild, everybody around her refusing to tell her what was going on.

"I pulled up in my vehicle to caution tape and police cars and Rusty's car, but no Rusty. I fell out of the vehicle, I was picked up by I don't know who, and taken inside."

"Was it a police officer, do you remember?"

"Have no idea."

"When you were taken inside, did you talk to anybody, or did someone talk to you or do you remember?"

"I remember, they sat me down in this office that they have, this little office room, I remember one of Sophia's [former] teachers, Katrina is her name, she came in, she was hugging me, couldn't let me go. No one was talking, no one was staying a word. No one would tell me what happened. And then eventually, Gary Cortellino from the Dunwoody Police Department sat down in front of me and started asking me questions."

"Do you remember how long that lasted, ma'am?"

"It felt like three seconds, but I have no idea."

"At that time did you leave the daycare?"

"Eventually my parents came from Roswell because I was on the phone with them almost the entire way to the daycare," she said. Then she put her mouth up to the microphone so her words were loud and clear. "I was on the phone with them on the entire way to the daycare."

"Yes, ma'am."

"They were keeping me company in the car," she said, adopting her lecturing tone, "because I was beside myself."

"Yes, ma'am."

"No time to call Rusty in there," she said.

Eventually, with the help of her brother and father, they tracked down the hospital where Rusty was taken.

"When you went to the Atlanta Medical Center, ma'am, did you find out what happened to Rusty?"

"They took me into what I call the Death Room. And sat in a chair and someone—I have no idea who—they came over and said that he came in with multiple gunshot wounds and that he was dead. I don't remember anything they said after that. I fell to the floor."

"You found out at the hospital that Rusty had been shot."

"That's correct."

"You say the Death Room. At that point, did they tell you or indicate to you that Rusty was in fact dead?"

"Yep."

"Is that the first time you found out he was dead?"

"Yep."

"And you found out he was shot?"

"Yep."

CHAPTER 17

The first day of the trial of Hemy Neuman was nearly completed and so far it had little do with him. Except for the early questions about the demon and hallucinations, there had been virtually nothing to build a case showing that Hemy was not so mentally ill at the time of the killing that he didn't know right from wrong. It was all about Andrea. Her tone—defensive, snarky, condescending, lecturing—stunned those in the courtroom.

The prosecution pressed on.

"Do you remember telling Tammi Parker in late December that you knew who it was that killed Rusty?" asked Geary.

"Yes," said Andrea. She appeared to become choked up. She had to regain her composure.

"Do you remember telling Tammi Parker in late

December 2010 that you knew that it was the defendant who killed Rusty?"

"Somewhere around the late December time frame, the twenty-seventh or twenty-eighth of December, I was in Florida," she began, and stopped. Looking down, she appeared to be fighting tears. "It was to be our tenth wedding anniversary. We were married in Florida at a synagogue in Florida. So I was down there with my family. On the twenty-eighth or so of December, I got a weird email from iTunes."

"That's not my question," said Geary, no change in his quietly relentless inquiry. "My question was: Do you remember telling Tammi Parker?"

"Yup, I told her that I thought it might be Hemy Neuman."

"Then did you immediately call police and tell them it was the defendant?"

"I started a draft email right after I got this mysterious email address, email from Hemy Neuman. He was in Florida at the time . . . the same time I was there. For all I knew, he was monitoring my email, knew exactly where I was, and so when I started the email to Chief Grogan on December 28, I had a discussion with my parents. What do I do? What do we do? Do I send this? What if he's watching my email? What if he's watching me?"

But she never sent the email. She didn't call police. She said she had given the detective Hemy's name way back on November 19, 2010. Her friend told her the idea that Hemy would have committed the murder was "ludicrous."

"I don't care what Tammi Parker said," Geary said.

"Oh, okay, well she's a very trusted friend and so when I explained to her and expressed my gut feeling that it might be him and she tells me it's kind of crazy and Mom is telling me that he might come kill you because he's in Florida, and we don't know what's going on, why don't we wait till we get back to Atlanta to tell the police. Up to that day, the police and I didn't exactly have the best working relationship."

"So you believed you knew who killed Rusty and you were going to wait until you got back to Atlanta to tell them?

"Yep! That's correct, for the protection of myself and my children I was going to wait till we got back to Atlanta to tell them, that's correct."

But she didn't tell police when she met with them on the afternoon of January 4, the same day that he was arrested.

"No matter that you knew who it was that killed Rusty?"

"And what was the difference? I couldn't believe it—it was even possible. I thought I was being stupid. Who would think that this would be happening right now? Whose boss kills someone's husband? I don't care, affair or no affair—there was no affair—who kills someone else's husband?"

She also didn't tell them that she had corresponded by email with Hemy in late December about a week before his arrest when she got the Bruno Mars iTunes song from him. This was the email asking if she planned to attend the office holiday party. Although she ultimately didn't, she had considered the idea, she told Geary. "I wanted to see those people and thank them for their support," she said. "And I wanted to hear it from Hemy's mouth directly. I was going to confront him myself."

And even when she was informed there was an arrest in the case, she didn't bring up Hemy's name. Geary played the audio recording of police at her house in which she didn't at first ask who had been arrested.

Asked to explain her reaction, Andrea shot back, "I'm asking are you sure that they have the right person. That's what I'm asking. That's it. How would you know who the right person is? I have no idea! All I was asking was: Are you sure you've got someone, are you sure that you know that you have the right person?"

Geary suggested she was sure when she talked to Tammi Parker the week before.

"I told Tammi, that's fine, that's what I said. I had a feeling that it was him." Andrea became agitated on the stand. She jabbed her finger at Geary. "But there's no chance that I thought I was right. It was unfathomable and unbelievable that it could be him, someone that proposed to care about me, care about Rusty, care about my family, be a normal guy, be my boss." She dropped her voice to a whisper. "And he murdered my husband."

With the prosecution examination complete, the judge called for a break. Andrea huddled in the hall with her lawyer and her father. When she returned a few minutes later for cross-examination, she held her head down and carried what appeared to be a photo of her family.

By now it was after 4:30 p.m. and Andrea had been on the stand since morning. Judge Adams, ever mindful of time, told the lawyers to squeeze in more questions. Hemy's attorney Robert Rubin brought her through her work and marital history, gently bringing up the possible strains in her marriage at the time she started working for Hemy.

"You were struggling to make it work for both of you?"

"Correct."

"At times he would get annoyed with you, especially when you were traveling?"

"That's correct."

"You told police he could be an ass if he was upset with what you were doing, correct?"

"With the way things were working? Do you want to say that again?"

"Did you not tell the police when he would get annoyed he could be an ass?"

"I don't remember saying that but I'm sure you could show me."

Andrea now made what most observers would later describe as a smirk. It was an expression she had off and on throughout the entire day. The jury didn't seem to appreciate it.

CHAPTER 18

Since this was the prosecution's portion of the case, Robert Rubin had had no idea who the state would call first to the stand. He had to come prepared to question any number of witnesses. For Andrea, the initial plan called for proceeding cautiously. To press her would risk alienating the jury. But her first day on the stand clearly left a bad impression. On day two of the trial, Rubin would become more aggressive, pressing her on why she didn't distance herself more from Hemy.

"I can't control what he said to me. I can only control what I said to him," she said. "I was doing the best I could to keep my job and keep everything together."

She was grilled on why, when she would describe Hemy at various times as a "stalker" and a "predator," she still traveled with him to the United Kingdom.

"Planning to go to a club, planning to go to a theater, going to a castle, going to a show—is that your definition of shying away from him?" asked Rubin.

"We all have different definitions. Like I said, going to London without seeing a show seems like a shame to me."

"Is that your definition of shying away from him?"

"It is."

Rubin rolled out more emails in which she'd alternately talk about betrayal and romance. Andrea acknowledged that at times she should have watched her own behavior, as when she went what she called "partner dancing" at the Pulse nightclub in Greenville.

"I realized the next morning it was not a good idea, that he did not know boundaries, that he was never going to let this go," she said.

The cross-examination ended with Rubin asking her, "You received the proceeds from an insurance policy?"

"Yes, sir, I did."

"For approximately two million dollars?"

"Correct."

The pressure on Andrea continued with the prosecution's questions on redirect examination. Andrea's answers were laced with apparent anger and disgust.

"Why were you protecting the defendant?" Don Geary asked her.

"I was not!"

"Why didn't you mention his name?"

"Have you seen what has happened to my life?" she lashed out.

"Have you seen what's happened to Rusty's?" the prosecutor responded.

"Have you noticed what's happened to my life since Hemy was murdered—" She corrected herself. "—since Hemy murdered my husband?"

* * *

The prosecution left it there, with Andrea getting her murdered husband confused with the killer. For more than a day, the prosecution and defense had gone after her as if she were on trial instead of Hemy, each trying to score points for their own purposes. Many would ask why she testified at all, though in reality she was in a difficult position. A refusal to testify could have brought the spectacle of her taking the Fifth in open court, something she clearly felt was unnecessary. Andrea took the position she didn't need to worry about self-incrimination since she had done nothing wrong. "Mrs. Sneiderman knew she was going to get beaten up on the witness stand," her attorney Seth Kirschenbaum told reporters. "She has always cooperated in this case, and she wanted to help the prosecution even if it meant being subjected to withering attack."

The final blow came when the judge told Andrea that she remained under subpoena and would not be allowed to watch other witnesses.

"I'm sorry," Andrea said, "I have to stay out of the courtroom?"

"At this point in time you're going to remain under subpoena and, yes, you're going to remain outside of the courtroom."

"I have to remain outside the courtroom for the remainder of the trial?" she asked in disbelief.

"I'm going to say this as clear as I can. You're going to come off that witness stand and you're going to remain outside."

Andrea went into the hall.

During a break in later testimony, it was the prosecution that asked the judge to let Andrea return to the courtroom. They argued she had a statutory right to be there anytime

Hemy was. Robert Rubin objected on the grounds she could talk to other witnesses, some of whom were close to her, and potentially "contaminate" their testimony. But the judge allowed Andrea to return and the trial continued, with Andrea watching from the audience section as the prosecution tried to make the case that Andrea had a liaison with Hemy in Longmont, Colorado, then lied about it to police.

Brady Blackburn, the desk clerk at the Hampton Inn in Longmont, recounted how insistent Hemy was about leaving flowers and chocolates in Andrea's room, as did two other clerks, Linda Powers and Ruth Ingraham. Lindsay Clayton, a supervisor at the hotel, testified about how Andrea requested a room change from two beds to one.

More witnesses talked about the second Greenville trip that Andrea and Hemy took when, a hotel representative testified, they had an adjoining room, followed by Pulse nightclub bartender Christine Olivera, who painted the most vivid picture yet of what both the prosecution and the defense were contending was an affair. Olivera recalled how Andrea and Hemy had become so steamy on the dance floor groping each other that she looked away.

"You said 'each other': Was each party doing the groping?" prosecutor Don Geary asked.

The judge interjected: "When you say groping, what are you talking about?"

"Groping," the bartender said, "like handling each other, like, you know, let's say, he had his hands on her rear end, she was hugging him. They looked like a couple, groping, like touching each other."

Geary asked, "At any time did you see the parties kiss?"

"Yes, I did."

"How many times did they kiss?"

"I would say about three times."

Again the judge asked for clarification. "When you use the term *kiss*, what is that?"

"Kissing, like, kissing, like a pop kissing, kissing like they were kissing. Not like making out."

"Was it lip-to-lip contact?" asked Geary.

"Yes, it was."

"Not on the cheek."

"No."

"How long did the kisses last?"

"While they were dancing, seconds. They were having their own moment. I didn't want to interrupt them, but they were kissing and they were being affectionate toward one another."

During cross-examination Doug Peters asked: "Miss Olivera, you described for us about the twirling and the dancing and the handling of one another, and I believe you indicated during that it wasn't just their hands making contact with each other's bodies, but there were times when they actually—their bodies actually rubbed together?"

"That's correct."

"And I think you've explained to me that there was some sort of grinding their hips together?"

"Grinding and his hands on her rear end and she was embracing him as well. It's kind of hard to describe. But they were very affectionate towards each other."

Further advancing the theory of an affair, Hemy's Realtor friend Melanie White recounted her conversations with Hemy about his marital woes and his affections toward Andrea, leading up to their trip to London, the timing of which stunned Melanie because it fell on Yom Kippur.

"What was his personality like, his demeanor like?" asked District Attorney Robert James.

"Same old Hemy."

"Same old Hemy? Had he spoken with you about any delusions that he had been having?"

"No."

"Did he seem depressed?"

"No."

"Same old Hemy?"

"Yes."

Except that this Hemy had become "infatuated" with Andrea. They had adjoining rooms, he told Melanie, and one night he went into hers.

"He said they laid on the bed and cuddled and did just about everything but have intercourse."

"Did he use those words?"

"No, those weren't his words."

"What words did he use?"

"That they kissed and they fondled each other and then she got up and went into the bathroom."

"Is that what he said?"

"Yes."

"Did he tell you what she actually did in the bathroom?"

'Yes, he told me that she went into the bathroom to 'finish herself off.' "

"Finish herself off?"

"Yes."

"Did you ask him what he meant by that?"

Melanie said: "I didn't have to."

"Well, why didn't you have to?"

"Because I assumed that that meant that she was going into the bathroom to masturbate."

In the courtroom, Andrea looked down.

According to Melanie, Hemy confided that during the second trip to Greenville the affection on the Pulse dance floor was part of a romantic night with a walk by a lake and a fine dinner.

"Did he tell you what happened once they ended up in the same hotel room?" asked James.

"What he told me was that she gave in," said White.

"She gave in? Is that what he said?"

"Yes."

"Did he tell you what he meant by 'she gave in'?"

"No."

"What did you believe he meant?"

"I believe he meant that they had intercourse."

Hemy's other confidante, Orna Hanison, recounted Hemy saying he had a woman in his life—the unnamed Jewish woman with kids—and seemed to be suffering a midlife crisis. Another witness, Jan DaSilva, spoke of how Hemy talked about having to get rid of the gun DaSilva sold him because of a problem with a mistress.

Through it all Andrea shook her head and whispered to her mother, becoming, it appeared, increasingly agitated. It came to a head when one of her best friends, Shayna Citron, was called. Recounting conversations in the weeks leading up to the murder, Andrea had been enduring marriage trouble, according to Citron, with the pair arguing over household duties and Andrea's travel.

"There was a time I was concerned for her marriage," said Citron.

Citron also recalled the day of Rusty's murder, when Andrea called her while Citron was in Arizona.

"She immediately at the same time was screaming to me that Rusty had been shot, and she didn't know if he was dead or alive and she was on the way to the hospital," testified Citron.

"Are you sure she said she was still on her way to the hospital?" asked Geary.

"Yes," Citron replied.

"And she told you Rusty had been shot at that time?" he continued.

Citron nodded yes.

Under cross-examination by Doug Peters, Citron said that while Andrea appreciated the professional compliments from Hemy, she claimed their relationship never went farther.

"Did Andrea admit or deny an affair with her boss at that time after the murder," asked Peters.

"Denied it," said Citron.

"Based on all of the time that you've known Andrea, based on your observations of her, her mannerisms, when she told you no, did you believe it?"

"No," said Citron, "but my heart really wanted to believe her."

"But you didn't believe her?"

Citron pursed her lips and shook her head.

Weeks later, when Andrea was in Florida, the women discussed the police sketch of the killer.

"And she expressed to you that in looking at the sketches, she kept seeing Hemy's face in those sketches, correct?"

"Not the face, it was the eyes."

When she finished her testimony, Shayna Citron walked off the stand and into the audience section of the courtroom. Andrea embraced her and kissed her. It was a long hug and the women walked out of the courtroom arm in arm.

It happened in front of the jury, the kind of demonstration that Hemy's lawyers had feared when they asked the judge to bar Andrea from the courtroom, and it created a kerfuffle. The next day, Adams took the unusual step of putting testimony on hold so he could huddle with lawyers for both sides and with Andrea's attorney.

"Yesterday," the judge then announced in open court, "after one of the witnesses left the witness stand, the court observed interaction by Ms. Sneiderman and that witness.

It appeared to be a hugging or some type of embrace. The court has to respond to that and give general instruction that no one is to interact with witnesses when they leave the witness stand in the presence of the jury or even outside of the presence of the jury in that manner."

Prosecutor Don Geary said Andrea's behavior had actually been much worse. During the testimony of other witnesses, Andrea kept up a running commentary in her seat. She said, "That's not true," and "That's a lie," and "You weren't there," possibly loud enough for the jury to hear, according to Geary.

"I almost turned and snapped and told her to shut up," said Geary. "But that wouldn't have been proper as well."

During the embrace with Citron, Geary said, a DA investigator tried to stop Andrea, but she pushed him out of the way. The hug, Geary contended, was "for show," because afterward Andrea confronted Citron in the hall, saying that she didn't believe her and that they weren't friends anymore. Citron would quote Andrea as also telling her that in light of the testimony, "I will do what I need to do." Citron called the experience "surreal" and didn't know if Andrea had been making a threat.

When Andrea returned to the courtroom, said Geary, "We told her: Do not go in our witness room. We got a look that I could describe but I won't."

He said that several other witnesses, including her coworkers at GE, asked the DA to keep her away from them. "She's not following our instructions," Geary said. "From what I've seen yesterday, she's not following the court's instructions. Everybody here has way too much into this to have her, on her own agenda, cause a mistrial. The state's purpose is to convict the man that murdered Rusty Sneiderman. I wish she could be here. I no longer have the opinion that she can be and make sure our trial is protected. We are moving to have her removed from the courtroom. Actually, we're moving to have her removed from the courthouse."

Hemy's attorney Robert Rubin reminded everybody that the defense had already asked for her to be booted from the courtroom, and said the prosecutor now "has certainly provided the court with sufficient reason . . . We would join in the court's motion."

The judge agreed. "I am going to direct that Ms. Sneiderman be removed from this courtroom, not have any direct or indirect contact with any witness or potential witness," he said. "I will say it as firmly as I can: Do not contact either directly or indirectly any witness or potential witness."

The rest of the trial would proceed without Rusty's wife in the courtroom.

Rusty's family later said they weren't surprised by any of it. "As a result of Andrea's actions yesterday," his brother Steven said in a statement, "today's extraordinary action is yet another example of Andrea's behavior that has been deeply troubling to our family for some time."

Shayna Citron had a different take. "I became frightened after she was banned from the courthouse because I was thinking back to what she had said." For years, they had been the closest of friends. Her children called her "Aunt Andrea." Now she wasn't so sure.

"When I learned that she was banned, I called my attorney," Shayna said, "and I called my children's school."

CHAPTER 19

The blowup over Andrea's behavior in court overlapped the main work at hand—determining whether Hemy Neuman should be found guilty of murdering Rusty Sneiderman—and witnesses continued to testify. Just after Shayna Citron left the stand came what would be the most emotional testimony of the trial.

"Mr. Sneiderman," asked District Attorney Robert James, "do you know Rusty Sneiderman?"

"Yes, sir," answered the witness.

"And how do you know Rusty Sneiderman?"

"He is my son."

Donald Sneiderman's face showed all the strain of the last fifteen months. He sat uncomfortably in the witness box though his voice was clear.

"Do you remember the day that he died?"

"Yes, sir."

"And what day was that?"

"November 18, 2010."

"How old was Rusty on that day?"

"Thirty-six."

"Did Rusty have any children?"

"Yes, he had two. A boy, two, a daughter, five."

"What are their names?"

"Sophia and Ian."

James didn't ask if Rusty had a wife.

The DA then showed Donald a photo and asked if he recognized it.

"That's a picture of Rusty."

"Is that a fair and accurate representation of Rusty while he was living?"

Donald grinned. "He had a bigger smile most of the time, but, yes, that's a fair representation of him."

Called in part to humanize the victim and show the emotional destruction caused by the murder, Donald Sneiderman described Rusty as a responsible man, "terrific" with money, a good provider for his family who died with $1.1 million in bank.

"How did you find out that Rusty had been shot?"

"Around nine thirty in the morning Andrea had called us and she called and said, 'Rusty had been shot.' She was so, so sorry, and that she was going to Dunwoody Prep to find out what had happened."

"Are you sure it was around nine thirty?" James asked

"Well, we had talked to Rusty over the Internet about nine, and he had taken Ian to school just a little before nine, so it was about nine thirty."

"And she said she was on the way to Dunwoody Prep?"

"Yes, sir."

Donald found out about his son's fate over the phone from a doctor at Atlanta Medical Center who said Rusty had been shot multiple times and did not survive. Donald and his wife flew to Atlanta, drove straight to Rusty's house to be with Andrea and their grandchildren, and made funeral arrangements.

"Do you recall the funeral?"

"It's kind of a blur, but yes," he said,

"At Rusty's shiva, do you recall meeting someone named Hemy?"

"Yes."

"Can you tell us how you met Hemy?"

"My wife introduced him to me, talked to him for about thirty seconds. I recognized the name, that Rusty had told me he was Andrea's boss, that he had tried to look for a job for him."

"Do you remember what if anything Hemy said to you?"

"No."

"Did he shake your hand?"

"Yes, sir."

"And did you shake his?"

"Yes."

"Do you see him in the courtroom today?"

"Yes, sir." His glanced to his left.

"Can you identify him for the jury?"

"He's sitting at the defendant's table," Donald said in a shaky voice, gesturing to his son's killer, "third one from the right."

The defense did not ask any cross-examination questions.

The prosecution, having established now that a second witness heard Andrea say Rusty was shot before she would have gotten that information from the hospital, now shifted the trial toward Hemy's activities surrounding the murder. Greg Gibbons, service director at Ed Voyles Honda, talked about Hemy bringing in his Honda Odyssey for recall service but not staying around for the quick repair. Christina Testa, the Enterprise Rent-A-Car manager, spoke of Hemy appearing "impatient," "fidgety" and "very uneasy" while waiting for his car. GE employees who had long known and worked with Hemy talked about a relatively normal day at work shattered by news of death. They spoke of how Hemy had rescheduled a morning meeting and wasn't seen until afternoon, after the murder, when he seemed normal. Nobody had ever seen signs of mental illness in Hemy and had certainly never heard him talk of an angel or a demon. The only hint of something going on between him and Andrea was that they seemed to sit next to each other a lot at meetings.

A security chief at GE brought the jury through Hemy's actions as recorded by the key-card readers and video cameras, showing that Hemy had sufficient time to leave the office, commit the murder, return the rental van, and get back to his desk—all without an alibi. GE's IT forensic examiner next brought the jury through Hemy and Andrea's travels together as documented in their forms seeking reimbursement for hotel rooms and wine.

The next witnesses were the people on the scene on November 18, 2010, describing the silver minivan racing through Rusty's neighborhood, then following his car into the preschool parking lot, the gunman in the fake beard calmly shooting Rusty dead before screeching away. The graphic descriptions of the shooting reverberated through the courtroom. Rusty's brother, Steven, cried as Aliyah Stotter said, "His eyes were still open and he was gasping for air. There was quite a lot of blood everywhere. He was laying on a slant, so you saw blood running from the school towards the pediatrician's office."

Once again, the trial boomeranged back to Andrea.

School official Donna Formato recalled getting Andrea Sneiderman's name from the daycare center's emergency information sheet and calling her.

"I told her that something had happened at the school, that Ian was okay, and that she had to come to the school right away."

"Did you not tell her that Rusty had been shot?" asked Robert James.

"No, I did not."

"Are you certain that you did not tell her?"

"Yes."

"Why?"

"Because I was worried for her to drive to the school knowing that her husband had been shot. I didn't want her to have an accident or anything on the way."

Then when Andrea arrived, her behavior at the crime scene struck witness Stotter as odd.

"One of the detectives was interviewing me right there when she pulled up," Stotter told DA James. "We actually had to move out of the way because she sped in so fast and barely put the car in park. So it was still kind of rolling a little bit. The doors swung open and she got out and she was just like screaming, 'What happened? What happened?' It was cold that day. I had a hoodie on. I put the hood up because I didn't want her to see me. I was crying. I was bawling. Later on, I told my husband, Craig, that it's really weird but she didn't have a tear in her eye. I told the detective that as well."

Emergency room doctor Mark Waterman also was taken aback by Andrea's behavior. The doctor, who came to court wearing his blue hospital scrubs over a T-shirt, recalled pronouncing Rusty dead, then going into the family waiting room where he "found the wife."

"What did you do?"

"I sat across from her, probably two feet away, and told

her [that] her husband had come in, had multiple gunshot wounds, and I just pronounced him dead."

"What was her reaction?"

"Not very emotional, not crying, screaming, not wanting to know what happened. In fact her first request was to ask for a child psychologist."

"Did she tell you why she wanted a child psychologist?"

"So that that person could inform her children of his passing."

"No screaming, no crying while you were there?"

"Not that I recall."

"Would you call that, in your twenty-seven years, normal?"

"Unusual to say the least."

The trial was barreling along—all these witnesses squeezed into the first four days—when the prosecution turned to the police investigation. Detective Andrew Thompson took the stand late in the afternoon of February 24 and brought the jury to the scene of the crime, showing security video footage of Hemy's van following Rusty into the parking lot. Thompson recounted the epiphany in the case—linking the stickers on the van windows to the possibility the van was a rental—then described the painstaking process of tracking down all the Kia Sedonas in Georgia and the Carolinas until finding the murder van at the Enterprise agency. The detective also spoke of the interview with Andrea the day after the murder and how she revealed that Hemy had hit on her, but said little of what police would later find out about them.

After the coroner described Rusty's autopsy—his family sat grim-faced, heads down during this testimony—Lieutenant David Barnes talked about the interrogation of Hemy. "It was a very long interview," Barnes said. The prosecution then played the entire five-and-a-half-hour video, the images of Hemy and the detectives grainy from the wall-mounted camera. The audio proved so bad that the video came with a closed-caption-style running transcript. The video consumed all of day five of the trial, with the judge breaking to allow jurors to stretch and snap out of catnaps.

Even during the testimony about Hemy's interrogation, the subject of Andrea returned. Barnes pointed to several of the things that Andrea never revealed: that Hemy had been with her in Longmont, the phone calls to Hemy the morning of the murder, that Hemy had given her the laptop at the shiva. Barnes spoke of his growing unease with Andrea when he and Deputy Chief Sides interviewed her after Hemy's arrest.

"When you talked to her on [January] 5, would it be fair to say you were pretty angry?" asked defense attorney Robert Rubin.

"Was I angry? No."

"Disappointed?"

"No."

"Confused?"

"No."

"Did you try to portray that you were angry?"

"Yes."

And while she did disclose more about her travels with Hemy, she still did not reveal her anger and guilt after the first Greenville trip, or sending Hemy photos of her daughter's birthday party, or dancing at the Pulse nightclub, or that she had cashed out a two-million-dollar life insurance policy on Rusty.

"You asked her specifically why it took her so long for her to tell you the defendant killed her husband?" James asked him on redirect examination.

"Yes."

"Were you satisfied?"

"I was not satisfied."

"At that point you became suspicious of Andrea Sneiderman?"

"Yes."

After the prosecution laid out its evidence about the murder weapon with testimony from ballistics expert Kelly Fite, the case against Hemy Neuman featured one last witness. On February 28, day six of the trial, FBI electronics examiner Chad Fitzgerald spoke of the secrets found in Hemy's iPhone. By showing which cell phone towers pinged his many calls, Fitzgerald could draw a map for the jury: Hemy in Norfolk with Andrea, in Denver with Andrea, in Greenville with Andrea. He texted her the same day he went to a gun show. On another day, he called a costume shop, then called Andrea, then called another costume shop.

He told the jury of Hemy's fifteen calls after killing Rusty—nine of them to Andrea's phone, one answered, the forty-two-second call at 10:43 a.m. while Andrea was on her way to the hospital. On November 19, 2010, the day Andrea spoke to a detective, there were two calls between them of about three minutes each.

Overall, according to Chad Fitzgerald, from May 1, 2010, when Andrea started working at GE Energy, through the day of her husband's murder, she made 1,426 phone contacts with Hemy—and 882 with Rusty.

Fitzgerald left the stand. The State of Georgia rested its case.

CHAPTER 20

Hemy's lawyers tried to keep Olivia Newton-John and Barry White out of the courtroom. As expected, the media jumped all over it after the revelation came out in a pretrial hearing just days before opening statements. Virtually every news report included clips of Newton-John singing in *Grease* and White booming "Can't Get Enough of Your Love, Babe." At the hearing, the defense asked that the judge allow only evidence that Hemy had visions, but to bar detailed questions about them. The prosecution objected. "When their report talks about six-foot demons that sound like Barry White and six-foot angels that sound like Olivia Newton-John, we have to prepare for the defense they led us into," said Chief Assistant DA Don Geary. "If he wants to say that's not what they meant to say in the report, we are so fine with that it's not funny." The judge sided with prosecutors; the evidence would be coming in.

Although Hemy pleaded not guilty by reason of insanity, the prosecution did not call any witnesses about Hemy's mental state. It didn't have to. The burden to prove he was insane fell to the defense. The prosecution's theory was that he knew full well the difference between right and wrong when he gunned down Rusty. It would wait to see the affirmative defense, then try to chip away at it through cross-examination and a rebuttal case.

As Hemy's attorneys laid out their case, their first push was to show that his mental illness was no laughing matter. To do this, they called Monique Metsch, Hemy's younger sister, to tell the jury of growing up with a father who survived the Nazi death camps only to bring some of the horrors home.

"He was a very angry man, so there was always fights or screaming," Metsch said, describing her father's double-scotch-fueled outbursts of violence. "You never knew how he was going to react. He was very erratic in his outbursts. We never knew how the evening was going to go."

Their father—though barely five feet tall but full of rage—would "always blame everything on Hemy," she told the jury, saying that he hit Hemy with an open hand. "It was more like rage, he was angry with God, he was angry with my mom." The slaps were "continuous," she said. Sometimes he also kicked and whipped both Hemy and her.

"I would be sitting at that table, and if I didn't finish my soup he would pull my head back," she said. "He once shoved vegetable soup down my nose."

After recounting other troubles in Hemy's life, from the boarding school to the marital woes, Metsch revealed the first time Hemy had spoken about a new woman in his life. He mentioned her in December 2010, the month after Rusty's murder, when Hemy visited his family in Florida for the funeral of his father's wife.

"He told me that he had befriended a colleague of his and that he had become close with her in the sense that, for the first time, he was able to really open up to someone about our childhood and talk," Metsch said. "He realized for the very first time that he didn't have that kind of communication with Reli but that this relationship was special because of that."

During cross-examnation DA Robert James sought to show that that while Hemy may have suffered trauma in childhood, it didn't translate to the sort of mental illness Hemy now claimed.

"Fair to say you knew your brother well?" he asked.

"Yes."

"Talk often?"

"Yes."

"Confides in you?"

"Sometimes."

"He told you about a woman?"

"To an extent."

"He didn't tell you about demons?"

"He did not."

"Barry White?"

"No."

"He didn't tell you about angels, Olivia Newton-John, did he?"

"No."

Next the defense called Dr. Julie Rand-Dorney, the psychiatrist who described her "forensic evaluation" of Hemy along with Dr. Peter Thomas. She noted that Hemy never spoke of seeing angels or demons, but did see one in the inkblot test administered by Dr. Thomas, who also testified. The test also showed "disorder, paranoia, weird magical thinking—if he would think about something it would come true," said Rand-Dorney.

"We explored what demons were and were they part of hallucination or delusion. It wasn't clear to us," she said. "We concluded it wasn't hallucination and that it was obsessive thought and he was tormented by those thoughts."

"Did he mention anything about Ian and Sophia Sneiderman being his children?" asked Robert Rubin.

"He told us he felt the children were in danger. He said . . . I feel like I need to protect them. When talking to me, it felt like in a more paternalistic way."

After Dr. Rand-Dorney recalled how she recommended "further exploration of confusion, possible psychosis, mood disorder, paranoia disorder," the expert who did that follow-up, Dr. Adriana Flores, took the stand to deliver testimony that served as the heart of the defense case.

Rubin asked her: "Did you arrive at an opinion whether or not Hemy is criminally responsible for the death of Rusty Sneiderman?"

"Yes."

"What is your opinion?"

"That Neuman is not criminally responsible for the death of Rusty Sneiderman."

"Why is that?"

"At the time of the shooting of Sneiderman, Neuman did not have the mental capacity to distinguish between right and wrong in relation to the shooting."

"What is it about his condition that rendered him incapable of distinguishing right from wrong?"

"He had a disorder, a mental illness called bipolar 1 disorder with psychosis," she said, adding, "He was manic in that phase of the bipolar 1 disorder, and he was experiencing psychosis. Specifically, he was experiencing some delusions."

Giving the jury a tutorial, Flores sought to dispel some

myths about bipolar disorder, telling them the swings from depression to manic behavior don't necessarily happen overnight. Somebody could be depressed for months, then manic for months more, or go for long stretches in a "green zone," when they're "normal" and "balanced" for the most part with some episodes of mania or depression.

While depression is marked by feelings of hopelessness and worthlessness, people in a manic phase, she said, have "racing thoughts" and are "abnormally active," operating at a high energy level with only two or three hours of sleep. They also experience "hypersexuality," she said. "Someone who is manic has very high sex arousal, a very high libido. Sometimes they get in trouble because they end up having sex with people, so it can get dangerous." This recklessness can extend to other aspects of their lives, including spending money or gambling. They can be agitated, irritable, and "hyper-religious," thinking they might be God. "They might be reading the Bible or the Torah," she said. "There's also talk of angels and demons."

The psychosis relates to a loss of touch with reality, perhaps due to delusions—feelings that are not real and highly resistant to change. Sufferers can have bizarre delusions, such as irrational fears of being poisoned by a neighbor, or the kind that Flores believed that Hemy suffered, what she called nonbizarre delusions. In this case, she said, he had two. One was an "erotomatic delusion." He had "irrational romantic beliefs about one's relationship with another person." The other was a "rescue delusion," an irrational belief that other people needed his protection and it was his job to save them.

"He had erotomatic delusions at the time he shot Sneiderman," she said. "He believed he was having more of an affair with Andrea Sneiderman than he was. He believed he was the father of her children, that the children were endangered, and that he was going to protect the children by killing Sneiderman and they, he would be, afterwards, with what he calls his family and his children, who are the Sneiderman children."

The order to kill, Hemy told her, came from the she-demon at the dinner party and that the angel returned a month later in the car. She stressed that Hemy never saw a physical embodiment of Barry White, only that he'd later describe the demon's voice as deep like White's; nor did he "see" Olivia Newton-John, but that the angel was "like" her but without the accent.

All the while, Dr. Flores said, Andrea was "pushing and pulling him," one moment expressing desire, the next pledging herself to Rusty. "It's very clear that they were having an affair," Dr. Flores said, but added: "It's the nature of the relationship they were having that he was delusional about." Hemy believed that his and Andrea's special, soul-to-soul connection meant they were destined to be together forever. What Andrea thought could only be gleaned from her hot-and-cold emails—she refused to be examined by Flores. "It's not all in his head because she was in fact having sex with him," said Flores. "Andrea fed into Hemy's delusions, manipulating him into believing what she believed and thinking what she thought."

Under cross-examination, Dr. Flores acknowledged that many of her conclusions hinged on statements from Hemy.

"Other than what he told you, you have no idea what he was thinking at the time of the crime?" asked Don Geary.

"If he in fact lied to me, I would be wrong. However, delusions are very difficult to fake."

"And if he's worried about the police, he knows what he did is wrong, doesn't he?"

She didn't immediately answer.

Geary pressed, "That's your opinion of the defendant's mental condition?"

"My opinion is that he—correct."

"You could be wrong?"

"I could be wrong," she said, "but I don't believe I am, though."

Geary asked her about Hemy's claims that he was driven to kill Rusty to protect the children.

"He never spoke to those children after the shooting, not even at the shiva?"

Flores rejected Geary's suggestion. "His first and second choices were (1) Protect the kids, and (2) become a family with Andrea and the kids," she said. "Everything I reviewed said that the mission he had was to protect the children."

But she acknowledged, "I cannot say with 100 percent certainty that what was in my report is accurate and my opinion is correct, but I believe both are correct based on my experience and testing. I do not believe I have evidence that is consistent with [Hemy] lying."

The defense wrapped up its case by calling its third expert, psychiatrist Dr. Tracey Marks, who reiterated that Hemy had suffered bipolar disorder with occasional delusional visits from demons for most of his life, never being diagnosed until after he shot Rusty. Her tests also indicated he was not faking a mental illness.

"He didn't believe that he was breaking the law," Dr. Marks replied. "He didn't see this as murder."

The cross-examination followed a familiar route, with Dr. Marks acknowledging she based much of her opinion on Hemy's statements to her and bristling at the suggestion that her conclusions could be incorrect. "I don't know if I've been wrong," she told Geary. "It's my opinion, so it's not as though there's someone who's going to determine if my opinion is right or wrong . . . There's not like there's an ultimate person who says, *Let me tell you after the fact that you're wrong.*"

On the afternoon of Thursday, March 8, Hemy declined to take the stand to testify in his own defense. It was almost 4 p.m., but Judge Adams once again told lawyers to call another witness whose testimony would spill into the next day.

The trial had just come off a two-day hiatus, the halt in proceedings abruptly called after a private session between the judges and attorneys, without explanation to the public. It was only after the resumption of testimony that an explanation was offered: The judge's mother had died. There would be no comments about it in court and Adams showed no change in demeanor, nudging things along with his usual impatience.

Before psychiatrist Pamela Crawford was to testify before the jury, she was grilled in a hearing by the defense, which objected to her testimony. Hemy's lawyers argued that she didn't have the credentials to be considered an expert. But despite her lapsed board standing and lack of license in Georgia, Judge Adams allowed her testimony.

Crawford returned the next morning, Friday, March 9, and told the jury that Hemy easily could be faking his mental illness. Somebody of his intelligence could lie to therapists and manipulate the tests. Before his arrest, Hemy showed that he could cope—and thrive—particularly at work with no mental impairment, thinking clearly, planning, and following through on those plans.

"It is my opinion based on the interview and based on the review of documentation and all the collateral information that Neuman would be considered under Georgia law criminally responsible for the death of Rusty Sneiderman," she said.

"In your opinion," asked prosecutor Geary, "when he shot Rusty Sneiderman, did he know the difference between right and wrong?"

"It is my opinion that there is no indication that he did

not know the difference between right and wrong at the time that he killed him."

The prosecution then went to the videotape, playing snippets of Hemy talking about seeing a demon who sounded like Barry White and an angel that looked like Olivia Newton-John only without the Australian accent, the testimony the defense had sought to bar. The clips showed that while these details emerged in his interview with Crawford, it was Hemy—not the psychiatrist—who came up with the names. They also showed the clip of Hemy saying that the first time he ever said he was driven to kill by visions was when he was in jail talking to his attorney while trying to come up with a defense.

The most chilling portions of the interviews came when Hemy explained his preparations to kill Rusty.

"I had gotten my marching orders and this was just another one of the things that I needed to do," Hemy was seen telling Crawford.

"What did you have to do to plan that?" she asked in their jail interview.

"Initially, like any project, the first thing that you do is say: What is the desired outcome? And you know the desired outcome is what I've been told and that is Rusty needed to die," he said, leaving the only question of how it would be done. "One, poisoning, two, would be him in an accident, a car accident. Stab him? Shoot him? So you go through the different concepts."

"Did you write them down?"

"No. I do all my planning in my head. I've always done planning in my head."

His project review, he said, led him to shooting as the best option. It would be, he said, "the cleanest way."

"So you got the gun?" asked Crawford.

"The first thing I did, I took a class on gun safety. I don't want to hurt anybody."

Hemy then led Crawford through his first attempt on Rusty's life on November 10, 2010, what turned out to a dress rehearsal, down to the disguise and use of a rental car.

"I put on a disguise and there was a road, a street parallel to their street, with a pedestrian walkway through the woods," he said. "So I had gone to their house at like 5 a.m., and the reason why I was in disguise was because in case something went wrong, Rusty wouldn't recognize me and Andrea wouldn't find out. So it was very simple. He knew my car. He also had seen my car a number of times, so the reason I changed the car was for the same reason.

"Anyway," Hemy continued, "I parked in the street and walked over to their house at 5 a.m, maybe 4:30 a.m. It was really early. I crawled through neighbors and made my way very quietly to the side of house. I just laid there and waited. I believed Rusty was going to take a walk and come back to the house. That was the plan, I was just gonna sit there and wait until Rusty came back."

"You got there at 5 a.m.?"

"Yeah, 4:30, 5 a.m.," said Hemy. "I just laid by the side of the house, where the air conditioner, gas, water is. Their house is on a hill so by laying down, people walking by the street wouldn't see me. I had a wig, a mustache. I had jeans, a shirt, and a coat, because it was pretty cold. So the idea was I would see Rusty drive away.

"First I made sure Andrea left with Sophia. Once that happened, the idea would be to have Rusty drive away and when he comes back, as the garage opens I would make my way into the garage and then shoot him."

The plan was foiled by a gas leak—which Hemy hadn't caused—a pure coincidence that spared Rusty's life for eight days.

"He smelled the gas so he came to the side of the house," Hemy said. "He saw me laying there. I think he thought

I was a homeless person. He said something. I mumbled something back. He went back to get Ian and started to drive away. I got up and ran away and back to my car, went through the pathway and drove away."

"How did you feel?"

"I didn't feel like it was a problem," Hemy said. "The next week I got a beard because he had already seen me with the mustache, so I got a different wig. I said I'll just follow him to the school and make sure that he drops Ian off at the school and that's it."

"And do it there?" asked Crawford.

"Yeah."

"Could you get away with that?"

"Yeah, once I put things in motion they happen. That's the way I work. Once the ideas are fostered, and I put all the elements in place, I can almost oversee it to make sure everything is taking place and intervene if I have to, but I'm a great, great executioner. Once a plan is in place, it's going to happen."

After the tapes were played, Crawford was cross-examined. Rubin attacked Crawford's credentials, but she insisted that while she wasn't allowed to write prescriptions, her South Carolina standing allowed her to conduct forensic evaluations in another state, though she did acknowledge that she had allowed her South Carolina board certification to lapse. And she said she was charging the state of Georgia three hundred dollars an hour, for a total of sixty thousand dollars.

As with other mental health witnesses, Crawford acknowledged that some of her opinion hinged on the truthfulness of those with whom she spoke, including Andrea, who denied having an affair with Hemy—a denial that Crawford didn't believe. She also said that the records of the marital counseling sessions between Ariela and Hemy were incomplete, and that she had relied on Ariela's accounts. But, she said, "Knowing that each person that I talk to may have their own bias, I take that into account. When you're talking to an estranged spouse, an angry brother-in-law, the information is important but it has to be taken into context who these people are."

As for Hemy's visions, "You're not contending that Hemy Neuman told you that Barry White instructed him to 'Come with me'?" asked Rubin.

"No, I'm not contending that."

"You're not contending that it was Barry White's voice that that Mr. Neuman heard?"

"No, I'm contending, what he said was that it was a voice like Barry White's."

"The same for the angel. He's not saying Olivia Newton-John told him to save the children?"

"No, he's not."

"He's not saying it was Olivia Newton-John's voice that commanded him to save the children?"

"No."

"He's saying it was a soft voice like that Australian actress in *Grease*, Olivia Newton-John?"

"Correct."

But there was nothing the defense could do on cross-examination to mitigate the power of the videotape and Hemy's methodical and seemingly clearheaded account of how he carried out his plans to kill Rusty. To cap off the state's rebuttal case, prosecutors called the jail's mental health director, Dr. William Jerome Brickhouse, to recount how Hemy only reported feeling suicidal after his legal team had announced the insanity strategy. He also didn't believe Hemy suffered bipolar disorder, only that he seemed to have the same depressed feelings that anyone else would have if suddenly incarcerated.

The defense then came back with Dr. Marks again, who

insisted that the prosecution's witnesses were wrong in concluding the defense witnesses were wrong. Dr. Marks added that her opinions cost considerably less than Dr. Crawford's: She'd billed just five thousand dollars. The prosecution did not cross-examine her.

With that, the testimony in the sensational case came to an anticlimactic end, the last of the dueling experts leaving the stand as some jurors struggled to stay awake.

Shortly before noon, the jury was sent home and told that closing arguments would begin the next day.

CHAPTER 21

At just before 9:30 a.m. on Tuesday, March 13, 2012, Robert Rubin stood before the jury and talked about what his client had done to the family of Rusty Sneiderman. "They lost their son, brother, father," he said. "There's emotion they are going through that hopefully none of you or us will have to deal with, and nothing we have said or done has been unmindful of the respect and empathy they deserve."

If only Hemy Neuman knew better, he said, if only he had the capacity at the moment he pulled the trigger to realize what he was doing was wrong. "In fact," said Rubin, "as bizarre as it sounds, he thought he was doing the right thing." Acknowledging that at first blush all this "makes no sense," Rubin opened his summation by reminding the jury what his experts had said repeatedly, that Georgia law does not hold a person criminally responsible if he doesn't know the difference between right and wrong at the time of the offense.

"We have to prove insanity," Rubin continued, the courtroom filled with family and friends of both sides, including Hemy's mother who sat behind him in the audience section. Andrea was still barred from the courtroom, but Rusty's brother and father were there. Rubin said the legal threshold for proving insanity was a preponderance of evidence—more-this-than-that. It was not, he said, the far more rigorous standard of beyond-a-reasonable-doubt faced by the prosecution to prove the murder charge. Rubin laid out the options that the judge would later enumerate: not guilty, not guilty by reason of insanity, guilty, and guilty but mentally ill. That last option held the power of a conviction, and he urged the jury to reject that as a "compromise." "Guilty but mentally ill is guilty," Rubin said.

Retracing the testimony of the defense's mental health professionals, Rubin said, "Hemy Neuman did not have the capacity to distinguish between right and wrong." Those witnesses came to that conclusion based on analysis of the documents and interviews with Hemy and others. Hemy's childhood trauma, his undiagnosed bipolar disorder with delusions, and his mounting personal problems all set the stage for disaster. To fail to see this, Rubin said, was to fail as a mental health professional.

He then launched a broadside against the prosecution's expert Dr. Crawford, tarring her as overpaid and underqualified and lumping her in with Andrea Sneiderman. "Two people got on that stand and lied to you in your face," he said. "One got two million dollars, the other got sixty thousand." Andrea Sneiderman and the life insurance policy and Dr. Crawford and her consulting fee—these were the twin villains in the case, Rubin argued.

"In June 2010, Hemy Neuman has dinner with Andrea

Sneiderman," said Rubin. "In June 2010, Hemy Neuman opens up to her like he never opened up before and tell her about his childhood. You saw on the clips. He tells her what he felt and how this affected him. Doug Peters will talk to you about his relationship and why his relationship with Andrea Sneiderman led to the death of Rusty Sneiderman."

And this co-counsel Peters did, with a fury. He branded Andrea an "adulterer, tease, calculator, liar, and master manipulator." Andrea, he said, intuited everything the mental health professionals would later diagnose. "Andrea knew Hemy was losing his mind," Peters said. "Sophia and Ian's daddy's blood is on the hands of Andrea Sneiderman. She is the person, the one person, who knew that Hemy was spinning out of control. She knew Rusty had been shot because she had primed the pump, planted the seed, stoked the fire. She knew that she was with someone who was sick." In the end, Peters said, "This case is about one bad—one really bad—woman: Andrea Sneiderman. The gun was in Hemy's hand, but the trigger, I suggest, was pulled by Andrea Sneiderman."

Peters sought to assure the jury that finding him not guilty by reason of insanity would still protect society. "Hemy will not go free. He will be held in the state mental institution," said Peters. "He is paying the price for what he has done. We wouldn't ask for anything else. A verdict of not guilty by reason of insanity is a verdict that speaks the truth. A verdict of not guilty by reason of insanity is a verdict that says Andrea Sneiderman is responsible for the death of her husband. A verdict of not guilty by reason of insanity is a verdict that says Hemy was used, Hemy was manipulated."

District Attorney Robert James had the final word, having waived the state's right to give arguments first. After a courtroom break, Hemy returned to his seat in apparent good spirits, smiling to his mother. But as James launched into what would be an impassioned summation, the DA insisted that this grinning face could not be trusted. "He's not insane. He's just evil," said James. "He's not crazy, but he's a co-conspirator"—Andrea being the other party, although not charged. "Why did Hemy Neuman shoot and murder Rusty Sneiderman on November 18, 2010? Ladies and gentlemen, I submit not because of some made-up, some contrived, some constructed mental defect. It's simple. Hemy Neuman killed Rusty Sneiderman because he wanted his wife, because he wanted his money, because he wanted his life. Period. That's it. That, ladies and gentlemen, is not insanity. That is not mental illness. In Georgia, in courtrooms, we call that good old-fashioned cold-blooded malice murder."

Taking the jury through the law as the defense had, James ticked off the various elements of each charged offense and argued that the state had proved them. The biggest was malice aforethought, the centerpiece of murder charges everywhere in the country. Hemy planned it like a work project, James said. "He intended to kill him and he in fact did kill him. That's crystal-clear."

The other legal element, he said, was Hemy's affirmative defense of insanity, a defense that James mocked. "I can go back three decades to quote Flip Wilson: The devil made me do it. The angels made me do it," he said. But under the law, James said, with an affirmative defense the prosecution need only prove that he committed the crime. Since the law gives a "presumption of sanity"—something the defense did not bring up, he noted—"We do not have the burden of proving he was not insane. We do not have to prove that he is sane. We don't have that burden. We have to prove nothing." It was up to the defense to prove insanity, and here they failed, he argued. Just because Hemy had a traumatic childhood or possibly suffered bipolar disorder didn't mean he failed to know the difference between right and wrong when he gunned down Hemy. James wasn't even willing to concede that Hemy was bipolar. Hemy's friends and co-workers all testified they saw no change in his behavior around the time of the killing. "Same ol' Hemy," said James. "That's all they said."

What might better explain Hemy's behavior was something else, James said. "He's having an affair," said James. "He's about to go to the room and do the horizontal mambo. Yes, it's great. What man wouldn't be like: *Woo, I'm about to have sex. It's great.* If that makes him insane, then half the men walking down the street are insane. Really? That's evidence of mania?"

Hemy lied to his friends, his family, his co-workers, and then, when he got arrested, to the mental health professionals. When the truth got too dicey for him, he claimed to have a faulty memory, said the DA. "Erotomanic delusions?" he said. "He's having an affair, full-fledged affair, holding hands and drinking wine. He's saying, 'I love you,' and she's reciprocating. What is he confused about? . . . If the relationship turns out exactly what he thought it was, he ain't crazy. He's correct."

It was a relationship so close, he said, that Hemy confessed to Andrea in the phone call shortly after the shooting. "Hemy didn't hide his crime from Andrea because Andrea already knew," James said. "How could she know thirty minutes after [Rusty] was shot that he had been shot?" He pointed to Hemy. "The only person who could've told her is sitting right here."

James wrapped up his argument by displaying two photos, one of Rusty alive and happy, the other of him bloodied and near death after the shooting. "This is a case about a real man. Look at him: flesh and blood. He did not deserve this. Rusty deserved a life," he said. "On November

18, 2010, the defendant Hemy Neuman did this. This twisted little man, he did this to Rusty Sneiderman. This is what he did and they had the temerity and gall to call him a good man. Good men don't sleep with other men's wives. Good men don't do what he did."

The jury retired for deliberations at 3:50 p.m. and selected a forewoman. After less than an hour, in their first decision, they sent a note asking to go home. The next morning, after about two hours of deliberations, the jury asked to review the videotaped interview in jail between Hemy and the prosecution's expert, Dr. Crawford. The panel was brought back into the jury room and watched and listened again as Hemy broke down in tears while recounting his childhood traumas and talking about Andrea. "I don't know," he said, "something about the connection with Andrea. Even with Reli, I was never emotional about it. It was just something that happened. With Andrea, there was this connection. She was listening to it. It was great. I opened up."

The jury deliberated for the rest of the day and for nearly two hours the next morning, when a question came out asking for the written reports of the mental health experts who examined Hemy. Since the reports had not been entered into evidence—only the witnesses' testimony—the judge turned down the request and told the jury to rely only on what they heard in court. The jurors took a lunch break and resumed talks.

At 1:45 p.m. on March 15, a message went to the judge. The jury had reached a verdict.

CHAPTER 22

It took about an hour to get everybody into the courtroom. Hemy's mother arrived. So too did Rusty's parents, Donald and Marilyn Sneiderman, and brother Steven with his wife, Lisa. Andrea was not there, barred by the court.

At about 2:20 p.m. the lawyers took their seats and Hemy was brought in by the bailiff.

Judge Adams made his usual big entrance and warned everybody to keep their emotions in check or leave now. He ordered that the jurors be brought in. Solemn and grimfaced, they took their seats.

"Ladies and gentlemen of the jury I have been informed by the deputy that you have reached a verdict," said Judge Adams. "Would the foreperson please stand."

A woman stood in the jury box. "Madame Foreperson, have you and the others reached a verdict?"

"Yes," she said in a clear voice.

"Is it unanimous and has it been signed by you and dated by you as the foreperson?"

"Yes."

"Would you start at the top of the form—and this is what's called 'publish the verdict' here in open court—read it in its entirety," he said, adding with a drawn-out "pleeee-ase." He then told her, "You may proceed."

The jury had two counts to consider—murder and the use of a firearm in the commission of a felony.

The forewoman began reading in a strong voice. "In the superior court of DeKalb County, State of Georgia, *State of Georgia v. Hemy Neuman*, defendant, indictment number 11CR1364-5, verdict form, jury verdict."

Hemy sat at the defense table, showing no emotion as always, in a navy-blue sweater over a light-blue shirt.

"Count one, we the jury, find the defendant as to count one"—the forewoman paused, her voice faltering—"guilty beyond a reasonable doubt but mentally ill."

Hemy pursed his lips, took his eyes away form the forewoman and stared down at the table, then slowly lifted his head up with his eyes closed. Rusty's father buried his head in his hand and seemed to cry. His brother appeared stunned. Hemy's mother looked down.

"Count two," continued the forewoman of the use-of-gun charge. "We the jury find the defendant as to count two guilty beyond a reasonable doubt."

Hemy stared back toward the jury, no expression now. Then he turned forward and closed his eyes and seemed to be talking to himself, as if saying a prayer. His defense attorney Robert Rubin grabbed his shoulder to reassure him.

The judge said, "I will receive the verdict in open court as published by the jury," and asked if the prosecution had any requests for the jury. It did not. But the defense asked that the jury be polled, with each panelist queried in open court.

Called by her jury number, the first juror—an older woman—stood.

The clerk asked, "Is this your verdict?"

"Yes."

"Was it freely and voluntarily made by you?"

"Yes."

"Is this still your verdict?"

"Yes."

The clerk went through the entire panel, nine women, three men, some answering sadly, some with resignation, some emphatically, but all the same: guilty of murder but mentally ill.

The jury was dismissed, their work done. The judge allowed a brief break. Wasting no time, he moved on to sentencing.

This was the time for family members on both sides to speak out, pleading for condemnation or mercy, making the hearing as much about catharsis as legal argument. The first family member to speak was Rusty's brother, Steven.

"I am here today," he said from a podium, "to speak on behalf of my parents, Marilyn and Donald Sneiderman, my wife, Lisa, my daughter, Samantha, and, especially, Rusty's children, Sophia and Ian," he said, pointedly leaving out Andrea. "During our investigation and the trial, my mother has repeatedly asked me, 'When is this about Rusty?' Unfortunately, I have been forced to explain to her this trial was really not about him."

As a lawyer, Steven said, he understood that. "But now it is important for you to know a little more about Rusty and why his murder and the subsequent loss of him from our lives is so devastating," he said. "There have been so many lies told to this court about Rusty, even to the extent of the defense shamefully equating my brother's life with that of this killer. So let's set the record straight."

Enumerating Rusty's qualities, he said his brother was "a good provider," "giving to others," "loving, "a devoted son," "a wonderful brother," "a great father." "All that love," he said, "silenced forever, because of that man." He pointed to Hemy but did not look at him.

In contrast, said Stephen, Hemy Neuman was a "man that left his family financially ruined while he vacationed with his lover on his company expense account." Hemy "abandoned his family to destroy another one," "subjected us all to this pathetic side show instead of accepting responsibility . . . even after admitting he shot and killed Rusty."

The question, said Steven, was why did Rusty have to die to satisfy Hemy's desires? "Was it just lust? Did he just have to have her and decided the rules of civilized society didn't apply to him? Was it greed? Did he think he could just step into his shoes and take what was Rusty's? Was it envy? Did he look at his own failures and shortcomings and simply could not tolerate what he saw in the mirror?" asked Steven. "It doesn't matter—any reason he and his lawyers could conjure up is absolutely ludicrous."

With emotion welling in his voice, Steven said, "He had no right to this! He had no right to anything my brother had built! Had no right to take Rusty from us, especially Sophia and Ian! . . . Every single day of our lives there will be a hole in our hearts and in our lives where Rusty should be. We all still reach for the phone to call him. We still expect to see him, Sophia, and Ian on Skype, especially on Sundays when we visit with my parents. Today, the pain of that void is almost unbearable."

All the court could do was is make sure Hemy is "confined to prison for the remainder of his days, forced to confront the hurt and devastation he has caused to so many," Steven said. "We ask you to show him the same mercy he showed Rusty and punish him in the only appropriate manner—life without the possibility of parole."

Steven took his seat, replaced at the podium by a woman about whom much was said during the trial. Hemy's mother, Rebecca Cohen, spoke only briefly. "Hemy has been a good son. I was always proud of him," she said, then added, "Not proud of what he did now. It was a big mistake. I beg of you to have mercy [on] him. Give him the opportunity of parole. Thank you for the time you dedicated to this case. I appreciate it. Thank you."

The last to speak was Hemy.

"Your Honor," he began, his voice full of resignation. "I prepared this statement several weeks ago to express my sense of loss for the death of Rusty Sneiderman. I do not think that anyone feels that anybody won here— everybody lost. I hadn't written this down but a lot of what Mr. Sneiderman said about Rusty is true. It is. He was a good man with so much ahead of him and I'm so, so, so sorry for their loss." He punctuated each word *so*.

"This is a terrible tragedy," he continued, "first of all, for Sophia and Ian, the Sneidermans—Rusty's dad, his mom, brother, Andrea should not have had to bury him. They should not have had to undergo the pain, the anguish, the sorrow, the loss, and as Mr. Sneiderman just stated, it goes on and it will go on forever. The Greenbergs"— Andrea's parents—"suffered the loss of a beloved son-in-law.

"It is also a tragedy for three other children, for Lee, Tom, and Addie," he said, mentioning his son and daughters. "And countless family and friends who saw a person they loved, admired, and respected—who saw him arrested and shamed, charged and now convicted.

"I am so, so, so sorry. I can't say it enough. I can't say

enough to all of you—to precious children, all five of them—to the Sneidermans, to the Greenbergs, my parents, the family friends and community at large—I am sorry from the deepest part of me, Your Honor.

"That's all I have."

He took a seat.

The judge, who had spent so much of the trial nudging and prodding and speeding the proceedings along, handed down a sentence in rapid-fire fashion.

"Mr. Neuman, would you stand with your lawyers, please." Judge Adams drew a breath and then continued with barely a pause. "Mr. Neuman, earlier this afternoon a jury returned a verdict as to count one, guilty beyond a reasonable doubt but mentally ill, which was the murder count. As to count two they also find you guilty beyond a reasonable doubt as to possession of a firearm in commission of a crime.

"Obviously I have had the opportunity to sit through many, many trials throughout my career, and this appeared—at least based upon all the facts and evidence, and I'm not commenting on that per se, but for lack of a better term—a planned execution of this individual.

"And at least I could not hear any justification on what this gentlemen, Mr. Sneiderman, may have done to provoke this result. And I fully understand you have indicated today that you were sorry for the tragedy. But at least upon the finding of the jury, and everything I've heard, this situation was brought about by your hands. And as a result of you killing this gentleman, Mr. Sneiderman, you're here in my courtroom and I have a legal responsibility to impose a sentence.

"And also I guess even during the course of the testimony—I think I heard testimony that you may have even attended the funeral of this gentlemen who you earlier shot and killed—and I fully understand you have apologized for the tragedy here in my court today, and I fully understand those words have been uttered, and they have been listened to, and the family members of Mr. Sneiderman will make a decision of whether or not to accept or reject those words that you uttered here today on March 15, approximately fifteen months after you took the life of Mr. Sneiderman.

"As a result of the finding of the jury and based upon all the facts and circumstances I've heard today, I'm going to sentence you to prison for life without parole. As to count two, I'm going to sentence you to five years in prison to run consecutively to count one."

He reminded Hemy that he had the right to file an appeal, then said, "At this point in time I'm going to direct Deputy Moore and his assistants to take you in to custody." He nodded to the deputy. "At this point in time, you may take him into custody and I will sign the sentence. Everyone else with the exception of lawyers remain seated."

A guard handcuffed Hemy behind his back. The metallic click could be heard throughout the courtroom. Hemy glanced at his mother as he was led away.

Hemy was barely back in his holding cell when attention immediately shifted back to Andrea. Absent from the verdict and sentencing of the man who murdered her husband, Andrea responded in a statement from her lawyer.

"Andrea is grateful and relieved by the jury's guilty verdict and sentence. Nothing can bring back her husband, but it is reassuring to her that, after all of the noise and distractions surrounding this case, some measure of justice has been done for Rusty.

"Rusty's family misses and mourns him every single day. But today, at least, the family can be comforted by the fact that his killer will spend the rest of his days behind bars.

"Rusty was an amazing man and a wonderful husband and father. He is missed every day by so many. The world is worse off without him.

"This trial has been extremely difficult for Andrea and her family. They need time to grieve and time to heal. As such, Andrea has no plans to make any further public statement at this time. We respectfully ask that the public and the media respect this decision in the interest of the rest of the Sneiderman family."

Others had plenty more to say. "The entire truth has not been presented," Hemy's attorney Doug Peters told reporters. "Hemy Neuman was as good of a man who ever walked this earth until he met Andrea Sneiderman . . . Andrea Sneiderman should be charged with murder in the first degree. I think she preyed upon him and used him to commit the crime."

Rusty's brother agreed. "We know she lied about her involvement with Neuman," Steven Sneiderman said. "We will have no peace until everyone involved in Rusty's death is brought to justice. It is clear to us that Andrea is covered in Rusty's blood. And there aren't enough rabbis in the world to wash that blood away."

District Attorney Robert James had just won the biggest conviction of his career and all anyone wanted to talk about was the next possible prosecution.

"Guilty is guilty," he told reporters. "Justice has been served here. I want to thank God that finally, after a year and a half or more, this family—a good family—is able to begin the process of healing."

But he acknowledged that his office would now have to deal with the "thousand-pound pink gorilla in the corner," as he called Andrea. "It's something we're looking at.

I know it's important to this family. It's important to America. But as a prosecutor I have an obligation to follow the facts . . . and make a decision that seeks justice."

Pressed on when he may make that decision, he said, "Stay tuned. When we know something, y'all will know."

CHAPTER 23

On Saturday, March 2, 2012, Donald Sneiderman had sent Andrea an email. The trial of Hemy Neuman was winding down with mental health experts debating Hemy's sanity at the time of the murder. It was a weekend break. Donald asked to visit his grandchildren for ice cream.

"Unfortunately, we are not available this weekend," Andrea emailed back. "You can try to schedule something for next weekend."

Two weeks later, with the verdict in and Hemy sentenced to life in prison, Donald asked again to see the grandchildren.

"This will probably be our last weekend in Atlanta for a little while," he wrote. "We would like to see Sophia and Ian on Saturday evening perhaps for ice cream again."

Andrea replied, "Don, I am sorry but tomorrow just

doesn't work with our schedule. We will set something up whenever you can in the future. We just can't make it this weekend."

In March 2012, after a year of frustrated attempts to see their grandchildren, Donald and Marilyn Sneiderman sued for visitation, invoking the language of the most bitter custody battles. A family devastated by the murder of Rusty Sneiderman now was being torn apart by his death.

"Prior to and subsequent to the death of the father, the grandparents had a loving, caring and consistent relationship with the minor children," said the petition filed in Fulton County court, the jurisdiction where Andrea now lived with her parents. "Subsequent to the father's death, the mother has unilaterally limited and most recently eliminated contact between the grandparents and the minor children." As a result, the petition contended, "The health or welfare of the children would be harmed unless such visitation is granted." The Sneidermans said they were also "ready, willing and able, should the court find it in the children's best interests, to accept primary custody of the children," the petition states. At the very least, Rusty's parents wanted a the court to appoint a guardian to "investigate and make a recommendation as to what is in the children's best interest."

Responding to the visitation filing, Andrea's attorney, Jennifer Little, told CBS Atlanta News in a statement that there had been "multiple in-person and Skype visits with the family, the most recent being immediately before the trial began" and that "we confirmed to them that Andrea is willing to schedule visits with her children, just as she has done in the past." Beyond that, Andrea didn't want to discuss the matter publicly.

"We believe very strongly that it is not in the best interests of the children for matters related to them to be discussed in the media," her lawyer said in a statement.

"Anyone who has their best interests at heart would recognize that this is a matter to be privately addressed within the family."

As they did with so much when it came to Andrea, Rusty's family disagreed. They continued to blast her in the media, adding a publicity campaign to the legal pressure on her. Hemy's trial had left Rusty's relatives convinced that Andrea had something to do with his murder and was now covering up that fact.

"We know that she's lied; we watched her lie on the stand," Rusty's brother, Steven Sneiderman, had said in a *Today* show interview the day after the verdict. "She lied about the nature of her relationship with the killer. She clearly had an inappropriate relationship with him. We know that she lied about critical information that could have led law enforcement to, you know, arrest him much faster than they did. We knew that she lied about when she knew that Rusty had been shot. And those [lies] raise giant red flags and raise a lot of questions for all of us as to what . . . happens here."

Steven's wife, Lisa, added, "The last time I spoke with her, we were speaking right after Hemy Neuman was arrested, and she indicated to me that she felt she was suicidal when she thought of how much worse this could get for her. I immediately was alarmed and I said 'What do you mean by that?' She said 'What do you think I mean by that?' and I knew immediately that she was in big trouble."

The *Today* show was not the only media appearance by Rusty's family. His parents expressed their doubts about Andrea in an interview on WSB-TV that had been taped before the verdict but aired after. Donald Sneiderman recounted a phone conversation with Andrea shortly after the murder in which he asked her if she had lied to police when she initially said she didn't know who could have killed

Rusty. Andrea responded by hanging up on him, Donald said.

"I thought she knew on January 4," he said. "I asked her if she had lied to me. All this whole charade has done is confirm everything that I thought. Nothing's changed my mind . . . I think she knew. I don't know what she knew."

While the Sneidermans went at each other, Hemy's wife went to court to finish off their marriage. On March 22, Ariela Neuman—already legally separated from Hemy—filed for divorce in Fulton County Superior Court. In the petition, she asked the court for everything the family had amassed during their marriage, from their home at 2208 LaSalle Drive in Marietta to "household furnishings and appliances and automobiles, banking accounts, investment accounts, retirement accounts and other property." Their "substantial personal debts" were the responsibility of Hemy.

But the petition said much more, listing as the grounds for separation what it called the "misconduct" by Hemy, including adultery, "the crime of moral turpitude"—being convicted of murder—and the "cruel treatment" of Ariela. She sought to return to her maiden name, Ariela Barkoni, asked for full custody of their minor child, their daughter, and wanted Hemy to pay for all costs related to the get, the Jewish Bill of Divorcement, "with a rabbi of her choosing." Struggling to make ends meet on three jobs and Hemy's small pension, Ariela acknowledged that Hemy's lifelong incarceration made it unlikely he'd ever be able to pay alimony or child support. But she added a just-in-case clause. "If husband's current financial position changes then the wife shall have the right to petition an appropriate court to recoup monies not paid since the date of husband's incarceration," it said.

The divorce action removed marital privilege that prevented Ariela from being compelled to testify, though her lawyer said she was prepared to take the stand against Hemy all along. "[The state] had enough overwhelming evidence of [Hemy Neuman's] sanity as well as his guilt, so they didn't need her," Esther Panitch told 11Alive news. "I didn't want her to be subjected to those ridiculous assertions that maybe she helped drive him insane or anything that the defense would've come up with."

A different situation faced Donald Sneiderman, who not only did testify but likely would again. One of the unexpected developments in the trial was his growing importance for the prosecution. Called primarily to put a human face on the toll of Rusty's murder, he had mentioned that during the tumultuous morning of the murder Andrea said in a phone call that Rusty had been shot. Interviewed after the trial, prosecutor Don Geary told the *Atlanta Journal-Constitution* that he had no idea that Andrea would say under his questioning that at the time of that phone call she still had no idea how Rusty had died. "It was the first time she had ever said those things," said Geary. His boss, District Attorney Robert James, added in the same postverdict interview, "We were surprised she admitted it . . . We did not expect her to be as forthcoming as she was."

In the days after Hemy's trial, prosecutors wrestled with whether they had enough evidence against Andrea. "We have strong beliefs about Mrs. Sneiderman's involvement," James told the *Atlanta Journal-Constitution*. But, he added in another interview with WSB-TV, "I'm a public official, and I hear what people say, and it's important to me what people think. But at the end of the day, when Mr. Geary and I walk into a courtroom with a case, he and I are satisfied that we have a good shot at proving that case beyond a reasonable doubt."

As a tactical move, the prosecutors had deferred a decision on charging Andrea until after Hemy's trial, gambling that she would shun taking the Fifth and testify. The gambit paid off. Andrea's two days on the stand—her sarcasm, defensiveness, and, in the prosecution's view, outright lying—could be another weapon against her in court. She presented herself so poorly, James believed, that a cold written transcript wouldn't do her appearance justice. So in April 2012, James took the unusual step of subpoenaing from WSB-TV the video of "the entirety of Andrea Sneiderman's testimony during the Hemy Neuman murder trial." Already shown live in the Atlanta area, the testimony could be presented to a grand jury. James didn't say when or whether that would happen, but Esther Panitch told 11Alive news that "every step that the DA takes to further investigate their case is a march closer to justice for Rusty Sneiderman and may result in the arrest of his widow Andrea Sneiderman for her role in not only his death, but also covering it up afterwards." At the very least, Panitch guessed, prosecutors would slap Andrea with perjury charges, using her own words and what the lawyer called Andrea's "level of arrogance" against her. "I think it would take a criminal charge to bring her back down to reality and realize that what she's alleged to have done is very, very serious," Panitch told the station. "This is not a joke. This is not a game. This is someone's life who was taken, and this is someone's life who will be affected by criminal charges, so the decision [to charge Andrea] has to be very deliberate."

As prosecutors pondered their next move, Andrea took her first substantive step to fight back. In a blistering response to her in-laws' visitation petition, Andrea's lawyers accused Donald and Marilyn Sneiderman of "litigation strategy" to see the kids and questioned the couple's true feelings about their grandchildren. She said that before the trial they visited the children twice a year for three days at a time. "They may love the children very much," said

Andrea's court papers, "but they have shown very little outward affection during their visits." Blasting Rusty's parents for their statements to the press, Andrea's papers said, "Clearly that was not in the best interests of the children for their grandparents and uncle to publicly make such terrible accusations about their mother."

Two weeks later, in early May 2012, the public squabbling over the children ended when the two sides reached an agreement. Appearing in public for the first time since Hemy's trial, Andrea sat near Rusty's parents in a Fulton County courtroom to finalize a visitation arrangement, the terms of which weren't revealed except that Rusty's parents would be required to temper their comments about Andrea if they wanted to continue seeing their grandchildren.

The deal offered only a momentary respite. About two weeks later Rusty's brother filed a wrongful death lawsuit against her, pinning blame for Rusty's murder on Andrea. The petition stated, "On November 18, 2010, Defendant Sneiderman, through her Co-Conspirator, Defendant Neuman, shot and killed Rusty Sneiderman as he dropped off one of his minor children at preschool in DeKalb County, Georgia." The lawsuit alleged that Andrea "utilized her illicit relationship" with Hemy "to manipulate and influence him to attempt to murder Rusty Sneiderman." Andrea knew that Hemy intended to kill her husband, the lawsuit alleged, and "actively and knowingly participated in the murder and the planning of the murder."

In a statement to the media, Steven Sneiderman said he filed the lawsuit "to protect the interests of Rusty's children for which he worked every day of his life to provide, to protect Rusty's legacy by making sure the truth about the circumstances surrounding his death are publicly disclosed and to try to bring closure, once and for all, to all of the issues that continue to haunt us." One of his attorneys, William Ballard, said that Steven would be seeking the millions of dollars controlled by Andrea, including the life insurance payout, "to make sure it all goes to Rusty's and Andrea's two children, and not to Andrea."

Despite the strong allegations, the lawsuit did not provide new evidence that Andrea had either had an affair with Hemy or been involved in the murder. Asked if he had such evidence, Ballard told 11Alive news, "I wouldn't have filed the case if I didn't think we were going to make the case."

The wrongful death case also brought another familiar face deeper into the case. Ariela Neuman's attorney Esther Panitch now also was representing Steven Sneiderman.

Andrea didn't let this go unchallenged. In her biggest move yet, she recruited a heavy-hitting legal team led by J. Tom Morgan, a former DeKalb County district attorney, and a lineup of some of Atlanta's best-known criminal defense lawyers. "We categorically deny each and every one of the allegations in the complaint filed today," her new legal team said in a statement. "We are looking forward to a vigorous and complete defense to ensure that Andrea is fully exonerated of these false accusations." The statement went on to say the lawyers were "disappointed" in Steven Sneiderman for filing a complaint "supposedly to benefit Andrea's children, when all he is now doing is forcing Andrea to incur legal fees that will, at the end of the day, simply take money out of the children's pockets."

In their response, Andrea's lawyers not only addressed the allegations but took aim at Panitch herself. "Steven Sneiderman and his attorney Esther Panitch have been attempting to try Andrea in the media for months," they said in the statement. "We look forward to vigorously representing her in a court of law where, for the first time, she will have the opportunity to tell her side of the story. We are also carefully considering our legal options regarding the

outrageous and libelous statements that have been made
to the media about Andrea, without the benefit of privilege, by various individuals."

As the civil litigation ground on, the DeKalb County District Attorney's Office had finally resolved the question of
whether it had enough evidence against Andrea. At 10:30
a.m. on Thursday, August 2, on a muggy Georgia morning, armed DA investigators and deputies from Putnam
County converged on Andrea's parents' house on Blue
Heron Drive. With her children in the house, Andrea was
arrested, handcuffed, and hauled off in a police car to jail.
She did not resist.

A grand jury had handed down a nineteen-count indictment. The charges included malice murder, criminal attempt to commit murder, insurance fraud, perjury, and
making false statements to authorities. By noon she arrived
at the DeKalb County Jail. Photos by a Fox 5 camera taken
from a distance through a chain-link fence showed Andrea
in profile, her hair thrown back in a hasty ponytail, surrounded by policemen. She wore white shorts, and her
hands were cuffed in front of her.

She posed for a mug shot, grim-faced, her mouth downturned, her eyes averted from the camera.

"Obviously she is in a state of shock right now," attorney J. Tom Morgan told reporters. "She was arrested with
the children in the home with her. She was not even allowed to say good-bye to her children." Scrambling to file
papers seeking bond, the former DA seemed beside himself. He complained that he had offered to work with authorities to turn in Andrea if she were indicted; instead they
sent "a SWAT team" to get her while her children were in
the house. The first he heard of her arrest was in a phone
call from a reporter. He signaled that Andrea would launch

a full-throttle defense, conceding nothing, not even an affair with Hemy.

"We categorically deny each and every one of the charges that were filed against Andrea today," Morgan said in a statement. "We are looking forward to a vigorous and complete defense to ensure that Andrea is fully exonerated of these false accusations. We are confident that, when an unbiased jury hears the facts of this case, it will be clear that Andrea is innocent."

At a press conference, DA Robert James said as little as possible. "My staff, my investigators handled the arrest along with the Putnam County investigators," he said. "My understanding is the children were not present." He declined to answer questions about the evidence against Andrea, leaving that to the indictment, which offered a detailed narrative, starting with Andrea's hiring at GE by Hemy, her business trips with Hemy, what the indictment called their "affair," and through the days before the murder. Rusty originally was to have been killed on November 10, 2010, the indictment said, alleging that it was Andrea who provided Hemy with Rusty's schedule and told him of a secluded path behind her house that he could use to escape. When that failed due to the gas leak alerting Rusty, Andrea gave Hemy Rusty's schedule for November 18, and the plot was carried out to its deadly end. The motive came down to money and passion. The pair "conspired together to murder Rusty Sneiderman so that they could enjoy a life together, eliminate Neuman's debt problems and fully benefit from the assets the Sneidermans had acquired as well as the proceeds of Rusty Sneiderman's life insurance policies," the indictment read.

Afterward, Andrea "misled police by indicating she was not in a relationship with Neuman," according to the indictment, even though she confided in Shayna Citron that she had suspicions about Hemy. This turned Andrea's long-time and once closest friend into the potential premier witness against her at trial, a role Shayna appeared ready and willing to take. "My client knew that she was not telling the truth," Shayna's lawyer, Jay Abt, told My Fox Atlanta. "You can tell when your best friend is lying sometimes. In this case, Shayna was able to know and understand that Andrea was not being truthful about denying a relationship with Hemy Neuman."

Rusty's family also issued a statement. "The arrest and indictment of Andrea Sneiderman is another important step in the pursuit of Justice for Rusty. This action, however, brings us no joy. We thank District Attorney Robert James, ADA Don Geary, Investigator Mark Potter and the rest of their team for their relentless pursuit of the truth in this case and we will continue to support their efforts in every way through the trial. We will NEVER stop fighting for Justice for Rusty."

But for all the detail in the indictment, it—like the petition in the wrongful death case—offered little in the way of new evidence. It didn't say how prosecutors intended to prove that Andrea gave Hemy the schedule for Rusty for either day he was targeted to die—whether it happened in an email or a phone call or in person. It referenced no evidence at all that said Andrea had any inkling that Hemy intended to kill Rusty or that Andrea herself had harbored such feelings. For all the emails presented at Hemy's trial, none came close to that. Nor did the indictment suggest that Hemy had provided new information or intended to testify against Andrea, a problematic scenario at best since his entire defense was that he was insane.

After nineteen days in jail, Andrea Sneiderman appeared before Judge Adams for a bond hearing on August 21, 2012. Her attorneys called a series of witnesses to show that Andrea had strong ties to the community and family and would not jump bond. Her father, Herbert Greenberg, took the stand to describe how close Andrea was to her children. "Her children have been the highlight of her and our life," he testified, the first person to say anything under oath on Andrea's behalf. "Before Rusty was murdered, every decision relative to the children was made by both of them planning together." Her friend Joanne Powers called Andrea "the best mother ever" and said, "Sometimes I'm really amazed at her patience." Her rabbi, Hirsh Minkowicz, described Andrea as an active member of the synagogue. Her friend and former sorority sister Tracey Carisch said Andrea is so rooted in the Atlanta area that she had turned down Carisch's suggestion to move to Chattanooga after the trial to get away. When asked if Andrea would be capable of abandoning her family and children if granted bond, her other friend Tammi Parker said, "Oh, gosh, no."

It was left to Shayna Citron's lawyer Jay Abt to present another side, recounting how Andrea was "threatening" toward Shayna at the trial, quoting Andrea as saying, "You're going to have to live with what I'm going to do to you." The statement, the prosecution suggested, showed that Andrea would be a threat to the community if sprung from jail. But Andrea had an answer for that, too. The defense called to the stand Joanne Powers, who also said she saw Sneiderman and Citron embrace in the courtroom. She said she went outside and observed Sneiderman and Citron sitting on a bench holding hands as though they were friends. She said she heard Sneiderman say, "I need people around me who trust me and believe in me and you don't believe in me so we can't be friends." Powers said Sneiderman's voice and demeanor were loving and kind, not threatening.

After hearing arguments, Judge Adams agreed to spring Andrea on a five-hundred-thousand-dollar bond with a number of restrictions, the strictest of which was that she had to remain under house arrest with her parents. She had to wear an electronic ankle bracelet that would alert authorities if she went outside the boundaries of her parents' home in Roswell (she'd have to pay for the device). The only time she could leave was to see the doctor or her attorneys. She also would have to give up her passport and those of her children. She could visit her parents, brother, sister-in-law, children, and rabbi, but could have no contact with any potential witnesses.

Two days later, on Thursday, August 23, her attorneys delivered a $250,000 cashier's check to the court—another condition was that half the bail had to be put up in cash. She raised the money even though as part of her arrest the prosecution had frozen many of her assets, including the two-million-dollar life insurance payout after Rusty's murder. The rest of her bail was secured by a bond backed by real estate. She had one request before being released; she asked to change out of the shorts and black top she had been wearing when arrested. The sheriff agreed, and at about noon she walked out of the jail in a smart black pantsuit, the cuff covering her new ankle bracelet.

Reporters converged on her, one of them asking, "Andrea, when your children get older and you have to talk to them about this—when they start asking about the situation and their father, what will you tell them?" She ignored the questions, got into a minivan with one of her attorneys, and drove off.

In the end, Andrea did not run away and did not try to intimidate any witnesses. She stayed and fought—against the prosecution's murder case, against Rusty's brother who continued to press his wrongful death lawsuit. She made court appearances and never wavered from declaring her innocence, though always expressing herself publicly through her attorneys. (Andrea to this day has not granted a media interview.) She would fight for more freedom. Soon her bail conditions would be loosened to allow her to attend Jewish services including Yom Kippur in September, Sukkoth services in October, and the lighting of the first candle for Hanukkah in December.

All the while, questions mounted about whether prosecutors had overreached. In October prosecutors formally turned over their evidence to the defense. At first look it appeared intimidating: 9,233 pages, ninety-one CDs of interviews, and a number of other video and audio recordings. But a closer examination showed that it was almost the exact same evidence prosecutors had used a year earlier against Hemy. There were the same witnesses, the same emails, the same phone records. The prosecution arguably could build a case that Andrea had an affair with a man who later killed her husband, but nowhere did it appear they had any direct evidence that she'd ordered Rusty killed or even wanted him dead. Nor was there anything between them suggesting they talked about the murder afterward. The prosecution case appeared to hinge on Andrea's behavior after the murder—her alleged lies about an affair, her apparent knowledge of the means of her husband's murder before it was officially revealed, and her demeanor on the witness stand at Hemy's trial. It could be argued she possessed a consciousness of guilt, but it was all circumstantial, a rickety case that Andrea's top-flight defense team savored attacking.

As before, however, the prosecution got an unexpected boost—from Andrea herself. Her behavior continuing to raise eyebrows. In November 2012, the case took a strange twist when Steven Sneiderman's attorneys suggested as part of the wrongful death lawsuit that Andera had begun a relationship with a man named Joseph Dell. Dell was among the many who had come to Andrea's aid since Hemy's trial, voicing their solidarity on a blog called "Friends of

Andrea," a forum to both support her and rip into the DA's office. According to jailhouse phone logs, Andrea had called her parents fifty-five times and Dell fifty-eight times. Recorded by the jail, one of the calls had Andrea asking Dell to move in with her parents, whom Dell called "Mom and Dad." On the day of Andrea's indictment, Dell called her and "is heard crying and professing his love for Defendeant Sneiderman," according to the court papers. "This bold romantic gesture is met by Defendant, who is apparently aware of the recording, with a response eerily similar to her handling of Neuman, 'I do not know what to say,' " the filing says.

The question soon arose over how long the alleged relationship had gone on. Steven Sneiderman's lawyer Esther Panitch wrote in a court filing that the relationship between Andrea and Dell had roots earlier. Dell separated from his six-months'-pregnant wife in June 2011, several months before the trial, around the time media reports had begun divulging details about Andrea's travels with Hemy. On the day that Andrea testified at the trial—February 21, 2012—Dell's wife filed for divorce. Dell was with Andrea at the courthouse, according to Panitch. "Despite the lack of finality in his divorce case, Mr. Dell was already well ensconced with defendant," Panitch wrote in her brief to the court, saying the divorce, which cited irreconcilable differences, wouldn't be finalized for another six months, in August 2012. When Andrea was arrested in August, Dell was in the house with her.

"What is known today about defendant's [Andrea's] relationship with Mr. Dell bears a striking similarity to defendant's relationship with the man who shot Rusty," Panitch wrote. "It is unknown when Dell became involved in Defendant's life but upon information and belief, it was prior to the murder of Rusty as Andrea and Mr. Dell arranged 'playdates' with their children." Panitch sought court permission to question Andrea to find out "whether Joseph Dell was the ultimate reason for manipulating Neuman to kill Rusty."

Andrea's lawyers in the wrongful death case strongly denied that anything involving Dell had a role in Rusty's murder. Andrea's civil lawyer Mark Trigg denounced that suggestion as "preposterous" and contended that Steven Sneiderman's attorney lodged it both to harass Andrea and to try to get Hemy to turn on Andrea. "It seems likely that the assertion at this late date that Andrea had another so-called 'paramour' is made in an effort to manipulate Mr. Neuman so that he will fall into a jealous rage, decide to no longer tell the truth in this regard, and finally provide something that so far is completely lacking: any direct evidence that Andrea Sneiderman was a co-conspirator in her husband's murder," he wrote.

The issue immediately spilled into the criminal case. It arose at a hearing that had been intended to focus on a completely different issue. Andrea had sought permission to leave house arrest to visit Rusty's grave on November 18, 2012, the second anniversary of his murder, for yahrt-zeit, the Jewish observance of the death of somebody close. At the last minute she withdrew the request, her prayers and lighting of the twenty-four-handle candle, fearing an invasion of reporters and TV crews. "It was going to be a madhouse," one of her lawyers, John Petrey, said. Instead, the hearing turned to the revelations from the civil case, with prosecutors suggesting that it was another potential motive for murder. Now prosecutors expanded their case from an alleged love triangle to something more complicated and sinister. "Evidence is starting to come up that might show that it was not for Mr. Neuman to be with the defendant but for someone else," prosecutor Don Geary told Judge Adams at a subsequent hearing in the criminal trial. "Mr. Dell might be that someone else." At the very least, the prosecution said, Dell was a potential witness at trial. And under the terms of Andrea's bond, she was not to have any contact with any witnesses while under house arrest. Geary sought to have all contact between Andrea and Dell cease immediately.

It was a hardball tactic, taking on Andrea not just legally but personally. If granted, it would leave Andrea more isolated. To suggest Rusty died because of this relationship was "incredible on its face," said one of her criminal lawyers, Thomas Clegg, and "has absolutely no bearing on any issue in this particular case." Clegg, however, tiptoed around whether Andrea and Dell had a romance, saying the "exact status of their relationship is best described as to be determined." Clegg portrayed Dell as something of a domestic helper. "She lives with her parents, but again they can't do everything on her behalf," Klegg told the judge. "She needs, quite frankly, some help and I don't see that there is any downside to allowing her to have contact with this gentleman." To add Dell to the witness list, and therefore remove him from Andrea's life, would cost her somebody to help pick up her children and care for them while she remained under house arrest.

Although Dell had apparently been in court with Andrea, few took notice of him and little was known about him until the court filing. On the Friends of Andrea website, Dell described his relationship with Andrea. "I hardly knew Andrea before her husband was murdered but I have gotten to know her and her family as an extension of my own," Dell wrote on September 28. "For anyone who knows Andrea, there is no mystery and no mystery man. The mystery man was Hemy Neuman: the mentally ill individual who was convicted of murdering Rusty Sneiderman. But the jury got it right and he is in jail for the rest of his life. The rest of the noise is an attempt to smear Andrea and any of her friends and family." He added in an apparent reference to Steven Sneiderman's lawsuit, "There are those who want to paint a picture and concoct a story about something far more salacious. I'm sorry to disappoint everyone but it just isn't there."

About a week and a half after the hearing, on November 26, 2012, Judge Adams issued a written ruling: "The Court . . . hereby DENIES defendant's motion and further ORDERS that the defendant have no contact with the witness Joseph Dell." Within days, the defense fought back, asking the judge again to remove Dell from the witness list. Arguing that there was no evidence Andrea and Dell had a relationship before Rusty's murder, the defense called the matter irrelevant and asked the judge to bar the state from bringing it up in court before a jury. The request came in a sweeping motion filed in early December 2012 to throw out all the charges against Andrea. Describing the indictment as ambiguous and confusing, the defense said it "fails to spell out what acts Sneiderman committed to warrant a murder charge."

This represented Andrea's biggest counteroffensive since police first began to wonder whether she had anything to do with Rusty's murder. It was accompanied by an aggressive publicity move. Although she again stayed away from reporters, Andrea's camp marched out a series of surrogates. While Andrea had remained close to some of her friends from before the murder—Tammi Parker among them—she had been joined by a growing circle of supporters drawn to her during and after the trial, connected via the Friends of Andrea website. Among them were a couple named Ryan and Elizabeth Stansbury who were at the forefront of Andrea's PR campaign that included interviews on *48 Hours* and in the local media.

"I think anybody who knows her for more than five minutes realizes that she didn't do this," Ryan Stansbury told WSB-TV the second week of December 2012. "It's been very difficult for her, for both she and her family." His wife added, "I think it's been a travesty that people are starting to show empathy to the villain, the murderer, the one that orchestrated this all on his own, and that's Hemy Neuman." Anticipating that prosecutors would show the criminal jury scenes from Andrea's testimony in Hemy's trial, Ryan also sought to explain why Andrea seemed to come off so badly. "Both the defense and the prosecution, for their own reasons, were both out to get Andrea," he told the news station. "They needed her to make their cases." The couple repeated their thoughts for the *Atlanta Journal-Constitution*, but this story also noted how the murder case had caused a rift not just among family members but also among friends. The case forced people to take sides: between Andrea and Rusty's family. "There's been a lot of angry emails that have gone back and forth between friends," Josh Golub, a radiologist who lived near Rusty's parents in Cleveland, told the newspaper. "Rusty would be so upset that his friends were fighting. He was always one to avoid trouble. He'd be trying to find a way around this."

Along with the media moves, Andrea's attorneys went after Hemy's wife, seeking a mountain of documentation, including scheduling calendars, diaries, and any papers that may relate to efforts to sell the rights to her life story. The lawyers portrayed this as an effort to amass evidence to help Andrea's defense, though many saw it also as a dig at Ariela's attorney, Esther Panitch, whom Andrea's civil attorneys had already accused of misconduct with her suggestions that the Dell relationship played a role in Rusty's murder. Panitch didn't take it quietly, blasting Andrea again and generating a headline-making revelation. Her papers filed in February 2013 quoted Andrea from her jailhouse conversations with Dell as talking about possibly selling her life story and asking Dell if "every day or every couple of days, you could jot a couple notes down."

"I know when this book comes out one day or movie or etc., it would be good for me to know in general what's happened out there while I was in here," Sneiderman said, according to the document. "I was thinking if Sandra Bullock wasn't so old, she'd be a good choice. I watched the 'Miss Congeniality' movie . . . I thought she kind of has my personality, so, you know, that would be a good choice, but I think she might be a little old, so we'll see." (Andrea was thirty-six, Bullock was forty-eight.)

In her court papers, Panitch wrote, "It is the height of hypocrisy that the same Defendant who has already chosen the actress to play her in the movie about her life would seek to impeach a victim of her own wretched acts. Notwithstanding the objection, Ariela Neuman has not sold her life rights or otherwise entered into any contract to sell her name or pictures, nor written a book, unlike Defendant's desire to do so."

Back and forth the battle went. At a February 2013 hearing in the murder trial, Andrea's attorney Thomas Clegg again sought to have Dell removed from the witness list. "Make no mistake: This is an ordeal. She is entitled to companionship during her ordeal," Clegg told the judge. District Attorney Robert James this time could only muster a shaky response. He finally acknowledged that he kept Dell on the witness list even though authorities had not contacted him. It was the first sign of a fissure in the prosecution's case. Seizing on this, Clegg snapped that James should "put up or shut up," to which James shot back that he didn't have to do any such thing until trial.

The defense next filed a motion in March, seeking dismissal of most of the sixteen counts against Andrea. They derided the perjury charges as "vague, uncertain, indefinite and devoid of specificity." Ditto for the counts alleging Andrea hindered the apprehension of a criminal, giving false statements and concealing material facts.

The prosecution countered that it had more evidence than most had realized. At a hearing in April, an investigator testified that records of Andrea's calls and texts with Hemy the day of the murder had been erased from her Black-Berry. The investigator said it was impossible to tell who erased them or why, but noted that other calls and texts between Andrea and Hemy before the murder had not been deleted.

Whatever boost the prosecution got was temporary. Not only did the judge rule that Andrea would be allowed to converse again with Joseph Dell, but buzz began building that the prosecution's case was crumbling. Twice after Andrea was originally charged the prosecution had to go back to the grand jury for new indictments, tweaking the lineup of counts. The essence of the case remained the same—that Andrea allegedly had something to do with Rusty's murder and then lied to authorities—but the tinkering with the charges sent a message of a lack of certainty on the prosecution's part. As the trial grew near, the situation grew worse for the state. The evidence James wanted simply never arrived. And in late July the word had gotten out. Local media outlets reported that the DA was planning to drop the most serious charge against Andrea, that of murder.

With a gag order imposed, neither side could confirm or deny the reports. This set the stage for a critical pretrial hearing where the prosecution would have to disclose its intentions. Televised live locally, the hearing was set for July 26—just three days before opening statements—and in the course of two tense hours in court tempers would fly. It began with lawyers debating a motion to allow the testimony of Hemy's friend and confidante Melanie White, the prosecution calling her observations relevant, the defense saying it would be too prejudicial.

When Judge Adams then asked about the second motion, the defense immediately called for a session at the sidebar. Several minutes of animated discussion ensued, the lawyers' words fuzzed over by the judge activating his static switch. At the defense table Andrea sat nervously, wringing her hands.

"All right, we're back on the record, Mr. James!" the judge boomed as lawyers returned to the seats.

"Yes, sir," said the DA as he walked up to the lecturn, "at this point the state would make a motion."

James asked to remove counts one, two, and three of the indictment.

"Mr. James," the judge said, interrupting him, "the way it's listed is count one is malice of murder, count two is felony murder, and count three is aggravated assault?"

"That's accurate, Judge," said James.

"Go ahead."

The prosecutor began tentatively. "Um," he said, "as is customary and I believe as is also required, um, I would tender a reason, um, to make this, um, to make this motion."

He noted that the court was aware that jurors had been called in and that he would "not be too detailed" about the evidence, but that his perception of the case changed after he went through the discovery evidence provided by the defense.

"After we received the second batch of discovery, we, the state, went back and reinterviewed most if not all of our witnesses in this case," he said. "I have an ethical obligation not to seek convictions but to seek justice, and I believe it would be unjust and unethical for the DA's office, for the state, for the district attorney of this county to go forward with a charge that I am not 100 percent sure someone is guilty of." Therefore, the DA was dropping the murder charge against Andrea.

Defense attorney Thomas Clegg couldn't disagree, but took a swipe anyway.

"There is no smoking gun in there leading anyone to conclude: *Wow, looking at this, all of a sudden I can say they don't have a murder case*," said Clegg. "I believe they have known all along they did not have a murder case. Be that as it may, I welcome at this time Mr. James's admission that he does not have the degree of certainty necessary to go forward with a prosecution for these counts. So I have no objection to the dismissal of counts of one, two, and three."

The judge seemed taken aback by the last-minute move. "Mr. Clegg, before you take your seat, obviously the court will have some say in this."

"I understand that, sir."

"And no one has presented to me a case that says the court must accept the state's motion."

The judge would call a recess without ruling. Afterward, a clearly rattled Robert James returned to the lectern.

"Your Honor, I'll make this very brief," he said. "What I was going to say I won't say. But what I will say is I've been prosecuting cases for fourteen years. I have never—as an assistant DA, as solicitor, and now as the elected district attorney—I have never indicted a case where based on the evidence I had in front of me, I did not believe that an individual was guilty of the charges that I was indicting them for. I have never tried a case, on the other hand, where I have doubts, or where I believed there was a possibility I could be wrong.

"That is why I'm before the court," he continued. "That is why I made this motion. I'm standing before the court and standing before millions of people, perhaps, asking for the court to [dismiss] right before the trial. I'm struggling to see how that lacks ethics. I'm doing what I think is right."

By the end of the day, despite his reservations, Judge Adams granted the prosecution's request. The Andrea

Sneiderman murder trial suddenly became the Andrea Sneiderman perjury trial.

The decision may have been a letdown for the national media—HLN had lost its marquee live murder trial—but the stakes remained high. Andrea still faced up to twenty years in prison. Her children could see her only behind razor wire and under heavy guard. All, Andrea maintained, for crimes she claimed she never committed.

CHAPTER 24

Opening statements began on a steamy southern morning on August 5, 2013, the cicadas buzzing in the trees outside the DeKalb County Courthouse. The trial had the feel of an afterthought. The national media left the story to the locals, who still gave it major coverage with live-streaming testimony, blogging, and tweeting. DA Robert James handed off opening statements to a newly promoted deputy, Kellie Hill, though he sat in court throughout the trial.

The jury that had been selected would not be tasked with deciding whether Andrea Sneiderman should be held accountable for the cold-blooded murder of her husband, but for not telling the whole truth to police and at Hemy's trial. She still faced decades in prison on the counts, which carried five-year penalties.

But the defense was emboldened. Thomas Clegg delivered a no-compromise opening statement signaling that this wouldn't be a reasonable-doubt case. "She ain't on trial for murder. No evidence suggests that she is," Clegg told the jury. "Everything will be based on inference, speculation, and a hunch. There is no evidence she has done anything wrong. It's a myth." Andrea was so confident that she turned down a last-minute plea deal, reportedly one year in prison.

It was up to DeKalb Assistant District Attorney Hill to remind everybody that there was still unfinished business. In an opening statement that built in passion, she told jurors that Andrea had a "forbidden romance" with Hemy Neuman that "ended in the murder of her husband."

"The evidence will show that she suspected Hemy Neuman immediately," said Hill. "And the evidence will show, ladies and gentlemen, that she lied." The lies, Hill claimed, "kept police from figuring out who shot her husband in cold blood outside her son's daycare." Near the end of the opening statement, Hill said that Andrea "took this very witness stand"—she smacked the wood railing—"and vowed to tell the truth. That is not what she did."

Over the next six days, the prosecution laid out a meticulous case, alternating clips of Andrea's courtroom testimony and police interviews with live witnesses. Each targeted statement came with a rebuke on the witness stand. Showing Andrea's trial statements out of order and in sound-bite form stripped them of their emotional punch; jurors at Andrea's trial didn't experience the same surprise and shock of her slow build to anger and sarcasm.

But the lies piled up all the same, the state argued as it sought to prove the 13 counts against Andrea. Prosecutors offered what it called evidence she hindered the apprehension of a criminal by deleting text messages and concealing her relationship with Hemy. They argued that she covered up her knowledge her boss had killed Rusty, using as evidence, among other things, their phone calls around the time of the murder. She concealed material facts, the state argued, by lying to police about a romance with Hemy, introducing their travel records, emails and testimony from the Pulse bartender and others.

Prosecutors played back portions of her police interviews seeking to prove she made false statements by failing to tell investigators she suspected Hemy until the very end of the investigation. It alleged she also made false statements to Lt. Barnes about having no idea what happened to Rusty when she arrived at Dunwoody Prep, bringing into evidence her alleged statements she knew Rusty had been shot before anybody, the state claimed, had told her that. Prosecutors argued she was lying when she told investigators she had made it clear to Hemy to stop chasing after her, that claim, prosecutors alleged, undermined by their emails. And prosecutors presented evidence she perjured herself at Hemy's trial by allegedly lying again about many of those same things on the witness stand.

As the prosecution built its case against Andrea, it injected drama into the trial, its marquee witness to present what the state would claim was the context of her alleged lies.

Impeccably dressed and accessorized, Shayna Citron walked to the witness stand in a black dress with plunging neckline and a silver necklace. Answering questions from Hill, Andrea's former best friend recalled their pleasant life when they were two young moms with great husbands in suburban Atlanta: the book club meetings, the playdates, the school activities, dinners at each other's homes, the baby showers as their children arrived.

Then came a lunch between Shayna and Andrea, a lunch like many others. Andrea was about to start her first full-time office job and wanted her friend's advice on office attire. "She was asking if open-toed shoes were okay in workplace or if flat shoes better option," said Citron.

Almost from the moment Andrea started at GE, Citron detected a change. A May 2010 dance recital in which Andrea performed—"Andrea is a very good dancer and always had been," she noted—was followed by a tense and uncomfortable dinner where Citron was stunned at seeing how her best friend acted with Rusty. "It was at that dinner that I saw for the first time that they were going through a rough time."

By September 1 things had gotten worse. When the women met at a restaurant for lunch, Andrea revealed that her boss had professed his love for her. This was the same anecdote that Citron testified about at the first trial, only now she could barely control her emotions on the witness stand.

"Did she tell you how she felt about her boss?" asked Hill.

Taking a moment to compose herself, Citron answered, "She said that maybe if she had not been married she'd be interested in him."

"Did she answer the question that you asked, What's going on with you and Rusty?"

Another pause, and Citron said, "There came a point in that conversation when I said, 'Are things that bad? Are you and Rusty going to get a divorce?' I couldn't even believe I was saying that because they had been such a good team. She said to me that she would never divorce Rusty."

This, Andrea told her, despite years of issues with him. "We started talking about how everything in their married life had always been about Rusty, whatever job he had, whatever problems were going on in his job, whatever the situation was with the boss or co-worker was, there was always something. It was always all about him."

Then she revealed something that shocked Citron. "She said that her parents never wanted her to marry Rusty."

"You had never heard that before?"

Tearing up, she said, "I had never heard that before."

"Did her parents tell her why?"

"Again because everything was all about him, and she had previously had a relationship with some musician and they almost would have rather had her marry him because he was more supportive of her."

The lunch ended on a traumatic note for Citron. "I thought, *Oh, my God, Andrea has checked out of this marriage*," she testified. Citron's voice choked, her face contorted with emotion. "When she was speaking about Rusty her eyes were dark and cold. When she was speaking about her boss—I did not know his name at that point—her eyes were sparkling."

Citron sniffled and reached for a tissue and dabbed her left eye.

Andrea watched her former friend intently but betrayed no reaction, her expression stony.

Court ended for the day before Citron finished. She returned the next morning, this time in a bright-red dress and a strand of pearls, with more accounts of conversations in which Andrea spoke of marital problems. The latest was an argument in front of the children, the first time this had happened, Andrea told Shayna. "She was particularly upset."

As she testified, Citron seemed to struggle to remain composed, finally breaking into tears when she spoke of a Halloween costume party. Andrea and Sophia dressed as mommy-and-daughter sock-hop girls in poodle skirts and bobbed hair.

"She looked amazing," Citron said. "She looked the happiest I had seen her in a long time, absolutely radiant and glowing. Even her complexion was just absolutely gorgeous."

Rusty was dressed as Fred from Scooby-Doo and Ian as Scooby. Rusty was "just wiped wiped out," Citron said.

"Did he look as happy as the defendant looked?" asked Hill.

"No," said Citron.

The party, the prosecution would later note, took place the same week that Hemy Neuman left his wife and started telling people he was sleeping with a younger woman.

On cross-examination, Citron turned steely, every attempt by J. Thomas Morgan to undercut her credibility met with terse and combative replies. There would be no more tears. Her demeanor would later be likened by the defense as a bad scene from the *Real Housewives of Atlanta*, and witnesses called by the defense would rebut her. Andrea's mother insisted her daughter and son-in-law had a strong, happy bond. Ben Nadler, who went to the same synagogue as the Sneidermans, said, "There was this little sparkle in her eye when she was talking about him and you could just really hear the pride." But Shayna Citron never wavered: There was trouble in the Sneiderman marriage, the kind of trouble that the prosecution said laid the groundwork for lies.

Testimony ended August 15 with Andrea telling the judge that she would not take the stand in her own defense, clearing the way for summations. After spending much of the trial as a second-chair lawyer, handling the occasional witness, DA Robert James—last seen explaining himself—was back in form. "You're a liar!" he said directly at Andrea during closing arguments as she looked away. "She's a manipulator. She's a deceiver," he told the jury. "If this was the street, they'd say she's got game."

Clegg wrapped up the defense case with the same stance as opening statements, conceding nothing. Andrea, he said, was a "victim" who had done absolutely nothing wrong.

The prosecution's case amounted to a "well-edited TV show" that lacked any real evidence. "Part of that woman's heart, part of that woman's soul was ripped apart and she will never get that back," he said. "The state of Georgia is doing all it can to take away the rest of her heart, the rest of her soul." Asking, "What on earth are we doing here," Clegg said of the prosecution, "They blew it, folks. They blew it totally. They blew it completely."

The jury retired that Friday to begin deliberations, returned after a weekend break, and by lunchtime Monday had a verdict. Judge Adams brought the jury into the courtroom and explained to the forewoman how to read the read the verdict, starting at the top of the form and reading it in its entirety into the record.

"You may proceed," he told her.

Sitting between Morgan and Clegg at the defense table, Andrea cast her eyes down, shooting nervous glances in the forewoman's direction.

"We the jury find the defendant Andrea Sneiderman, count one, hindering the apprehension of a criminal," she began, "guilty."

Andrea's head dropped and she stared at the table.

"Count two," continued the forewoman in a strong voice, "concealment of material facts: guilty."

Andrea now breathed more heavily.

"Count three, false statement, guilty."

On it went: guilty on a total of nine counts, not guilty on four. The form was shown the prosecution and the defense for their approval. The jury was polled and each panelist affirmed the decision.

As the trial moved to sentencing the next day, the extent of Andrea Sneiderman's fall came into stark relief. Once a promising young manager at a major corporation, with a successful husband, a beautiful big house, and an active social life in one of Atlanta's premier suburbs, Andrea was now led into court by a bailiff, not through the front door, but from the prisoner's entrance, paraded in front of the pool camera. Gone were the smart sweaters and blouses and skirts. She wore an orange jumpsuit with DEKALB COUNTY JAIL stenciled on the back.

It was the same uniform that Hemy wore on his first court date.

She had on no makeup. Her hair was pushed back behind her ears. She took her seat at the defense table, embraced Clegg, and faced her fate.

Sentencing meant victim impact statements. Steven Sneiderman, whose wrongful death lawsuit against Andrea was still pressing on, lambasted her "pathetic narcissism" and called her a "common criminal" who despite the lack of a murder charge still should be blamed for Rusty's murder. "Without her lies and betrayal," Steven said, "Rusty would still be here with his children." Andrea's friends came to her defense, imploring the judge for mercy for the sake of Ian and Sophia. As Andrea wept, Elizabeth Stansbury quoted Ian as telling her, "Miss Elizabeth, I can't see my mommy, but she's not dead."

In arguments before the judge, DA James sought twenty years in prison; Clegg asked for five years' probation.

Finally it was left for Andrea Sneiderman to speak for herself. She walked up to the witness stand. Twice she braced herself with her left hand as she went up the two steps, then turned and raised her right hand to take the oath. Her mouth was downturned. Her voice choked as she spelled her last name for the record.

"Mrs. Sneiderman," the judge began, "you have been found guilty of various charges by a jury and you do have a right to make a statement on your behalf before a sentence is imposed." He also told her she had a right to appeal. "At this point in time you are more than welcome to make a statement, you don't have to make a statement, it is completely up to you. Would you like to make a statement to me at this point in time?"

"I would," she said.

"You may proceed."

She folded her hands in front of her and read off a paper.

"Your Honor, I'm here to ask for your leniency for the sake of my children," she said in a shaky voice. "I am going to try to find the words to describe what it's been like—an indescribable and unimaginable three years.

"I met Rusty when I was eighteen. We fell in love and began our futures together. After having children I worked from home, and GE was my first job back in an office environment. It was an exciting and terrifying time for me. I didn't know what to expect. At first I thought my boss, Mr. Neuman, was a nice guy taking an interest in me as his new employee. He was showing and teaching me the business, and I was appreciative. I believed he controlled my career and I let him therefore control my time and too much of my life.

"I wanted to do well and I thought that being nice to him was the answer. One of my greatest regrets will always be allowing this predator into my life or not being stronger for not dispelling his advances sooner."

She sniffled and continued. "I viewed Mr. Neuman as a mentor, a kind and helpful man, a father of three. I never thought Mr. Neuman was capable of this murder. As time went on our friendship grew, so too did my reliance on him at work. The line of appropriate conduct clearly blurred. In hindsight I should have told Rusty about his advances. I should have quit my job and filed a report with HR and hid from Mr. Neuman. There are so many reasons that I didn't. Yes, I was flattered by what seemed like harmless attention. I thought I could handle him. I thought he was just a man being a man, and the things that I did like introducing him to Rusty and sending him pictures of our happy family—they all backfired.

"I didn't know this mild-mannered executive was capable of killing anyone. In hindsight knowing now that Mr. Neuman is a murderer, I wish I would have immediately opened my GE emails and gone through them as this court has done for signs of what can now be seen as an obsession with me.

"What I remembered as isolated inappropriate and insignificant comments tell a different story when read in chronological order and with the knowledge that Mr. Neuman killed my husband. I am shamed by and apologize for my emails. I regret sharing anything personal with this man; allowing him to get too close to me on a personal level was a complete betrayal as I've never shared my personal feelings with any man other than Rusty.

"But I want to be clear. There was no physical romance between Mr. Neuman and me. No sex. No kissing. Nothing other than putting my head on his shoulder to cry and holding his hand on one occasion to comfort him. I was never leaving my true love, Rusty, and our children, and I made that clear. Especially in October of 2010.

"After November 18, 2010, when Mr. Neuman killed Rusty, I stopped sleeping, I stopped eating, my life was misery without Rusty and if not for my children I wanted to die. I felt those exact same feelings when visiting Rusty's grave site with Sophia and Ian last week for the first time in a year."

Andrea struggled now to speak, her voice choking with emotion.

"Despite my state of mind following the murder, I did nothing to obstruct justice in any way. I gave the police names, passwords, access to all of my personal and GE computers and phone information," she continued. "When asked on November 19, 2010, if I knew anyone interested in breaking up my family, I said yes, and immediately gave Mr. Neuman's name to the police. At the time I felt great apprehension about giving the name of my boss, someone who I thought was a friend, to the police as a murder suspect. But I was asked a question and I answered it truthfully.

"I later took the stand at Mr. Neuman's murder trial because I wanted to prove that he was sane. I did not prepare for my testimony. I didn't review any emails. And I ignored all of the people who told me not to testify."

Staring at James, anger in her face, she said, "I was shocked when the prosecution began attacking me and making me the focal point of Mr. Neuman's trial. Without an attorney to object to the inappropriate and irrelevant questioning, I fought back and I tried to defend myself."

She turned a page and then looked at the judge. "I'm embarrassed when I watch the tape of my testimony and I feel it does not represent who I am.

"Hemy Neuman has already robbed my children of their father and his love," she continued, breaking down. "Rusty is no longer here to play baseball with Ian or to carry Sophia on his shoulders. He will never have the chance to raise his children. He should be at Ian's bar mitzvah."

She coughed and sniffled. "He should be there to walk Sophia down the aisle. He should be there the day they graduate from high school and college. He will never get to sit at the head of the Passover table again, or with his grandchildren. He deserved to have that. There is an entire history that's been erased by Mr. Neuman.

"Sophia and Ian desperately need me to help fill that role for them. They have already suffered so much. Since last August, they've had no parent to join them at school events, to take them to the playground, or to go have an ice cream all because the state wrongly charged me with a murder that I had nothing to do with and would do anything to undo."

Andrea began to cry. "Sophia and Ian have been punished enough. Please, let me go home to my kids. Mr. Neuman changed my children's lives forever by killing their father. Please don't make them live without their mother. Thank you."

The judge said, "Thank you," and looked toward the lawyer tables. "Mr. James, anything?"

"No, sir," said the DA.

"Mr. Clegg, anything else?"

"No, sir," said Andrea's attorney.

"You may come down, ma'am."

She braced herself again as she walked down the steps and back to the defense table.

After a recess, the bailiff signaled that the judge was ready to give a sentence. Judge Adams burst into the courtroom and slammed the door behind him. Family and friends filled the room. Rusty's brother and sister-in-law were there, as were her parents. Andrea's parents and a number of friends sat on the other side of the courtroom.

"Hi, good morning again, you may be seated," the judge said. "As I indicated, the court will not tolerate any outbursts one way or the other. If you do not feel as if you can control your emotions, you may want to step outside. This is zero tolerance. I'll give you a moment to remove yourselves, if you wish. You can stay if you wish, but you don't have to."

After reviewing papers in front of him, the judge said, "Mrs. Sneiderman, would you stand, please, with your lawyers." She and three lawyers stood. "Mrs. Sneiderman, a jury has returned verdicts . . . and as a result of the jury verdicts, I have a responsibility to impose a sentence . I've listened to all the lawyers and the parties and the witnesses throughout the day and also reviewed the law as it exists in Georgia, and I will impose the following sentence at this time."

He paused.

"As to count one," he said, "I will sentence you to five years. As to count two, five years. As to count three, five years. As to count six, five years. As to count eight, five years."

It kept going. Five years for each guilty count. But at the end he said, "I will give you credit for the time you have been in custody and also the time you have served under house arrest." He also did not run the terms back-to-back. "This will be five years to serve on each count, I will render them concurrently. I'm not going to run them consecutively. I'm going to run them concurrently."

He looked at Andrea. "Any questions, ma'am?" Andrea, standing stone-faced, had none. "At this point in time, I will have you taken into custody."

Clegg tried to speak, but the judge interrupted him. "Take her into custody. Step out of the way, lawyers, do not obstruct. This woman will be taken into custody." She was handcuffed behind her back and led out of the courtroom past the pool camera.

"Anything else?" the judge asked. "All right, the court is in recess!" Judge Adams banged the gavel and strode to his door. He was a step outside his courtroom with his back to everybody before the bailiff could finish shouting, "All rise."

CHAPTER 25

The Lee Arrendale State Prison greets visitors with a cheery colonial-style sign on a post that would seem more appropriate for a southern diner than an institution with a history of violence and controversy. Located in the northeastern corner of Georgia, about eighty miles from Atlanta, the prison sits near the one-square-mile town of Alto, population twelve hundred, in the foothills of the Appalachian Mountains. "Warm hospitality is offered to visitors who venture to this beautiful section of the state," says the official website for Habersham County, which touts the region's "fine dining, quaint shops, outdoor recreation and fine arts." Cool and wooded, it's the kind of place to which busy Atlanta residents would escape on muggy weekends in the city.

Built in 1926, originally as a hospital for tuberculosis

patients, it was converted in the 1950s to a prison for men ages eighteen to twenty-five, including children sentenced as adults. A population of the state's most violent criminals, combined with chronic understaffing, proved incendiary. The Law Office of the Southern Center for Human Rights called Arrendale a "violent and troubled institution" for the young inmates, including an eighteen-year-old man who was raped and strangled to death in 2004 not long after he had written to his grandmother about his fears of prison. "Rapes, stabbings, chokings, and beatings with locks, broomsticks, trash cans and other objects left many of these young people with severe head injuries, lacerations, bruises, broken teeth and other physical injuries as well as severe psychological trauma," the center reports.

Things changed beginning in 2005 when the state converted Arrendale to a women's institution. The first batch of 350 female inmates arrived in 2006 from crowded jails around Georgia, and tensions eased. The prison earned marks for creating the state's first all-woman fire department, made up of inmates, serving the surrounding towns. The inmates now were known more for their high-profile crimes than any troubles in prison. The "antifreeze killer" Julia Lynn Turner, who murdered her police officer husband and later her fireman boyfriend by spiking their food with antifreeze, was among the first to arrive (she later died in another jail in 2010). The Grammy-nominated rapper called Da Brat—real name Shawntae Harris—landed in Arrendale on an aggravated-assault guilty plea for smashing a rum bottle over the head of a hostess at Atlanta's Studio 72 nightclub on Halloween night in 2007.

DeKalb County district attorney Robert James had requested a twenty-year sentence for Andrea, but after her five-year sentence expressed satisfaction in the term. "Mrs. Sneiderman is on her way to jail as I believed she should be in the first place," he said. "Two families have been torn apart. This is a very sad situation," he continued. "In America you cannot lie to police and you cannot lie to a jury. It's difficult for me to feel sympathy when someone asks for mercy but they're not willing to admit fault."

Andrea arrived in late 2013. Her time behind a fence and razor wire in a dormitory-style building promised to be short. With credit for her year of home confinement before trial and good behavior, she could earn parole as early as spring 2014. But even that was too much time for Andrea, who petitioned for bail. "This is a fight Andrea Sneiderman is going to win," said her new lawyer Doug Chalmers, brought in for the appeal. Her legal team would cite what it called legal mistakes made by Judge Adams, including allowing the testimony of Hemy's friend Melanie White, which the defense said was objectionable hearsay. Andrea's camp argued that she should be free while the appeal was being filed. She could help her attorneys on the criminal case, be with her children, currently in the care of her parents—and continue to do battle with her in-laws in court.

Rusty's family was not happy that the murder charges had been thrown out and that Andrea would serve relatively little time. "Our family has determined that we have no choice but to continue to litigate the pending civil lawsuits against the defendant to the fullest extent possible under the law," they said in a statement. One of the actions, a wrongful death case, alleged that Andrea "knew that her co-conspirator intended to kill Rusty Sneiderman" and that she "actively and knowingly participated in the murder and the planning of the murder." Another action was over the more than two million dollars in Rusty's life insurance money that had been paid out to Andrea. The state had frozen the funds during the criminal trial and now Rusty's family wanted the money to remain out of her hands while they pressed a wrongful death lawsuit.

In fall 2013, Andrea appeared in prison garb in an Atlanta civil court to argue that the money was rightfully hers because she ultimately was never tried for murder. Incarceration only stiffened her resolve, and the legal wrangling remained rancorous as her attorneys took shots at the DA's office for dismissing the murder counts at the eleventh hour. "Representatives of that office swore under oath that Andrea Sneiderman was guilty of murder," said one of her lawyers, Mark Trigg, at one hearing in September 2013. He added, "When it came time to put up or shut up and prove the allegations before a jury, they shut up." Esther Panitch, representing Rusty's family, asserted that Andrea "does not appear to be suffering or in great need of those funds. She has literally sacrificed others to obtain Russell Sneiderman's property and without intervention she'll continue to act in furtherance of [her] ultimate goal, which is to keep as much money of his as possible and away from her children." The session typified the emotionally charged tone between Andrea and her detractors after the trial. As Andrea sat at the counsel table, her mother wept in the audience. A fed-up Fulton County judge Doris Downs tried to bring some calm to the proceedings, warning both sides to "cool things down." She cautioned, "As hotly contested as I'm sure this whole issue is for both of your clients, you all have got to bring the clear cool heads to the table, otherwise we can spend all of the money litigating."

By year's end, cooler heads did prevail. In December, both sides abruptly reached a settlement in the wrongful death case. With the litigants now agreeing to remain silent publicly, a number of questions remained, including the fate of the insurance money. Rusty's family had sought to have the funds placed in a trust for the children; how much control over those funds Andrea would now have as part of the settlement was left unstated. The reason for the Sneiderman family's retreat was never revealed. Everybody vowed to remain mum about the settlement. Certainly the interests of the children loomed, the bickering and attorney costs a detriment to their well-being and financial futures. But another factor likely came into play—the simple lack of evidence. It was the same problem that plagued prosecutors.

And it invited the same question. Was the evidence missing because Andrea ensured that it would never be found?

Judge Adams may have ended the criminal case with a sharp rap of his gavel but that didn't quiet a nagging sense that business was left undone, that gaps were left unfilled, that months of investigation and litigation had still failed to resolve key questions. Among them: was Andrea a greedy and a manipulative conspirator to her husband's murder? Was she the victim of overzealous prosecutors, inept cops, and spiteful in-laws? Or some other possibility? No court now apparently seemed destined to resolve those questions.

Had this been a murder trial, Shayna Citron would have been the star witness, not just for her emotional testimony but for providing the critical element to a prosecution case: motive. Her accounts of tension in the Sneiderman household propel the theory that Andrea solved her domestic woes with murder. Using her feminine wiles—a prosecutor may well have argued—Andrea duped the mentally addled Hemy Neuman, blinded by love and torn asunder by her romantic teasing, into doing the dirty work and taking the fall. With no hard evidence against her, she would walk off with a couple of million dollars. In the end, the prosecution could have said, Andrea was undone by her lies and arrogance and the fact that she blurted out her husband was shot long before anybody told her so, to, of all people, Shayna Citron, the former BFF she treated so shabbily after the murder.

It was a tidy and compelling storyline, and DA Robert

James seemed poised to present it before a jury up until literally hours before the start of trial. Even now aspects of it ring true. Andrea likely was unhappy in her marriage, much more so than she was willing to admit, evidenced by her behavior after she left part-time home employment for the big leagues at GE. She described the transition as "terrifying." It upset the delicate balance of power and responsibilities in the marriage, left her both disoriented and, possibly, more vulnerable than she might otherwise have been to the attentions of another man. She acknowledged being flattered by Hemy's attentions, his respect for her professionally, and his apparently genuine interest in her feelings. Andrea also seemed to savor being his confidante. She would try to paint herself as naive. And from much of what she told the judge at sentencing, she did seem genuinely unaware of the consequences of developing a personal relationship with her boss. She said she saw him as a friend and mentor, a kind father of three. She didn't say he was also a husband.

Whether she was the driving, manipulative force in this relationship remained less clear. Andrea offered several strong denials. Hemy possessed the power, according to her. He controlled her career and therefore her life. The best she could do was go on the defensive, and in this, she said, she failed. She seriously downplayed his behavior. She called it "harmless attention" and his declarations "isolated inappropriate and insignificant comments." She thought he was a man being a man and that she could handle him. Her biggest regret, she said, was not repelling his advances and running off to tell Rusty and the HR department.

But even a cursory review of the emails, combined with Andrea's steely demeanor in court, suggests she was selling herself short in front of the judge. She was no helpless waif; nor was she, it appears, an evil seductress. She looked instead like a woman in over her head sometimes, more in control in others. Before GE, her office had been her home, and most contact with co-workers was via phone or email. Now she was navigating her way through a strange and scary new world of work intermixed with male–female relations, overcome with emotions that were new, perplexing, and frightening.

As the relationship deepened, she acknowledged that the "line of appropriate conduct" had become "blurred." At first she suggested it was Hemy crossing those lines, not her. But the emails suggested that this was so much more than a randy boss hitting on her. She appeared fond of him, respected him as he respected her, and she was excited by the prospect of travel, dining out, drinking wine, dancing, and visiting overseas, all on the GE AmEx.

How close did they ultimately get? The Pulse bartender recalled kissing, butt grabbing, and close dancing. Whether it went any farther is impossible to tell. Hemy wavered on whether they had actually had sex, giving differing accounts to friends and mental health experts and finally just throwing up his arms and professing to a faulty memory. Andrea flatly denied it: "No sex." But, she spoke of the "complete betrayal" she committed of "allowing him to get too close to me on a personal level" and sharing feelings with him in a way that she had never done with anybody but Rusty. Her pained emails after a fateful business trip suggested that the feelings ran even deeper than she was willing to admit even at her sentencing, and that they conflicted her.

What the emails didn't reveal was any evidence of a murder plot. Nowhere did Andrea tell Hemy to kill Rusty. Nowhere did Hemy offer. Not a single witness could recount either Hemy or Andrea speaking of wanting Rusty gone. That scenario, under close inspection, made less and less sense. She could be mad at him, but how would killing him solve anything? The insurance money? They were already wealthy; she didn't need it. To free herself of Rusty's self-absorption and job-hopping? Shayna Citron painted a vivid image of an unhappy woman poised to have an affair—but murder? Shayna never heard the word, and neither did anybody else.

Lacking a "smoking email" and a clear motive, the leap to suggesting Andrea recruited Hemy as an assassin became a big one. Andrea predictably said she had no idea her mild-mannered engineer boss had the heart of a killer. But so did everybody else at GE, who had no reason to lie. In fact, it appeared the only one who thought Hemy capable of murder was Hemy. He put on such a front that virtually nobody saw the slightest indication of his inner demons. Outside of his sister, nobody even seemed to know he had emotional problems, much less severe bipolar disorder and delusions. Even Hemy's own long-suffering wife denied having any knowledge of his mental issues. Nor, did it seem, did Andrea. There was no corroborating evidence—no emails, letters, testimony—that Andrea had a clue. Accepting the suggestions that she was a manipulator, Andrea may have seen in Hemy an escape from a troubled marriage or a pawn for promotion or a weak man to push around to boost her own ego. By the end she may even have worried about attentions and what motivated them, and as she distanced herself from him could have detected some of the psychoses that would later play such a big role in his trial.

Still, the investigation uncovered evidence that raised troubling questions and couldn't go unexamined. Had she gone on trial for murder, Exhibit A would have been Andrea's purported knowledge that Rusty was shot before she had been informed of this. She had related this information to Shayna. In a fictional murder mystery this would have sealed the suspect's fate. How else could she have known unless she had arranged it? But in reality, a defense attorney could have shredded this evidence. The defense would only have had to step back to the chaotic scene at Dunwoody Prep in the hours after the brazen attack. A lot of people were coming and going, a lot of people were saying a lot of things. Rusty's father was told over the phone that Rusty had been shot, but he couldn't remember by whom. Couldn't somebody else have told Andrea?

A homicide investigator—Gary Cortellino—talked to her at the school. He would deny later that he told her that Rusty was shot, but at a murder trial Cortellino's credibility would come under attack. This was the same Cortellino, the defense could note, who professed he never heard Andrea mention Hemy's name when she was being questioned at her home two days after the murder, when the tape recording showed she did. Could he have said it and forgot? Or did it slip out? Or could somebody else have said something at the preschool? A lot of people heard shots. That Andrea couldn't pinpoint exactly who said it to her and when would be a flimsy foundation for a murder case, particularly one lacking any of the documentary evidence of a conspiracy.

The more compelling circumstantial evidence was the phone records. The fact that Hemy called her at key points—when he was out buying the gun, for instance, or heading to a costume shop—would be hard to ignore. But these were calls to her from him, and it wasn't known what they said. Had any of the calls been followed by a text or an email that mentioned "gun" or "disguise," even cryptically, a case could be made that Andrea must have known what he was doing. Lacking that, it seemed to be more smoke than fire.

This left the most provocative evidence, the phone records showing Andrea's calls to Hemy the morning of the shooting. Andrea's attorneys suggested she was merely calling Hemy to tell him she would be out of the office for an emergency. Here is where the relationship between Andrea and Hemy becomes relevant. Andrea may not have considered Hemy insane, but she received numerous emails in which he professed his love for her. He had proposed to her. Whatever the extent of their physical relationship, they had become much closer than Andrea would admit for a long time. It was possible that Andrea reached out to him as the friend she always said he had been, looking for somebody, anybody, to talk to, as she did when she called Shayna Citron shortly after the murder.

But there are other possibilities, ones that may strike to the heart of the case and explain so much of Andrea's subsequent behavior.

The moment she found out Rusty was dead, apparently violently based on the police response, she could have feared that Hemy had killed him. The word *crazy*, which she'd use to describe him after his arrest and which she may, in the back of her head, have always suspected, may now have flashed like a big light-up sign. The evidence suggested that Andrea and Hemy had ended whatever relationship they had before Rusty's murder—at least from Andrea's standpoint. The emails had stopped, she and Rusty showed signs of getting closer again. But Hemy may not have been ready to let it go. Had she wondered that very thing? And now that Rusty was dead, had that wonder turned to terror?

The idea may still have seemed preposterous to her, as she would later claim. And so she may have called him not so much to confront him as to confirm if he was in the office, to hear him tell her that he had been there all morning, that he had an alibi, that her fears were irrational.

It may not have taken much to convince her.

When the detectives asked the day after the murder if there was anybody trying to break up her marriage, she provided Hemy's name. She did this knowing he was still her boss, that she could be wrong about fingering an innocent man who had been a friend, that she could be exposing an unflattering chapter in her life in a case generating wide media attention. She would return to this point over and over. And while she did also mention others, from Rusty's business associates to the exterminator, the name Hemy Neuman came from her mouth and was memorialized on tape. It wasn't her fault the cops blew it.

But it set in motion an avalanche of complications that would ultimately bury Andrea. Within weeks police had arrested him, and it was clear they wanted full disclosure—and still she resisted. The longer she held on to the details of her travels and conversations with Hemy, the worse it got for her. Her recalcitrance fueled a frenzy. The more she dodged and weaved and eventually clammed up, the guiltier she looked, and the harder police pressed. Authorities don't like to be challenged—anybody who gets pulled over for speeding knows not to argue with the cop—and Andrea violated every rule. Her behavior at trial, and on the witness stand, seemed to be the last straw.

By Andrea's trial it had become a zero-sum game. "There is no evidence she has done anything wrong," her attorney Thomas Clegg asserted in opening statements. She had her attorneys draw a line in the sand while forgetting one important thing. While there may not have been evidence beyond a reasonable doubt that she was murder conspirator, she did plenty wrong when the stakes couldn't have been any higher. The defense couldn't make good on its promise to the jury.

The final question, then, was not whether she lied, but why should she?

In the lead-up to Hemy's trial, Andrea's character and behavior drew the attention of mental health experts. Many of the findings reflected poorly on her. Psychologist

Adriana Flores, hired by Hemy's defense, suggested Andrea was a woman who had toyed with the emotions of a disturbed man. "It is a pattern of pushing him away and pulling him forward, pushing him away, pulling him forward," she had testified. "Neuman is already delusional. She was giving him signs that were there. That's what makes it more concerning. He already had this thought that children were his and he'd have a relationship forever and ever. It's not all in his head because she was in fact having sex with him," said Flores in her testimony. "However, she was giving him cues that were very much real."

Flores's opinions came with a proviso: She did not speak with Andrea, who refused to be interviewed. The prosecution's witness, psychologist Pamela Crawford, did talk to her but appeared to have been left with no deeper insights. The interview was conducted under poor clinical conditions—Andrea's attorney was in the room—and Andrea skirted details about her relationship with Hemy. "She maintained throughout my talking to her that [there] was no physical contact," said Crawford, who finally gave up asking her about a possible affair. "It was clear to me that she was not going to acknowledge anything to do with having a romantic relationship. I wanted to try to get information from her and did not want to close the information down, so I did not want to push her on that." When Crawford was asked if she had considered testing Andrea's veracity, she said, "No, what I did was get information from her. I was trying to get info about Hemy Neuman, I didn't with her in the interview, take emails to see if she was truthful." That didn't stop Crawford from forming a conclusion: "I thought it was unlikely she was being truthful from the information that I had."

For all their probing of Hemy's motivations the mental health experts never cared much about Andrea's. They fulfilled the mandate of bulding a case for or against

Hemy Neuman and somewhere along the line larger truths got ignored. Andrea emerged more as an abstraction than a person, one more factor shaping Hemy's sanity like his troubled youth or financial woes. Nobody was interested in what Andrea felt or why she felt it. Had the mental health experts dug deeper, they may have found those motivations behind the behavior that cost her so and provided some answers to the questions that continue to bedevil the case.

At 12:22 a.m. on Monday, June 16, 2014, Andrea Sneiderman walked out of prison after serving 22 months of her five-year sentence. She left with a fat bank balance, custody of her children, the support of her parents, and an uneasy truce with her in-laws. But it will never really be over for her. The rest of her years promise experiences few can ever comprehend. She can start over, but the events surrounding her husband's murder are forever preserved in a digital world that forgets nothing. Everything she did and said is but a mouse click away, to future neighbors, future employers, to her children.

And always will linger the question: If it weren't for her behavior—in Greenville and Longmont and London, over email and text and cellphone—would Rusty still be alive?

Were there truths too painful for her to confront—to her family, to the police, to herself?

For now, she insists the institutions of authority spared her no mercy for her trauma and stripped her of her liberty for crimes she says she never committed. "I want to go back to the life I had with Rusty," she told the judge at sentencing. "This is not a world I understand anymore." And yet, for all her bitterness toward the justice system, "I am determined to raise my children to be happy, productive citizens of this country." To the end, she remained a woman wrestling with contradictions.

* * *

One hundred and thirty miles due east of Atlanta, on the outskirts of Augusta, stands the Augusta State Medical Prison. Like the Arrendale women's prison, this place of punishment is located in a pleasant community of trees and friendly folks—visitors are greeted by a sign reading, WELCOME TO GROVETOWN, A COMMUNITY THAT CARES. A century ago the rich of Augusta fled the stifling heat and swampy diseases of summer for vacation homes in Grovetown. Though called a medical prison, Augusta is no quiet hospital. An analysis of prison reports and state Department of Corrections data by the *Augusta Chronicle* found that Augusta State Medical Prison ranked among the highest in the state for serious attacks between inmates. In the summer of 2011 one inmate was stabbed to death with homemade shanks in the prison yard. Nobody is immune from the violence. Guards and even nurses, the *Chronicle* wrote, "are routinely slapped, punched and harassed by inmates."

Hemy Neuman's mug shot taken upon entering the prison shows a man with close-cropped hair, gray and thinning, head tilted to the left, eyes wide, with a curious almost whimsically resigned expression, as if he's saying, *What can I do?* It was a stark change from his trial. He looked more like the incarcerated mental patient he'd become than a high-level corporate manager he had been. "He's surviving," said his attorney Robert Rubin. "He's on medication. He's not being mistreated in prison. He's trying to make the best of a very bad situation. He's actually a very easygoing guy." Hemy's home was now a barracks-style building, not a cell, and he had not fallen victim to violence. It was behind these walls that the question of whether Andrea conspired to kill Rusty would be posed. Before her trial, the prosecution made overtures to Hemy. Locked up for life, he had little to lose, it would seem. If he would turn on Andrea, now would be the time. He didn't. Andrea had nothing to do with the murder. Hemy acted alone. He never wanted her to know it was he who pulled the trigger four times. That's why he wore a disguise and rented a van. He didn't want her to be mad at him.